Ann Belford Ulanov

Back to Basics

Ann Belford Ulanov

Back to Basics

DAIMON
Verlag

ACKNOWLEDGMENTS

My warm thanks to Christopher McFadden for his skills and his kindness in bringing my manuscript to good presentable form to be sent to the publishers. My warm thanks to Patricia Llosa for her amazing facilitation of finding the owner of the beautiful Cézanne painting, Portrait of a Woman (1902-1906), and my gratitude to its owner for his generous permission to show it to all of us (Chapter 5). Again warm thanks to Patricia Llosa for locating the source of permission to include Paul Klee's The Serpent Goddess and Her Enemy (Chapter 9) for all of us to see. My warm appreciation of Michael Wilhoite's talent as a photographer and thanks for the photo he created. My warm thanks to Robert Imhoff for his great gifts as formatter and for cover design and for Robert Hinshaw, Publisher of Daimon Verlag for his steady presence and deliberate pace in bringing this book into the world.

Cover art by Barry Ulanov
Photograph of the author by Michael Wilhoite

The image by Paul Klee, "die Schlangengöttin und ihr Feind/The Serpent Goddess and Her Enemy" (1940) on page 263 appears with permission of Zentrum Paul Klee, Bern, Image archive

Copyright © 2022 Daimon Verlag, Einsiedeln

ISBN 978-3-85630-786-8

All rights reserved.

Contents

Introduction

The corona virus reached New York City in January 2020 and broke into collective consciousness by March when we all went into lockdown. In lockdown I discovered I seemed not able to desert my city in its forlornness. I did not want to abandon it. Collective anxiety was palpable and steady, and increasing, partly because we could not see an end to lockdown which actually meant the virus. As always in crises, New Yorkers revealed their latent kindness to each other and I wanted to be part of it.

During my lockdown in the city, and continuing when I moved four months later to the country and then back and forth between two locations, it soon was very clear to me each of us had to do our personal work, whatever that was. We could easily succumb to fear morphing into jolts of terror – this wasn't just getting sick – this could kill you. We could drift into aimlessness to avoid that threnody. We could even drift into the collective anxiety and be pulled out to sea.

We needed our personal work to anchor us, to bolster us, to keep our personal footing and orientation. What could that be? Countless variations occurred – get a dog (adoption agencies were sold out); learn to bake bread; take on educating our children at home and in support of online teaching from their schools; make a conscious point to help our neighbor (my neighbor checked on me with a pleasant irregularity); construct meetings with friends on zoom; clean the closets; try to work on the anger that came up with loved ones in close quarters. I began to write; it was necessary. Five chapters were written during winter and summer of the 2020 lockdown (1, 2, 4, 8, 9). Four of the chapters had been done a few years before the virus (3, 5 6, 7). Unlike writing most books where one keeps a steady pace, this one was interrupted more than once. The collective anxiety continued and had new variations: worry about our threatened economy, trying to gain access to getting vaccinated, and most recently the threat of the mutated virus named pandemic D. I have only now been able to bring the work to conclusion August 2021.

These many months in 2020-2021 have been accented by what I see as a four-way crossroad that makes evident the upending we all have experienced of facing what feel like new crises or new versions of old ones. In such a tumult we need the basics, not as return to yesteryear, but as alive and growing, here, now and into the future. The four, as I see them, are: the pandemic that threatens lives everywhere and makes fact that we are neighbors in this suffering with people in every direction across the world. The saying, 'no one is safe until we all are safe' is true. The virus threat makes us live that truth both personally and together. The second factor is the challenge to government, in America to the structures of democracy – of every citizen's right to vote freely and in the attack on Congress meeting to certify the 2020 election and the rivaling interpretations of cause and remedy of those attacks. Other countries show their versions of challenge to foundational rights of citizens to speak freely, to elect their leaders and a splitting of interpretations equally severe of the failure to secure those rights. The third factor is a change in collective consciousness about the systemic nature of racism in our country. We have worked on that wound, with some success, but its healing is incomplete. The murder of George Floyd, I suggest, broke open deeper and wider this racial wound. The opportunity of this crisis is that we know about our wound in a more immediate way, personally and in collective news, arguments, discussions, new groups forming. It is here up front. The fourth factor is the bursting out of new symptoms of climate change that are here now of exploding fires, extreme floodings and huge storms and pollution of air, extinguishing heat waves, droughts, and growing consciousness about the preciousness of water and its feared decrease.

Religious upheavals surprise because twenty-five years ago it was forecast we were entering a post-religious age. It is not 'post.' Religion, spirituality, cultural symbols of meaningfulness are implicated in every aspect of the four-way crossroad. They are upended and forming new forms. Many of the political battles are rooted in opposing versions of the gods. The economic flailings that result from all this disorder makes it hard to see new forms emerging and where to find them.

In the midst of such turmoil, we need to root our feet again in basics of each of our professions. I speak here for and of depth psychology, meaning the clinical practice of analysis including the unconscious and our psyche's soul dimensions.

Back to Basics we must go. To the fundamentals and their evolutions in this book. Basic does not mean a hard-set, immutable definition treated as sacrosanct with the consequence of bullying everyone to sign on, or else. I mean something elementary, formative. Each chapter takes up in practice and in theory requisite aspects of psyche and with attention given to soul.

By basic I do not mean something fixed and unchangeable. I mean something elementary, rudimentary, a dynamic underpinning or ingredient that is formative for vital human life with self and with others and with whatever we recognize as of ultimate presence and importance, an image of God.

What forms its basicness? Its going on growing does, like a yeast that forms the miracle of bread appearing that we eat up and live by. These prime elements go on in a core liveliness and transform a life connected to it and is itself transformed by such connection.

What accounts for that? The authors of human activity do, in building things, doing the job, making something beautiful, surviving the suffering, doing writing or dancing or hearing or painting or composing mathematical formulas, or, whatever, who get transformed by the prototypal ingredients. They get hold of an epiphany and it gets hold of them; and both are changed. They tell us about this interpenetration – and they make something of it that clicks with us too. We see something in what they see; we hear it in a whisper; we catch its scent and then understand those tales of, Sell all you have to get this field, this pearl. This is the necessary thing which is not a thing at all but the original dynamic in everything. We get the point, and like the point that begins geometry by extending into a line, then into a plane then a structure imperative in everything, we catch this indispensable idea, combination, gist at the center, this *sine qua non*.

What is the basic that goes on going on, each one changed by it, changing others but the 'it' is still traceable? What is an image of that? Here is one person's dream that comes close to show a version of it (albeit in unconscious language): the dreamer is lying flat on the back, legs straight up perpendicular to the body, feet pointing to the heavens, lying atop the round globe of the earth. Precisely at the core of the dreamer's abdomen muscles there is a fastening of that nucleus with a line down thru the back securing the body to the earth and with that line extending downwards through the earth to the core of the globe. The dreamer's center is fastened in a sure link to the globe's center. The two are anchored, personal to cosmic, cosmos to individual.*

* All references throughout this book to analysands' material comes with their permission to include it and my gratitude to them for their generosity.

The chapters show a circling round and round again some basic themes in Jung's work to see the same symbolic process from different angles, its Manyness and Oneness taking new forms. The chapters can be read right through to follow the point I am making to connect to basic sources that are fructive now. Or one can read around according to which chapter prompts your attention.

Jung embarked on an originary approach, set sail, as that first letter of the first word in his *Red Book, Liber Novus,* illustrates in his tiny painting of a big ship leaving the city, leaving the harbor to explore unknown waters. And bring back what he finds. Jung's work makes possible doing this work by stirring up the depths in his readers who must then set sail too, and, *Deo Volente*, bring back what is found to share with others. I wish for you a strong voyage and safe return.

Ann Belford Ulanov
New York City and Woodbury Ct. 2021.

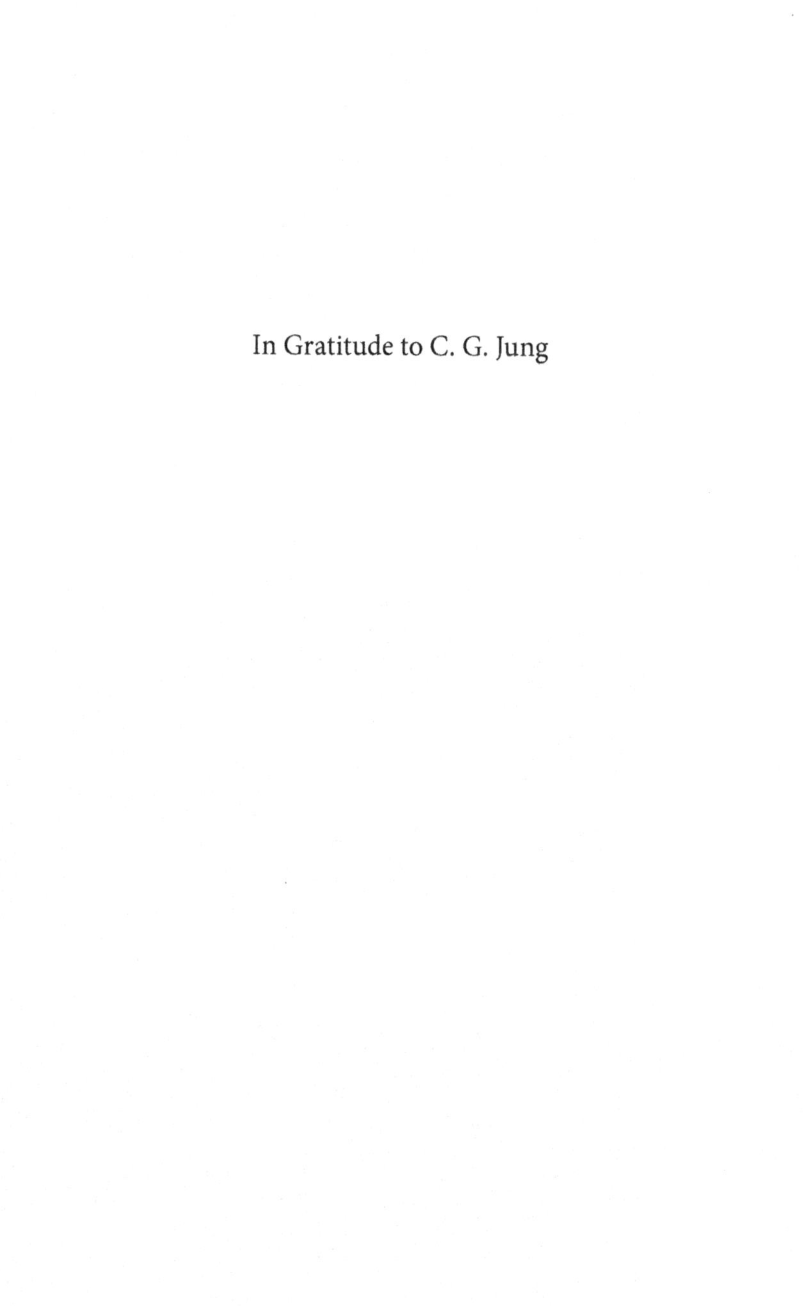

In Gratitude to C. G. Jung

Chapter 1:

Two Points of View

Two Projects

Two points of view pertain to practice of analysis and the theory underlying it. In this chapter the thesis emerging from years of work with analysands and the work of theoretical reflection, and from my own level of development, can be simply stated. Two projects go on in our psyche continuously and simultaneously, an individual personal one and the project of the psyche itself, so to speak, that reflects the influence of the collective dimension of society, historical era, culture, archetypal dominants.

The personal project draws on the raw material, the stuff of our actual individual life, its context in family, pivotal relations with others, with our conflicts, contemporary cultural influences, body embeddedness or its lack, and with our devotion or its lack, to what unfolds in our own growing. Jung calls the project our process of individuation. It becomes more than less conscious to us and includes aspects of what Jung calls our personal unconscious and most specifically, "the mousetrap of our complex" (Jung 2008, p. 4). From the overview of our life and what we have pursued over the years, we can see the dominant complex around which smaller and associated ones have gathered into a repetition of a major theme: what has bedeviled us as a false truth, and what has emerged as a unique true path.

Complexes are normal and make up our personal psychic structure, conscious and unconscious. Examples are ego; even it is a complex; persona, shadow, and so forth (See Jung 1933/1960, paras 755-758; see also Jung 1939/1954, paras 290-292, 296, 302 re individuation). The one that signals our major life struggle puts a bag over our heads, kidnaps us, interferes with our ego functioning and leads us astray. Such a complex reveals and defends against something frightening that needs to be included as a necessary part of ourselves.

As analysts we gain from reflecting what is the major complex of each analysand with whom we work, and of ourselves too. Around what personal problem has the struggle consisted, and which archetypal constellation emerging in that problem have we each been working on, or, by which have we been worked over? Analysands can name the bedeviling false truth: "I should have tried harder;" "I should have known;" "I don't understand, my mind blanks;" "I could go crazy at any moment;" "I must not make my mother suffer;" "I can't find my place in reality;" "Anger bursts in me;" "I left my body;" "I haven't got the goods."

From such "mousetraps" have developed categories of the Diagnostic Statistical Manual of the American Psychiatric Association written in more "objective" language than our personal names for what strafes us all the time. But that "objective" language is always in danger of objectifying the persons to whom the categories are applied. 'Oh, she's a borderline; oh, he is schizoid.' A delicate touch is required to perceive through these diagnoses the sufferings that afflict, but never define a person.

The project of the psyche, albeit carried on in our psyches, feels strangely impersonal, general, collective. It connects to what we do not know, to what is unconscious. Our dream, for example, although dramatizing our personal conflict, may also exhibit a remote quality, presenting a human "existential question without any reference to the ego" (Jung 2008, p. 362). Such a question belongs to all of us and spirals us down to such basic queries as, Where does consciousness come from? In what does real love consist? What heals a sense one is disintegrating? In this bad thing is there a seed of good?

In response to an anguishing problem, the dream often simply presents an unguessed image or implied statement of fact as if the unconscious says, this is such as it is. We cannot ascribe to the unconscious human intentions or anthropomorphize it as guiding father or wise mother: "It is pure nature. It just happens this way" (ibid, p. 413). For "The unconscious means we don't know it; it is profound, abysmal ... we have said nothing, except that we don't know" (Jung 2019, p. 247).

Jung also writes however, psyche seems goal oriented with a purposive nature (Jung 2008, p. 4). In a dream for example, a friend sends a letter to the distressed dreamer containing "remarks about redemption" that are at once commonsense advice to the dreamer's disintegrated state but in language that evokes the sacred, the holy, as if conveying there is an "intelligent agency at work in his unconscious" (Jung 2019, p. 247). This is not a theory but a description of a psychic fact observed in the dream and of its healing effect on the dreamer: "it is simply a formulation of actual experience" (Jung 2019, p. 247).

Further, contact with this project of the psyche exerts a healing effect. It sets our personal struggles in a larger bowl of the human story. It strikes a spiritual note:

> "If this supra-individual psyche exists, everything that is translated into its picture-language would be depersonalized,

> and if this became conscious would appear to us *sub specie aeternitatis.* Not as my sorrow, but as the sorrow of the world; not as a personal isolating pain, but a pain without bitterness that unites all humanity. The healing effect of this knows no proof." (Jung 1960, para 316)

Our personal experience of that paradoxical personal/impersonal aspect of psyche grows as we engage in the individuation process coming to be all of who we are. Nestled in our dream's depiction of my problem is a general human problem not reducible to the raw material of my 'stuff,' but as if extending into primordial realms there already from the beginning. Jung hypothesizes "an unrecognizable center from which dreams emanate" rather than a clear causal sequence that originates the dream (Jung 2008, p. 10).

> This unrecognized center emerges in "a thinking in primordial images, in symbols that are older than the historical man, which are inborn in him from the earliest times, and, eternally living, outlasting all generations, still make up the groundwork of the human psyche ... It is a question neither of belief nor of knowledge, but of the agreement of our thinking with the primordial images of the unconscious ... the unthinkable matrices of all our thoughts." (Jung 1933/1960, para 794)

Jung likens these images to "psychic organs" and says he might say to a patient "'Your picture of God ... is atrophied, consequently your psychic metabolism is out of gear.' The ancient *athanasius pharmakon*, the medicine of immortality, is more ... meaningful than we supposed" (ibid).

Their Interweaving

Consistent attention to the two points of view shows their interweaving and gives a felt sense of the larger whole of a personality. The individual project circles around personal conflict that centers suffering and its potential healing. For example, one analysand summed up the major conflict as being erased, not noticed as existing in her ownmost reality. This lack of interest and recognition she actually was there and was worthy of notice existed from birth as the emotional environment she was born into, rather than resulting from e.g., traumatic loss of a parent, who loved her and then was dead from sudden illness or accident. She discovered her being alone as if annulled in the midst of others. This emotional fact shocked her to her core. She dealt with it as if it was a card life dealt, simply the way things were, her personal issue to struggle with and assume responsibility for. From long work in analysis emerged a chunk of aggression left undeveloped. Learning to endure and assimilate great anger at being treated as if she was not, led to using that aggressive energy to acquire agency: to stand up for and with herself, "staying steady with myself, no longer allowing or colluding with erasing these erasures of me."

In the midst of personal anguish, taking hold of her extreme vulnerability to rejection and reaching clarity about the theme of erasure, images emerged of a different sort, arising from she knew not where, typical, says Jung, of archetypal symbols popping up in the midst of personal turmoil. The dreams were really visions in contrast to the more usual personages and plots, climaxes, denouements. Pictures simply appear. Here are some examples: "four standing shapes of radiant light, golden, bright"; "a circle formed by naked people standing close together with arms embracing each other's shoulders define the circle's circumference by leaning back on its rim with their bare legs and toes pointing to the empty center of the circle"; "three figures: an abstract upright long shape of light, and a red thick small circle with empty space in the center, and a third figure combining these masculine-like and feminine-like shapes, not as an intercourse but the long shape of light now horizontal and erect like a phallus originating within the center of the red circle and pointing out to the right; the dreamer asked is it pointing in the direction of consciousness – the masculine anchored in the feminine and the whole getting conscious?; "a large square with multiple tiny differently colored squares inside its frame."

In this brief sum can be seen a mixture of abstract seemingly impersonal images with some hints of personal material – the embracing naked humans, the linking of masculine and feminine. But the contrast stands out. She is pursuing healing of a lifelong wound of being erased and the analysis and the personal dreams work on this tirelessly it seems and repeatedly. The other images – square, circle, light – call to mind collective symbols in the history of symbolism, They just happen in dreams often without personal associations and point to the psyche's project, so to speak. A parade of images – circularities, quaternities, masculine/feminine, arrays of colors, geometric designs suggest some kind of integration process proceeding over the years.

Jung, I believe, was particularly fascinated with such collective symbols, those primordial images that belong to humankind. They present basic human difficulties of being alive, of how to prepare for death, of how consciousness emerges from the unconscious and can be overcome by it, of a process leading toward wholeness even though it never reaches perfection or conclusion. Combing through symbols of religious dogmas and rituals, cultural icons, myths, legends, alchemical stages, Jung understands them to be concerned with this individuating process. Jung has great knowledge of symbols and shows tremendous interest in their collective shared references across time and differing historical periods, their archetypal patterns, yet he sees these going on in a person's particular personal life.

I am especially interested in where the two viewpoints meet, the immediate moment now with the timeless, the specific locale with the largeness of the vast cosmos. I call the meeting a nexus point as a way of focusing on its vital importance (see chapter 8). Such moments, where the two projects touch, radiate numinous intensity that mark a life and can change it. Jung stresses the importance of such moments for the experience of meaning which makes life liveable.

In commenting on the *prima materia* as found everywhere "the cheapest thing in the world" yet "nothing less than the source of life", Jung notes that when "the patient realizes the extraordinary importance of this story, the real meaning of it, he crosses the Rubicon … we use that metaphor when we make a fateful decision, make up our minds to go across, saying, 'I will risk it'" (Jung 2019, p. 192). The danger is we will not risk it: "If we encounter a situation that requires our wholeness, and fail in this situation, we will have forfeited our wholeness. For we have to put ourselves completely in it, at the risk of being consumed by the fire" (ibid, p. 201).

Further still, in such moments we experience the two basic human projects meeting. The actual details of our finite personal events interpenetrate with the infinite beyond us. Jung writes, "In all of life's highest points in which we face life completely, we also have the feeling of the meaningfulness of life … [that] is always linked to the feeling of eternity" (ibid). But to participate in the meeting and the meaning it confers, we have to contribute our bit, tiny, but essential. This comes from not just consciousness but a peculiar quality of consciousness: "If you do not want to miss the moment, you have to be absolutely attentive. You constantly have to be alert. This means a constant devotion is necessary, a particular exertion of consciousness for healing an unborn state … by reflecting and paying attention." (Jung 2008, pp. 437-438)

To further this quality of devoted attentiveness, let us look more closely at the effects of the meetings of the two points of view.

Seeing Differently

Keeping the overview in mind that two projects direct our becoming who we are in the world, we are nudged to seeing differently. Consciousness has one vector and necessity and the unconscious another as best we can tell because it is what we do not know. Both are needed, indeed required, to live a life knowing life is also living you. Through both those vectors together, fulfillment lies. For example, the banal is just as much a part of our wholeness as is the startling archetypal image. We need the personal associations to the problem or to the dream, our social and embedded-in-the-body context, our psychological situation and particular motivation. Jung remarks, "For practical treatment, it is useless to talk of archetypes and bearskins" (ibid p. 108). It does not help to disclose mythological references; those are just "theoretical tools" (ibid, p. 275). We need to look at the therapeutic issue from both sides – the personal and the psyche's project and not subsume one into the other.

Take the symbol of bread as the archetypal mainstay, the fundament of nourishment, even as the bread of heaven in Christian Eucharist ritual. It only clicks with us, bestowing terrific energy, if we also have already translated the primordial bread image into *my* bread where I tasted its particular meaning for me, like my grandmother handing me a warm piece, or with friends breaking bread together, or of learning to bake it myself. The idiosyncratic meanings bread holds on a personal level--chewing it with pleasure after school, inhaling its scent baking in the oven – meet its primordial image as basic food for survival. Then the impersonal symbol bread opens a door to a profound experience. If I go through that door; I do not know about it, I live in it, it lives in me. Bread has come to me and fed my soul. Or, instead, I have forsaken it, bypassing it in gluttony or in rushing into identifying myself as the powerful bread-giver to others, falling for the first temptation that Jesus resisted in the desert. Receiving I am fed life-giving bread by another, pulls up dependence on the provider and through that personal experience a felt dependence on a Source beyond us feeding us. That basic food given and received allows me to accept my dependence. That yields gratitude. The negative can equally mix the personal and general and exert a profound effect. Associations to no bread, or only dirty hard scraps, touches Scarcity, not Source. That marks us with abandonment, not nurture.

Another example. Jung's notion of Self describes his theory of the total personality including conscious and unconscious, a center ordering the whole that may bestow abundance or a force that can overpower ego. We find primordial symbols of Self down through the ages – castle, city, fountain, garden, stone, diamond, hammer, sword, Word. But each of us needs to find *my* Self for the psyche's (so to speak) promoting Self to make any sense. The collective ageless symbol of this center means little more than intellectual knowing if it does not click with each of our personal experience of a center in us bigger than what we used to think of as us, which turns out of be only our ego. Our idiosyncratic symbol of Self links the primordial into our particular lives. And our particular detail grounds the mere concept into the image's livingness. As Jung says, we build a hut to house the divine.

The traffic goes both ways: the god shows up in our peculiar hut and our hut offers a location for the god's streaming aliveness. Integration means mulling over, attending to what forms such interchanges take and lassoing them into daily living and giving them back to the center from which they arrived. Where and how and in what form did this totality touch us and change our view to a vastly larger context? From whence are we granted a glimpse of where we fit into its expanded compass of reality, that indicates we might have something to contribute to it? We need the particulars of our human experience in order to house the flame, the water, the rush of air, that which plants us deep in earth of primordial image that has informed the human family, as if there before the beginning, touching us now, breaking in on us, blessing us, menacing us, a big event that exceeds our experience and beckons us to see the whole picture. We work to accommodate its penetration and filtering through our whole body, and body of knowledge, even our present culture. Neglecting this work is to leave the big event untethered, unhoused. It is alive, however, and will make its presence felt – blasting our consciousness to bits? Causing a nervous breakdown? Bidding us steadily in gentler terms to greet it and give it a place to live?

The personal and impersonal interpenetrate and bring close the finite with the infinite. For example, Jung is eloquent about facing the shadow in us – those impulses, thoughts, emotions, pictures we want to avoid as a threat to our ego ethics and ideals, flinging us out of the good into the bad. Or out of the bad into the good, mixing up our division of good and evil. The shadow,

> "that tight passage, a narrow door whose painful constriction no one is spared who goes down the deep well. But one must learn to know oneself in order to know who one is. For what comes after the door is … boundless expanse full of unprecedented uncertainty … no inside and no outside, no above and below, no here and no there, no mine and no thine, no good and no bad … where all life floats in suspension, where … the soul of everything begins; where I am indivisibly this *and* that; where I experience the other

in myself and the other-than-myself experiences me." (Jung 1939/1959, para 45)

Thus "our concern with the unconscious has become a vital question … of spiritual being or nonbeing" (ibid, para 51). We need both points of view to navigate a life of our own in relation to life with others in the world and in relation to the beyond.

The personal project with all its problems, plots, events, both joyous and sorrowful, anchors us in space and time. The psyche's project opens that door on the boundless infinite. Here we experience the piercing of space/time barriers in the psychoid dimension of psyche where conscious differentiations and definitions no longer rule. Here we are touched by a level that belongs to every one of us. All that is, belongs to this moment, squeezing the whole into the narrow particular event. Opposites dwell together, and are distinct, not merged, not blurred: life and death, terrible and wondrous, abundant and stark. If able to bear this sense of everything there bubbling and quiet, chaos is also experienced as abundance (Ulanov 2017, pp. 41, 48, 52, 65).

On the chaos side, an analysand repeatedly stymied in her work, feeling disorganized because overwhelmed, illustrates the disarray: "Too much is going on and I cannot see everything whirling around me and so fast I cannot see what the things are. I am at the hub of the wheel and fear all is going to collide on me. If it gets too close or too big, it could destroy me, kill me, shred me. It would pull out my hair. I am bald." And then the fatal question: "What's wrong with me? I can't even make a list of what needs to be done. I get so panicked I just have to go away, look at a movie, disappear." That repeated difficulty reaches all the way to feeling basically flawed and in threat of extinction.

The rest of us who do not have this particular disorganization difficulty, nonetheless if we have looked into the 'deep well' of our shadow, resonate with this terror of being basically flawed, under threat of whirling into nothingness. We too will feel helpless. Like this analysand with the whirling chaos pulling all her hair out, leaving her bald with no resource of simple thinking, we too confront our inferior function, that missing fourth that the psyche's project seems to promote toward consciousness. This analysand said her incapacity was her thinking that she could never get hold of. If she managed to do a list, she soon misplaced it, hence could not use it to order and stop the whirl. Unlocated and unreliable to be used, the undependable thinking pulls out all her potential growing thoughts, leaving her bald, hairless, thoughtless, exposed to the fear of going into overwhelm. Added to this inner disarray, she faced a lack of validation and support of her work from her supervisors. Instead, they required her to hand in additional reports on the sequence of tasks in her duties.

The Fourth Function

The problem belongs to all of us of the inferior function as the missing fourth of our four functions of thinking opposite to feeling, intuition opposite to sensation, as Jung sees it. One function will be deemed superior and the habitual way of relating to self and world; a second, also well used but definitely secondary to the first superior function; a third still less developed but to some degree still available; and the fourth really inferior, not easily developed let alone used effectively. It is slow, clumsy, unadapted to conscious customs and purposes (see Jung 1921, paras 763-764; see also Ulanov 2007, pp. 168-173; Ulanov 2014, pp. 87-102).

We suffer this 'incapacity,' Jung's first name in his *Red Book* for the inferior function left undeveloped in us. His is feeling, he says. Hence its redemption means developing concentrated noticing and tending its manifestations and personifications, (whereas for my patient, I believe, it is thinking that needs to develop to catch her from falling into an abyss of chaos.) We all suffer fear of such threat of overwhelm breaking out of us in wailing, despair and anger at facing such a substandard thing in us. We get summoned to that task and feel helpless in confronting it. How to pull it into consciousness to be used, along with the three functioning capacities, this missing fourth that is called in alchemy renegade, wild, that runs away, will not join, yet is also the One superior to all the others.

That paradox of being inferior and superior simultaneously stems from the fourth function residing in and being left in the unconscious, penetrated by all that is there – archaic energies, historical relics, former ways of residing in symbol or ritual seemingly outgrown by our developing consciousness and discarded as 'primitive,' but still active unconsciously as primordial thoughts, impulses, affects and imagery. We glimpse this archaic 'language' in idiosyncratic gestures of hastily making a cross or engaging in a disgusting secret habit or a compelling apotropaic ritual that cannot be traced to any cause in our personal past. We see, for example, through smell not sight – something fishy about the economy or get an intuitive inkling a pandemic is coming before salient facts are known.

Jung makes the pivotal point: the fourth is different from the three functions capable of becoming at our conscious disposal; it is different not just in degree of development, but different also in kind. The fourth function, the missing one, is immersed in unconsciousness and its collective nature. We cannot just detach it from the unconscious and make it conscious because it has been penetrated by the unconscious and resides there. When we touch the inferior function, it is not separable from its embedded state in unconscious but brings the whole unconscious with it. It cannot just be lifted up to consciousness and function like the other ones already somewhat habituated and adapted. It is like lifting the floor of consciousness and upsetting the basis of the conscious mind.

We feel threat of a total collapse of consciousness, its destabilization, and we react with hatred. I mean hatred. We want to kill this alien incapacity, pronounce it 'nothing!' get rid of it. Like my patient, we fear it will pull out all our hair and shred us. Or dreams will feature the dream ego taking aim to shoot this enemy, to make it not exist. Goethe in *Faust* pictures it as the devil – that brand of intellectualizing that picks to pieces and kills the value of ordinary feeling relatedness. As Jung puts it, "The devil is the disintegrator par excellence, the destroyer" (Jung 2019, p. 260).

I think of Riccardo Lombardi (psychoanalyst, psychiatrist and doctor of medicine) who works with patients suffering from psychosis. They, he says, suffer from a primitive mind-body split. They hate their body and disembody themselves because the pain that they cannot bear has been lodged in the body (Lombardi 2016, pp. 131, 135-137). But living disembodied means forsaking space/time location in the here and now, uprooting finite life. This is a danger, not a solution. Like my patient who has to leave her disorganized work entirely and go look at a happy ending Hallmark movie to recover from the inwardly attacking accusation that basically, "something is wrong with me," other analysands describe a similar alarm. One said, "My mind is slipping sideways;" another said, "I'm a scared little boy running from terror;" still another says, "When I look inside me all the way down, there's nothing there." Confrontation with the inferior function bringing up the entire unconscious lifting off its moorings, upends the foundations of the human mind. As Jung puts it, "the whole system shakes" (Jung 2019, p. 264). Hence we reject the inferior function in us.

But the fourth function is also the One, superior to all the others, the rejected stone that becomes the cornerstone. What is at stake is the whole risk of life; and it comes to many of us as it did to Jung's dreamer and to Jung himself, despite fear and danger he "felt it came up to him, and he had to face it no matter what the risk was" (ibid).

The psyche's project presses to include all that belongs to us, the inferior too. This comes to each of us. We get to respond yea or nay to such a confrontation. With it, we are called to concern for the whole, for seeing multiple points of view, and that God (or what we put in place of God) could present in any form. I think of an anguished question a widow (with a brilliant superior thinking function) asked her beloved partner now dead. In conversation that felt real not invented, the widow asked, but how do I know you are not just my unconscious speaking, and the partner retorts, how else am I going to reach you except through the unconscious, implying that is the best way to circumvent all the arguments and reasoning the widow can fall into and be tortured by. I laughed when I heard this truth so simply put. We need both projects to live from the basics.

Disidentification of the Archetypal and the Actual Object

A task we all face, with good and bad results, in multiple variations, is separating an object from the archetype. Let the two projects – the personal individual and the psyche's – be differentiated, not identified. It is an ordinary part of development eventually to distinguish the mother, or father, from their archetypal images. Let the actual parent be a real person and let the archetypal image be a real image. Each has its powerful impact.

The archetype and the person are NOT identical (Jung 2008, p. 72). If they are, the child is threatened. As one man experienced, one can get trapped in the earliest infant archetypal bond as he remained with his father and lose one's mortal life.

His parent would take his son into his bed in the early morning at the son's earliest ages of 1-3 years forming a blissful merging full of eros. In the face of that numinous experience, no actual partner of either sex could ever measure up, leaving the little boy without a life partner as adult man. This inability in various forms was impotence – physical, sexual, in achieving what he set out to do, in committing to a job, in handling his inherited money. Robbed of robust personal life, when an archetypal event appears, we lack the raw material with which to deal with it, work it through, able to choose to let it go, having enough good stuff of finite experiences to filtrate the intense beam of archetypal mana. Blown away, breaking down, or lured to destruction (see chapter 2), we miss the blessings of finitude and feel exiled from the infinite.

To identify the archetypal good mother, the great one of unconditional loving with one's ordinary mother, or, if she herself falls into identification with that image, leaves the witch side of the mother who devours to roam free and come up anywhere. (Ulanov A. and Ulanov, B. 1987, chapters II and VI). She feeds on the child, blood-sucking their consciousness away from human congress into the desiccated woods, where nothing grows and bones lie about. We need both worlds – the personal with real people we cherish and come up against, and the archetypal with real primordial images that constellate basic psychic patterns that influence our living. We need to differentiate the two energies; they may interpenetrate but should not persist in a state of identity. Let the archetypal penetrate, bid, impress, beckon, turn up, but not eclipse daily fare. And let daily fare know about those events of wonder, wrestle them, but not be encapsulated in them, not locked in grudge and letting your whole life slip by unfulfilled, taking so long to get the point that it is hard to see there is a point anymore. Like the creator of geometry the point is the beginning, turning into a line, then a plane, then describing a level or a bounded object. All life grows up.

A third example of identifying the archetypal with the person, and the psyche's project with the personal aim is the mix-up that happens when the anima or animus is used by the ego to relate to outer reality in the world. More specifically, we lose the real function of the contrasexual factor to relate to the unconscious, as mediating between ego and Self. If instead projected onto and identified with a real person in the world, serious negative results may happen. One becomes obsessed with or possessed by the object with which the anima or animus is projectively identified. That can lead to emotional and physical abuse as the object carries one's projected ideal and must be punished for deviating from it.

More simply put, the contrasexual factor is archetypal and ill-suited to function in down to earth ways with a partner who also has demands from their ownmost life, from children, from taxes. Further, if dominated by the archetypal, we miss the wonders, the blessings of relationships where the persons involved are full of their own contact with their unconscious as it beams through their daily interactions but does not substitute for them in such crude forms as always being right, dictating the spiritual truth, or in mood swings and guilt makings (for examples see Ulanov A. and B. 1994, pp. 5-9, 68-80).

If the anima/us fulfills its function as relating to the unconscious, the personal project is enriched by steady fueling from unconscious psychic project and the psyche's project gets housed in ordinary living, not kidnapped, but recognized as going on in one's life too. People speak, for instance, of finding their vocation. "Looking back," as one man said, "I see I was where I belonged;" he had followed his destiny. The psyche's project, often shown in dream images that express ancient human patterns, even cosmic ones, and types of transformations all of which prove helpful references for the personal problem the individual is trying to solve (Jung 2009, 362-363).

An example of the benefits of seeing two points of view is recognizing how when we are conscious and unconscious we seem to experience time differently. If we have living access to both viewpoints; we have both senses of time. Jung puts it, "Consciousness is: *this* time, *this* here and now. Consciousness wants to let everything appear as a *here and now.* The unconscious ... is an eternity, a timelessness, and has no intentions regarding the here and now. Accordingly, the values are also on a quite different level." (Jung 2008, p. 80)

If we accept both experiences, our sense of time is expanded. Consciousness follows a chronological sequence "in temporal succession ... in the unconscious ... everything lies together" (ibid, p. 360). That heap of all angles and tenses together suggest to me the abundance of the psychoid level. Contact with that psychoid level of abundance can relieve our fretting about time running out and not enough time to do the task at hand. Like my patient suffering disorganization and losing even her list ordering the tasks to be done, we see we are proceeding according to a conscious sense of time. Priorities are strictly in order of first, second, third. But the unconscious sense of time is nudging through and reorients the whole scheme. It may also bring a felt sense of plenty, even of liberation from the one, two, three dictating schedule, or the chaos that threatens if she fails to keep up the tempo. Instead, there are many ways to take up tasks, and the possibility of reordering to begin with the most appealing and accessible step. Then the rest of the tasks miraculously begin to fall into place. The disaster of messing up the preordained order and feeling a failure dissolve, giving way to the value of what might be enjoyable.

Different views of death become visible by recognizing the two projects going on in us. For consciousness death is the end, the finish, the liberation from woes, the period at the end of our sentence. The soul leaves the body which is no more, decaying into 'remains.' For the unconscious, death is "something other than what we think" and turns up in many different ways (ibid, p. 343). Jung writes, "Psychologically correct thinking … always retains its connection with … the depths of the psyche, the tap-root … nature prepares itself for death" (Jung 1945/1960, para 808). Death is the beginning and the end, the earth from which we are born and to which we return, from dust to dust in the ritual words of religions. It is not cessation but the narrative of the immortal part that Jung says is the collective in the unconscious that lives on, while the mortal part ceases. It is as if the unconscious wants to convey in image or dream: "'You will have experiences of an immortal one, namely experiences of the collective unconscious,' because the collective unconscious is the immortal substance in man. Conscious is mortal … but our mind is based upon a layer of the psyche that is everywhere and always there … we might call it the immortal part of man" (Jung 2019, p. 315). To repeat, "The collective unconscious is not oneself – it is collective like an objective event an objective fact. That is a fact, that is not a projection, it is not an opinion, and moreover it does not belong exactly to my own psyche, despite the fact that it influences my psyche" (ibid, p. 174).

Amplification and Interpretation

In practice, how to work with materials that come up in every analysis shows the different emphases aligned with these two projects in which we are engaged. Personal amplification draws on an analysand's particular associations to a dream image or a specific conflict or hope that surfaces in the session. This is not just general talking that will be drawn to whatever complex threatens to be a 'mousetrap' to the analysand. Attention is directed to focus on the specific item on hand – to this table that surfaces in a memory of the conflict that exploded sundering the man's relation to his father when sitting across that table; that table also appeared in a following dream when a man he did not like (a shadow figure) sat across from him; that table the man suddenly said is like the analyst's table serving as her desk. These directed associations amplify the total psychological context out of which this item surfaced – environmental, relational, social and the transference/countertransference field (Jung 2008, p. 275; see also Winborn 2019, pp. 107-108, 125-127). We also note in what forms did the emotional associations to the table come forth – shouting, weeping, moping, silent stubbornness, rage, grief, remorse, love? What is the body expressing while the tale is told? Hyper-breathing, holding his breath? Jumping up and striding around? Jung calls personal amplification a gathering into consciousness the living time and space details of what the analysand is telling. The aim is to gain understanding of the subjective meaning of the table, the world it opens up through dream image, memory, transference.

Archetypal, or earlier called ethno-psychological, amplification (Jung 2008, pp. 28, 136) gathers parallels from human endeavors in mythology, religions, symbology, history, folklore, ethnology, nature itself (growth patterns of the tree, of animals, of earth, air, water and fire, social movements, cosmic references) that are pertinent to the specific item, task, dream image, and archetypal image around which the mousetrap of the patient's complex circles. Such motifs present as if there before beginning to note a beginning, there *a priori.* The relevant motifs set the individual problem or talent in the larger setting of objective human patterns and possibilities. The healing effect of this objective psyche, albeit unconscious but there in our collective history, sets a personal problem in a larger human context. Jung writes, "Just take a look once at how much ill persons suffer if they do not find expression for their inner contents, and how much it means to them when they find a mythical expression for them" (ibid, p. 139). This view tries to see "What nature herself tried to do to that man" (Jung 2019, p. 245).

If we stay only on the personal level, then it only gets more personal round and round with ego strategies to fix the problem. But they do not work and only make us feel more entangled and hopeless.

Jung is criticized for archetypal emphasis as if it rises above the nitty gritty of the work of analysis into intellectualizing about archetypal motifs. His theory can be misused that way. But that is to misunderstand what Jung is getting at, I suggest. We are released from isolation in our madness or even in our smaller neurosis when we see our struggle is a version of a human struggle that many have suffered and worked on. We are pushed beyond ego deflation of isolation and humiliation of having such a problem. We join the community of this tribe. (See Ulanov 2001 as example of belonging to the Ivy League of violent poison ivy). We are pushed beyond ego inflation that our schemes can manage life and we will crack the code. Here we join the other sufferers and learn to listen in to what psyche's dreams and symptoms, may be aiming toward.

There is a compensatory function of the unconscious to the entanglements of consciousness and we may learn to trust in it if we perceive its patterns through the ages. The psyche is self-regulatory like the body. We may relinquish desperate attempts to control the outcome and wait instead on the psyche speaking its language of image, affect, impulse, growing toward a renewal, even a rebirth. Jung is not avoiding the personal except in setting it into a larger bowl of human suffering and tales about it where "dangerous destruction and ineffable creativity touch each other" (Bisagni 2021, p. 821). Even further, we glimpse life itself working toward initiations of a wholeness that includes all our mistakes as well as our best efforts and original perceptions and formulations. The point here is that the personal project and the psyche's project both matter and get included in ordinary analytical work, the tiny penetrating the whole and the huge wholeness penetrating the tiny of each of us. Jung sums up the two projects in his approach to the dream: "I stay with the original image. I understand nothing of the dream ... I amplify an existing image until it becomes visible" (Jung 2009, p. 28). Personal amplification seeks "the subjective meaning of the dream;" Archetypal amplification looks into the "universal image" and for that "we have to know what is in the storeroom of the human mind" (Jung 2009, pp. 26-28).

If we keep both projects in mind in the work of analysis, a symbolic process becomes visible. On the personal level our vexing symptom, for example, shows as well a symbolic representation of what we push out of consciousness because it is too painful and/or indicates a direction toward healing. Hence the concrete thing we want to be rid of also manifests as a communication from our depths to our conscious mind and enlists our participation. Further, the symbolic process itself enforces action, which may be a surprise. It is anything but wordy intellectualizing. It is anything but rising out of the body to airy thoughts detached from actual relationships to others and to collective consciousness. Symbolic processes demand we "dive in" and voluntarily as that turns a danger into the less dangerous. "You can never individuate if the process does not happen in reality" (Jung 2019, p. 333).

Jung writes, "Symbolic thinking is thinking by doing ... that somehow has to do with the sequence of life ... The dream leads us into an action, into an experience, that no longer corresponds to conscious experience ... we again live in that kind of instinctual experience that is characteristic of the nature of unconscious activity. We experience archetypal situations ... that human kind has experienced from time immemorial ... We go there to get something. As a rule, it is a valuable treasure ... this is about bringing up an archetypal value" (Jung 2008, pp. 161-162). Symbolic thinking connects with ethics of everyday life. And we always come up again against the wonder of this life – the eyelashes of a giraffe, the fear of the appearance of huge shaggy wild goats taking over a road in a town in Wales, running up and down it and gobbling the hedges lining the way while the citizens shelter in their houses due to lockdown in the pandemic. We must never lose our capacity to laugh out loud at the seriously funny in life.

This chapter was written during the pandemic spring 2020. Material from it was presented to the Montreal Jungian Society April 2021, to senior candidates of the C.G. Jung Institute of San Francisco May 2021, to 23rd Conference "Faith and Knowledge in Analytical Psychology" Ural Association of Analytical Psychology and Psychoanalysis at Yekaterinburg Russia, and to Jung on the Hudson July 2021. All these presentations were on zoom.

References

Basagni, F. 2020. "The landscapes of the minus: hatred, adolescence, and the paradox of growth" *Journal of Analytical Psychology* vol. 65, no. 5, pp. 818-838.

Jung, C, G, 1921. *Psychological Types Collective Works* 6. Trans R.F.C. Hull. Princeton, N.J.: Princeton University Press.

— 1933/1960. "The stages of life" *The Structure and Dynamics of the Psyche Collected Works* 8. Trans. R.F.C. Hull. Princeton, N.J.: Princeton University Press, paras 749-795.

— 1939/1954. "The development of the personality" *The Development of the Personality CW* 17. Trans. R.F.C. Hull. Princeton, N.J.: Princeton University Press, paras 284-323.

— 1939/1959. "The archetypes of the unconscious" *The Archetypes of the Unconscious Collected Works* 9:1. Trans. R.F.C. Hull. Princeton, N.J.: Princeton University Press, paras 1-88.

— 1945/1960. "soul and death" *CW 8*, paras 796-815.

— 1960. "The structure of the psyche" *CW* 8, paras 216-342.

— 2008. *Children's Dreams: Note from the Seminar Given in 1936-1940.* Eds. Lorenz Jung and Maria Meyer-Grass. Trans. Ernst Falzeder with collaboration of Tony Woolfson. Philemon Series. Princeton, N.J.: Princeton University Press.

— 2019. *Dream Symbols of Individuation: Notes of C.G. Jung's Seminars on Wolfgang Pauli's Dreams.* Ed. Suzanne Gieser. Philemon Series. Princeton, N.J.: Princeton University Press.

Lombardi, R. 2016. *Formless Infinity Clinical Explorations of Matte Blanco and Bion.* Trans. Karen Christenfeld, Gina Atkinson, Andrea Sabbadini and Philip Slotkin. London and New York: Routledge.

Ulanov, A. and Ulanov B. 1987. *The Witch and the Clown: Two Archetypes of Human Sexuality.* Asheville N.C.: Chiron.

— 1994. *Transforming Sexuality, The Archetypal World of Anima and Animus.* Boston: Shambhala.

Ulanov, A.B. 1996. *Attacked by Poison Ivy: A Psychological Understanding.* York Beach Maine: Nicolas-Hayes Inc.

— 2007. *The Unshuttered Heart: Opening to Aliveness and Deadness in the Self.* Nashville, Tn.: Abingdon Press.

— 2014/2019. "The inferior function" *Knots and Their Untying Essays on Psychological Dilemmas.* Einsiedeln, Switzerland: Daimon.

Winborn, M. 2019. *Interpretation and Jungian Analysis.* London and New York: Routledge.

Chapter 2:

The Lure of Destructiveness

Lure is a strong word. A word usually followed by the other words – to lure 'away,' or 'into' (Webster's dictionary). Here it means to entice with some form of bait and to attract back again with a promise of reward, like a falconer with food for the circling hawk. I use it as a strong word, including to ensnare, trap, enthrall. For I link it here with destructiveness that can bind us in a spell. The 'lure' is its fascination. But the shock is that we are vulnerable to falling into destructiveness again; it could happen, even though we dread its happening. We are half aware of a danger we have semi emerged from, yet here! now! it could happen again! How could this be any 'reward'?

Fascination and Dizzying

Fascinated, lured to the power of destructiveness, we sense we could be complicit in bringing it about, whereas before it happened to us like a thunderclap from the outside. Then, we discovered we had fallen into, or suffered from the impact of an event, with no understanding how it had come about. Only that it was horrifying, a disaster rendering us helpless. But now, fascination alerts us we could be captivated again but this time with the knowledge we participated, did what we did not want to do. It crops up again, hits us from outside ourselves, and yet also results from something inside ourselves. The space we won between it and ourselves is there, yet still too small. We are too near its power to trip us up to make a terrible mistake. It is not our intentional 'accidental' happening, but nonetheless something that could occur, as if we are overpowered by its allure. Dread fills us.

Examples are various: not putting in the word 'not' in the sentence so that it reads we want to do X. Somehow hitting the delete button and it obliterates the carefully crafted report for the critical business meeting, or proposal for resolution of community conflict meeting, or the checks electronically deposited into the bank account, so that the valuable thing disappears. Or, somehow before we know it, sticking the drug filled needle into our vein again, or gulping down the oblivion making pill again; or, bypassing thought, just looking at the feared email; or with careful thought but no sense of its meaning or consequence, making the finely delineated cut on our arm, or, just stuffing into our mouth the binge food once more. The terrible 'mistake' could occur! The limits we built as safeguards hold but threaten to break. It is not being overrun by blind impulse, for we know the slipup could happen; we hang as if suspended in terror over this chasm into which we could fall. We are attracted back again as if into a pattern that had held us captive. Its power to seduce has weakened but not disappeared. We cringe at the thought we could find ourselves doing the very thing we would do everything to avoid, flee.

This emotional field calls to mind Kierkegaard and Tillich building on S.K., both emphasizing the "dizzying" effect of falling into existence. Kierkegaard writes,

> "Dread is the dizziness of freedom which occurs when the spirit posits the synthesis [of body and soul], and freedom then gazes down into its own possibility, grasping at finiteness to sustain itself. In this dizziness freedom succumbs. Further than this psychology cannot and will not go. That very instant everything is changed, and when freedom rises again it sees that it is guilty. Between these two extremes lies the leap, which no science has explained or can explain." (Kierkegaard 1957, p. 55)

We leap into our own possibility and into consciousness of being spirit which is soul united with body. Spirit is a living synthesis of body and soul that Kierkegaard sees as our true nature, and sin leaps in through excesses in either direction – too much soul seeking at expense of body living or too much indulgence of body at the cost of soul. Our innocence is ignorance of being determined as spirit. In this innocence

> "there is nothing to strive with ... But what effect does nothing produce? It begets dread. This is the profound secret of innocence, that at the same time it is dread. Dreamingly the spirit projects its own reality, but this reality is nothing ... Dread is a qualification of the dreaming spirit ... The reality of spirit constantly shows itself in a form which entices its possibility, but it is away as soon as one grasps after it" (ibid, pp. 37- 38; see also pp. 27, 33, 39).

In innocence dread manifests itself as thirst for adventure or the mysterious. Soul and body exist in innocence but not united except by spirit, so spirit is there in innocence but disturbs it as dread of possibility of "*being able*" (ibid, p. 40). Dread "signifies two things: the dread in which the individual posits sin by the qualitative leap; and the dread which entered along with sin, and which for this reason comes also into the world quantitatively every time an individual posits sin" (ibid, p. 49).

Thus coming into existence, our freedom making the leap, also means coming into awareness of good and evil, here under exploration of the theological notion of 'original sin.' Theology cannot do without psychology or it stands above the depth of existence where we are in it, in good and evil in the daily turn.

Tillich links coming into existence with falling into sin, and freedom as the means by which we belong to the infinite but are also excluded from it because we are finite. Thus our freedom is finite freedom. We move from an essential potentiality to existing actually but estranged from our total nature which includes relation to the infinite but in a freedom that is finite. We live "excluded from infinity to which [we] belong (Tillich 1957, p. 31). We are driven beyond "dreaming innocence" of "non-actualized potentiality" by consciousness of our finitude which we experience as anxiety [dread] of being a mixture of finite and infinite "a mixture of being and non-being, or of being threatened by non-being … freedom is united with anxiety" (ibid, pp. 34-35). "In the state of innocence freedom and destiny are in harmony, but neither of them is actualized." We are anxious of losing our potentialities by actualizing our self and losing our existence if we do not actualize our self. "He [sic] stands between the preservation of his dreaming innocence without experiencing the actuality of being and the loss of his innocence through knowledge, power, and guilt, The anxiety of this situation is the state of temptation" (ibid, p. 36).

Kierkegaard and Tillich are exploring the large universal issue of good and evil, sin and guilt, infinite and finite, and on the level of individual choice and refusal of choice. They each give many arresting examples of these themes which show a background influence on the lure of destructiveness I am describing that happens to individuals. Behind the specific lure, there is the mystery of good and evil and their relationship. Kierkegaard describes objective and subjective dread, dread of the good, the dread of evil, shutupness. Tillich describes existential estrangement individually and collectively, estrangement as unbelief, as hubris, as concupiscence.

For Kierkegaard sin is condition, not caused by a single act. But the act gives evidence of the condition into which we have fallen and from which we need liberation by a source outside ourselves. Living in spirit, of our body and soul united, our mortal and eternal natures together, is living in the good. Disturbance, or worse, fleeing from that synthesis is what we know as evil up close. Tillich recognizes this wholeness of infinite and finite as our true self from which we become estranged when we fall into existence. We live estranged, our society is estranged: "Man [sic] as he exists is not what he essentially is and ought to be. He is estranged from his true being … [implying] that one belongs essentially to that from which one is estranged" (ibid, p. 45). Evil is the disorder of this estrangement, felt as exile, emotions of hostility, acts of perjury. Estrangement does not replace sin in Tillich's thought, for sin recognizes "the personal act of turning away from that to which one belongs" (ibid, p. 46).

My emphasis on lure of destructiveness is one small subset of this larger universal condition that happens to each of us as potentially living spirit as unity of body and soul but failing to do so. We fall into a condition where we struggle to become actually a unity of body and soul, of living our ownmost life fully, not falling into unlived life as if dead before we die. Further, as Jung tells us in *The Red Book*, that unlived life keeps the dead in a restless unpeaceful condition. Because they did not live what they should have they are driven to seek the answer why (Jung 2009, pp. 349-352). Kierkegaard talks about our struggle to live as spirit in a unity of body and soul. Tillich speaks of conscious union of essence and existence and essence under God. Their focus takes us right to the mystery of relation of good and evil.

What I am describing is particular to some individuals. I have not found the lure to destructiveness in all my analysands;

there may be moments in each case, but not a captivity. That moment echoes the large human condition and the existential question we all face, namely the power of evil facing us. The lure I am focusing on threatens destructiveness to self or to other or to a vision of a whole life. Seduced by attraction into specific destructiveness idiosyncratic to each of us yet there as possible for all of us annuls our sense of agency. It effects destructive results like falling off the wagon of the alcoholic or the relapse into a former and now conscious enthrallment to harmful actions toward self and others.

This subset of being caught in destructiveness is worth considering as it casts light on the existential questions even if we want to ignore good and evil and their relationship. Mysteriously enticed into some 'mistake,' something wrong we do, we need to remember Ricoeur's insight in examining Job's plight: we cannot reduce sin to the scandal of fault. The 'mistake' echoes possibility of doing something wrong, grievously wrong and destructive but we cannot indulge self-excoriation for our "badness." That just adds blaming to the excess or the minus of the fascinating action or attitude that snared us. Evil is mysterious, as is good, not a problem permanently fixed and disposed of. The subset of lure of destructiveness dwells within the background of good and evil and their relationship as a frightening, beguiling, terrible, repellent yet hopeful interweaving in myth and legend. Here is the serpent whose serum is poison yet related to a seed that will blossom out of the affliction. The magical pharmakon of the doctor as medicine man is redemptive, yet if too strong a dosage, lethal. The serpent's bite is fatal yet linked to the birth of consciousness of new beginning, marked off from the old now labeled as before, prior, whose destruction makes space for rebirth or its failure.

In sum: the lure of destructiveness pulls, fascinates, terrorizes we will land again committing even if not meaning to the mistake fatal to one's self, one's work or relationship. Something actually happens, not just by omission but involving secret – less than conscious – participation and action. We do it and dread we will do it and experience all the horror of what doing it will make happen. Yet it happens to us!

An analysand who successfully climbed out of alcoholism and for over a decade stayed not only sober but free of desire to drink, when in a new place with new people and anxiousness about fitting in at a small dinner party, remembers saying to a waiter asking what she wants to drink, Oh, I'll have what she is having, gesturing to her neighbor. That 'innocent' glass of wine reproduced an entire destructiveness again. She 'came to' many hours later naked and collapsed in her shower. Helplessness, utter and devastating, ensues, hopelessness that once again we are in it and will never get out of this injurious pattern.

Other examples involve more worried anticipation – a physical clenching – did I do it again? Oh my God if I pressed delete when I did not see it and was avoiding it – is the poem all gone? Did I mistakenly click and 'log out' all my files instead of just 'shut down' to close the computer so my entire file of work vanished? Did I once again not notice where I put the wallet? the keys? Am I locked out now a second time? Did I vow to keep my mouth shut and out darted the sharp arrow of criticism that once again felled my mate? Did I blank out when driving and not see the car coming from my left? Did I fear I would start screaming in this tense racial meeting so I dictated what everyone should be doing? Did I turn my face away again from my small child trying to look me in the eye? Am I again just going to disappear from connection to others, just not answer their communicating, not show up, even though I know it will hurt them? Will I just blurt again instead of reflect? Cut off instead of work through, become a stone?

Our vigilance feels like a persecution and it fails; we are taken over. Jung describes what produces such a takeover: "we are possessed by an affect … because we completely identify with it. For in the affect we can *totally* be what we feel. That is why it has something fascinating about it." But, Jung adds, that is a childlike state where "we forget we are also the other" (Jung 2008, p. 98). We are captive: "But what possess us is an autonomous complex, which has seized power over the whole or a great part of the psyche" (Jung 2014, p. 141). Hence the nonchalance, without any remembering of the hard work of getting a self free of drink; hence the careless dismissal of the effects of our falling into a ruinous pattern again; hence the not knowing enough the emotional truth hiding in the lure that needs to surface and be faced, the emotions we neglect to notice. Caught in the lure, we are not in our bodies, not in space/time embodiment of our finite lives (Jung 2008, p. 184). We need to step out of the primordial into the limits of finitude, into life.

Soul matters

In the transference/countertransference field, we need to look at what the Self is engineering by this state of luredom (see Ulanov 2007, pp. 189-192). This is different from working out personal issues in relation to the analyst who carries our projections of parents or of their opposites. This is to do with being and nonbeing and what functions for the analysand as the spirit or the transcendent god in which conscious and unconscious, finite and infinite, body and soul unite and foster the project of our becoming more whole. It concerns what the analysand believes about the ultimate. We might say this is a soul issue.

Jung writes of loss of soul when the lure shows up in the form of anima or animus complex put into a person who appears in an analysand's life. Yet Jung comments that destruction can also happen if the man falls prey to the anima and marries someone who does not correspond to that type (Jung 2008, p. 315). If sexuality is involved too then the combustion is powerful, even explosive. But anima or animus may be projected into a mentor, a political leader, into someone who seems to promise the key to what life is all about, to a love and even more a service to something beyond oneself. The catch is to get the inner anima/us and the outer person differentiated and connected with oneself. If the sexual sizzle and extravagant libido that the animating projection constellates does not fuel the partnership it can lure one away from it. Not on good terms with this anima/us personification of the unconscious, the commitment to the other person falls dead, or withers and one is drawn off course from full living of desire. Or one may wander into serial liaisons as if hunting for the lost soul but come away feeling one has wasted something precious and been unkind to the partners (the original one and the subsequent ones) one chose.

The anima or animus functions to communicate with the unconscious. It positions a bridge of communication between ego and Self; it does not negotiate well in the real world (see Ulanov A. and B. 1994, pp. 10-13 and notes 10 and 11). In a man's case, if he is not attuned to this function the opposite problem may erupt where his anima wants him all to herself, so to speak, and sabotages through moods, touchy misunderstandings, narcissistic wounds, the actual relationship to another person. She hogs him to herself. I discovered this in one analysis through the shock of feeling jealous of the man's new love relationship which he all but wrecked in berating his beloved for her former partner choices and her 'unconsciousness'. I was shocked because the jealousy felt emotionally real yet not mine. It was incomprehensible to me as I was in love deeply with my husband. It was as if I was carrying something intensely alive but not *my* jealousy, though it lived in me.

After much work on myself it hit me: I was carrying his anima reaction to his new love (Ulanov 1982, pp. 68-85).* It was

* Three levels of countertransference are noted by most schools of depth psychology. The first are analysts' 'normal' idiosyncratic styles of response

as if she was yelling, what about me? What do you think you are doing going off with this new woman, and ignoring me. No! Hence the nasty words and moods and negative judgements welled up in him to burst forth attacking the new person. But the issue was his unconsciousness of his own anima relationship, so to speak, and 'her' function to connect him with his experience of the unconscious in himself.

This is an odd but deep tangle with narcissism different from its more obvious presentations. This is a private narcissism often in people of talent, ambition and accomplishment. There is an odd inflection in their self-presentation, having to put themselves first; on hearing another's work as if to say the other's work confirms their own. They lasso the other into serving their own work. The dazzle of the narcissist shows in this attitude of I got there first or I already know about this. They refuse the other's otherness and their own need to learn something they did not know that somebody else does know. This is a soul issue, not a persona one as their talent shows well; this is like a refusal of the something more beyond the ego. The ego armors itself with what it appropriates from the other rather than regarding the other's otherness and serving what transcends the ego.

We traced down the explosive rage and wounded humiliation to roots in embarrassing doubts. Was he as good as her former partners? Could he trust his judgment to give himself into this new relationship, as he was still haunted by the breakdown into divorce of his previous marriage? Did he make another perilous choice by falling in love with her and was her judgement faulty?

---

and work. The second is an area where analysts have more work to do on unresolved conflicts in themselves that intrude on the work with analysands. The third, called 'objective' are responses evoked by the analysand's behavior and personality that provide analysts with valuable clues to what is going on in the patient. Jungians note a fourth category of countertransference, where a patient's transference activates an archetype-centered process of individuation in both analysand and analyst (Ulanov 1982, p. 73).

What did he deeply believe in this big experience about love? Was he up to it? What if he was wrong in his feelings about her? And what about his neglect of tending his own woundedness instead of attacking hers? What about his own connection to the animating soul connection to living? Was he tending that?

Once these questions surfaced and occupied our attention in the sessions, my 'jealousy' evaporated. It was as if we turned to his anima and her life in him, no longer just giving all attention to his new relationship. 'She' had her place in his attention now. We faced the task of making room for both relationships – to the new woman who captured his heart and to the anima function within that began to function as a bridge to his experience of the Self. Jung notes that when anima or animus begins to function, its personifications disappear.

Three relationships caught our attention. The connection between him and me flowed with more simple ease with my jealousy dissolving; he began to take notice of the anima part I had been carrying for him. Connection between him and the new woman grew and thrived, and connection between his conscious ego and the anima functioning to relate him with the Self began to take its shape. Further, a fourth was added to our attention: relationship between his daily life and the intense sense of meaning, emotional purpose, soul connection to meaningfulness, indeed, a kind of enlistment into service of what transcended and interpenetrated the unfolding of the three relationships.

I remained impressed by the intensity of soul demands and the peril of neglecting them. This was serious business to get connected to the larger dimension of falling in love and the unity of claiming as much of Self as one could stand and meditating on being initiated into service to something beyond oneself. Technically speaking, through a process of projective identification I was for a while holding an anima part missing from his conscious engagement. It got lodged in me. As

I became aware of this unconscious communication from this anima part of him, so outraged at being eclipsed by his absorption in the new relationship, I could speak for her, the anima, and use it in conversation with him. When relation to this bridge to a deeper engagement with himself began to lodge in him, some changes happened. A connection became more visible between lambasting and humiliating his new beloved for having numerous partners before him, connected with his anima lambasting him for neglecting to pay attention to her, and he unloaded this barrage of scolding criticism onto his partner. Building these connections brought relief to all three of us – him, his new partner and me and maybe a fourth too, the anima now playing her rightful part lived as an effecting function, may we say between him and his soul.

Paradoxically, tending to himself relieved much of the hidden narcissism whereas neglecting himself meant that deep need to put himself first and appropriate the other to fuel his self-assurance remained paramount. An inroad was made on that self-seeking and his capacity increased to see the otherness of the other – whether of the new woman across the table from him or the anima function within him. The other was allowed to be there as other from himself with a free standing view or knowledge apart from him. He did not always immediately appropriate the other's insights as a footnote to his own. And I learned of this strenuous process where the analyst is host to an emotion or need very alive within the analyst but not actually their own property but the property of their analysand. The analyst holds it for a while, carries this package, so to speak, until it can be returned to its rightful place in the analysand.

This is an occupational hazard of the analytical profession, very strenuous and demanding work to understand what is going on, but also an example of the intimacy of limits analyst and analysand share. The degree of change profited the new relationship too, leading to fruitful longstanding commitment.

We might say all three of us experienced relief in this process, or perhaps actually four of us if we include the personification of the anima with which he now had to engage. We could say the lure was to soul, but to get there one had to forge through destructive outrage and harsh judgement both within and without and discover that engagement dug up hidden narcissism and that made more space for love.

Animus examples can run along similar lines when a woman becomes aware more than less a particular kind of man is poison for her, a 'bad boy' in popular slang, destructive to her and yet she is lured while knowing better. Where is the spirit of the animus left out so she does not receive its communication from her unconscious, from the Self to her ego and meets it instead in a person outside herself? Where is a consolidation in her awareness of her ego perceptions, needs, wishes, communicated to the animus, so to speak, from ego to Self.

She knows and she does not know about this unvoiced communication going on in her. The animus personification gets projectively identified with the man whom she knows from experience with him is not to be trusted, let alone depended upon. For instance, when dining with her in a restaurant, he flirts with the waitress and gets her number to call her later. My analysand is outraged and deeply hurt simultaneously; he is untouched by her emotions. Yet here she is, still beguiled, lured by something in him to have a go at it again. She feels drawn to him as if he has some spirit, some angle of seeing, some commanding sexual ease, some bid to what is outside her conventions and mores, outside her consciousness toward something more that feels ultimately important. He carries the heft of that unconscious communication that feels to her as if something valuable can be found. And there is also a lot of fun and intelligent conversations back and forth between them in this relationship. She is unusual, with flair and beauty and her work as an artist.

Like the man in the above example, she feels this is a soul issue, about the very meaning of loving someone or something beyond oneself. Maybe her date does possess some spiritual magnetism in fact; she needs to have all her wits about her and go forward also protecting her vulnerability. She is not a masochist. She needs to have more conscious contact with her own masculine thrust, her own steady intent to reach this valuable insight or spiritual meaning she senses but cannot articulate. She must go right at it, not be tempted to byways and diversions into wasteful action. She knows and she does not know. She must inquire what is it here that draws her. We work on this elusive soul element repeatedly in our sessions.

I have been astonished by instances of this masculine assertion in a woman in analysis. Jung puts it, "masculinity means knowing what one wants and doing what is necessary to achieve it" (Jung 1928/1964, para 262; see also Ulanov 1971, pp. 256-257; see also Ulanov 2013, p. 11). In this example, in suffering once again this luring man's betrayal, this woman uncovered a long forgotten but still bleeding wound of loss and abandonment. We discovered the link between her feeling utterly abandoned by him repeatedly that drove her to suicidal thoughts, and an experience of an entire loving and being forsaken at the beginning of her life.

She lived being loved and emotionally held by her grandmother when her own parents deposited her at one year old in their parent's care. Two years later the beloved grandmother died and no one told her. Suddenly, she, now three years old, was deposited again to the wayward parents. The present abandoning by the luring man engaging simultaneously in affairs with other women while in affair with her, reached all the way to that wound in her earliest years. The abandonment that made her feel suicidal was the link between the present and the past, as was the loving all-out, as a child does and as she did with him. That love given and received was the treasure with her grandmother and then cut off without explanation in the shock of being whisked away because grandmother died. But she did not know it; she felt only utter bereftment. The present abandonments out of the blue by the man pressed hard on the deep bone-bruise of the ancient abandonment out of the blue, the loss of love when a small child. Later she understood intellectually that death parted her and her grandmother, but the underlying wound had not been experienced consciously, or its truth known, that her grandmother did not suddenly disregard her, but had been taken by death. The wound bled unconsciously all these years until evoked by the repeated being left by the man.

Finding and feeling the deep suffering of her earliest years weaving into her present life also made sense of her 'dizzying' behavior, her continued fascination with this man and her lack of protecting herself much as a child is unable to do. Some days it felt as if she was engineered to go through this lure to find the treasure hiding in it. Claiming her loving and her grief, working to integrate them into their rightful places within her, she felt a greatly enhanced capacity to live. The power of the lure toward him faded. The swift nearness of loving and death added something to her work as an artist, the thrum of those creative and destructive forces meeting.

The analytical work focused on developing communication between the animus personification by the man and her ego wants. The lure to destructiveness symbolized by the man occurs in that gap of communication between the two persons and inwardly between ego and Self. That is a deep place hard to find at first, a secret soul here but not secured. That conversation with animus, with ego and Self contents meeting, engenders communicating bit by bit both her ego needs and aims and what the Self says. It can create a turmoil even a heated conflict. Each side of it must fully lay out its position and let the conflict sharpen to a razor's edge if need be. Such an impasse is important; great values and belief about the whole of life are at stake. In that bad and painful and hurtful relationship in what feels evil also lies some power to attract. In this analysand's example, the treasure of claiming all-out-loving can shed some of its suffering to live again. Getting more conscious of her early experience of the vulnerability of such a big good of that loving that was inexplicably gone, unnamed, that death cut off, introduced her as a small girl to the mixture of transience and ultimacy, of loss and of not losing the capacity to love. Integrating the implosion of such forces and making sense out of the lure, strengthened this woman's path of individuation; it fed her artistic work.

If we can simultaneously hold in consciousness the warring opposite views, let them be at war, repeat the points again on each side, and again as long as is necessary, and let it be, not solve it by rubbing out one of the sides, something will happen; the gap between them will act as door or portal or space for something else to appear and astonish. Instead of falling into the lure which operates in the gap and spells its binding to a false solution, too hasty and too imposed, not grown, something new, not invented but appearing on its own will settle the war, lift it to another level. Jung calls this that appears the transcendent function (Jung 1916/1960, para; see also Ulanov 1996, pp. ix-xii; see also Ulanov 2007, pp. 199-203).

Transition

The psyche's project manifests itself in our experience of the transcendent function which arouses our wonder as well as questions on a personal level. Both 'projects' are involved. We may wonder what the Self is engineering in this lure to bring oneself to a new anchoring between ego and animus in the woman's case above and between anima and ego in the man's case above. Those terms – anima, animus – are clumsy. Jung himself said, a sign of madness, but they aim to make something obscure and fantastic accessible. Jung writes, "Take ... anima and animus. No philosopher in his senses would invent such irrational and clumsy ideas. When things fit together it is not always a matter of philosophical system; sometimes it is the facts that fit together. Mythological motifs are facts; they never change; only theories change" (Jung 1975, vol. 2, p. 192; see also Ulanov A. and Ulanov B. 1994, pp. 1-5, 10-12). The mixture of good and bad in the terms themselves echoes the condition of good and bad in real life. Can we distinguish them without getting entrapped in rigid definitions that turn out to define us – oh that part of me is bad; that public senator is evil. Can we distinguish them enough, making space for less trammeled confusion, and for more robust living?

Jung names the consequence of the transcendent function as a new attitude, image, realization or action that dissolves the war between conscious and unconscious in the offering of something original. If, however, the development takes place in the unconscious and never makes it across the gap into consciousness, it is alive there in the unconscious and makes itself felt to consciousness in a way that intrudes, implodes, presses, like an impending nervous collapse, or depression, or a sense something is there but cannot yet cross the border into awareness. That 'something' may manifest in a patient bringing masses of material to a session as journal notes or a great heap of dreams so we cannot get at what is the nodal point. Jung writes, "you will get completely dizzy" (Jung 2008, p. 404) recalling Kierkegaard's dizziness at the border of the eternal crossing into the mortal, or Tillich's dizziness where in our finite freedom we long toward the infinite.

The lure to destructiveness is itself a transition from being entirely caught in the 'mistaken' action and also a coming enough aware through allurement that a hesitation inserts itself. Dread fills that pause; we could make the same 'mistake' again! Yet we feel free not to, we could not! Yet we feel hobbled, as if with one foot still tied into the old hasty action that slides us into the soup again. A gap yawns between can do and cannot do, between potentiality and limit, or is it a space in between? We disregard our being enticed: Oh just get this over with, do it. And there we are again, fitting too much into too little time. For example, while talking to a loved one on the phone, an analysand finds she is also trying to erase unneeded messages from her cell phone. But in the divided attention and the haste to get a pesky chore done, she unwittingly erases all the important vital instructions she laboriously took down in a previous call of an exercise procedure to deal with her extreme physical pain. Falling into the gap, despairing how could I do this, so careless with the things that might help me! A barrage of self-attack ensues.

The lure to destructiveness is a genuine space of transition from entrapment to freedom, or at least more freedom. But this space is beguiling and confusing. It seems bad but as if hiding a good – the stone, the ju-ju, the pharmakon, the diamond. We also get aware of the lure's power by resisting its destructiveness through repeating instructions in consciousness, a sort of process of imprinting: I could pause, feel the threat and not succumb to it. As if teetering on a chasm's edge, I could step over into ruin again, but I do not. I repeat the mantra 'I am free not to succumb to temptation' but it repeats right next to feeling the breath of I could fall again, once again go into annulment. In the lure to destructiveness, we become aware that the unconscious exists and can intrude as threat, and that consciousness, right on its border can find passage to freedom from threat. We feel the breath of each beast – unconscious and consciousness – simultaneously, that the good is somehow there in the vicinity of the bad, that the precious goal to be pursued, the inestimable value of the treasure, the ultimate good that is there somewhere to be discovered feels as if near, hinted at.

The man in the above example, in the midst of wrecking the new love relation with a barrage of righteous disapproving anger discovered that to make it right he had to find the good in himself. Where did he lose that animating connection that imbued him with faith that his life was worth living: he had good to give? Losing sight of his soul, it yelled at him through the jealous anima personification, saying in effect, what about me? You belong to me, you owe me! He, unconscious of it, projectively put it into me and I had the bewildering work of finding out who was jealous of whom and for the sake of what? I emphasize that because it is hard work to sort out the threads of appropriate linkings. We could have gone wrong in several directions. *He* needs to look in, not out, to the woman in himself, so to speak, recognize his unconsciousness of the enlivening good within. Then the promise of his new relation to the woman without might blossom, liberated from his own hidden sabotage, the bad within the good opportunity. In fact, it did blossom into sustained happiness and commitment. And I was relieved from my proxy role to a more sane ease. For the woman above, the lure of the bad fellow faded and anchoring in her own capacity to love showed signs of blossoming in her work as an artist. Finding the meaning of her attraction to the bad relationship freed her agency.

But the odd thing is that the precious substance, the good, is everywhere – the garden, the fountain the *aqua permanens,* the *lapis exilis* to cite alchemical symbols of it. Jung writes, it is "the cheapest thing … you find it everywhere. It is thrown out into the road … the most unassuming thing … with no appearance, no show at all, a vile thing" (Jung 2019, p. 285; see also Ulanov 2001 for a striking example of good in bad). Further, neither the personal project of individuation nor the psyche's project of luring us into that goal is simple nor obvious. Jung writes, "individuation or concentration of human personality does not happen in a schematic way, but in a … complicated, and individual way ... it is exceedingly difficult to find a rule or regular course for it" (Jung 2019, p. 288). And we can lose it!! Miss that brass ring and go round and round the carousel and never grasp it. The impersonal tone of the psyche's project looms here: "the psychological process is a piece of nature. It is like a plant, like a tree or an animal; You have to study its nature" (ibid, p 294). And still further, "The process goes on without you, if necessary. There are plenty of people in whom the individuation process, with mandala dreams and all the most beautiful stuff, just goes on without consciousness even. There are plenty of lunatics with the most wonderful individuation dreams, and nothing comes of it because there is nobody home" (ibid). We need to respond, to let the impact hit us. The lure pulls, beguiles and tempts. Its threat of bad knows about some hidden good too. It may be that lures happen as a way the unconscious makes its project known. It cannot get through to us directly, so it tantalizes with fascination.

Dangers

Dangers lurk. I mention only a few. They are real and perilous and all together amount to evasion, inattentiveness, or simple bad luck. On the positive side, however, isn't it amazing that a human being goes through such grappling with good and bad forces and struggles to make something lasting and even joyous? How amazing we can do this or even think of attempting it, that we are capable of imagining and relating to these strong psychological and soul forces. (Raff 2000, pp. 228, 245-248, 258; see also Rovelli 2016, pp. 63-64, 67-68, 71-75, 78; see also Atwood 2019. pp. 1-2, 42-44). We are so made that cosmic vistas are things we think about, or we can perceive that we do not invent thoughts but rather receive them and dare to think them and choose among them. We can mull on deep wells of meaning and find words to speak of them to each other and to the others not here yet but in the future. This is the hope of any teacher. Then there is the profession of analysis. What an odd and wonderful occupation of our thought and feeling and sensing and intuiting what life is about and wanting to derive theories to express and bring about that life. How extraordinary the human venture is – what people are capable of enduring and creating.

A principal danger is our reaction to original insight that emerges from wrestling with the lure to destructiveness. It emerges like the pearl of great price from the hard shell of the oyster. We prize it and can even shape it into a summary statement or attitude. For example, we have been able to make into a psychological experience a shocking trauma so we need not live forever captive to it in PTSD; we can escape it defining who we are. We fell for the lure and into destructive attitudes and experiences. We came through to greater respect for the power of the unconscious and for finding a way destructiveness is part of livingness.

The danger is we can hold too tightly to the precious pearl and make it into an immutable rule for the rest of our lives and for everyone else too. Then a living experience gets concretized into a definition that defines us. The lure is not the same for everyone, nor is it fixed in stone. Its process is similar among us but the danger is precisely because the precious resolution of it rescued us, we want to fix it in stone, not to lose it again. No, it does not work that way. We can lose it by holding too fast to it. The danger is we can become entrapped by our very understanding of what the problem and its solution are and make them into a rule to apply to living situations and that kills them.

One interpretation of Toni Wolfe's later life, when her relation to Jung changed, exemplifies this danger. She did not follow him into his interest in alchemy. She tried to persuade him against pursuing it as ruinous to his reputation and as deserting the complex psychology they collaborated on together. Jung went his way; he said he felt always compelled to do so (Jung 1963, pp. 345-346, 356-357) and the feeling changed between them. She felt their emotional closeness ended when their joint work on complex psychology reached its end, as did the sharing of strange images of his compelling fantasies recounted in *The Red Book* that she had received and helped him understand.

Unrequited love can turn hard, adamant like concrete. Healy says Toni wanted Jung to marry her and he refused. Feeling level between them shifted. Healy cites a significant dream of Jung's (December 1923) as does Sonu Shamdasani in his introduction to Jung's *Black Books* where his anima appears and he saw that she had died and did not know it yet (Healy 2017, p. 203; Shamdasani 2020 v. 1, p. 96). Jung's mother had died around the time of that dream and Jung associated her death with the anima falling silent. Healy suggests that Toni in these later years sneered at love as a fraud, turned her back on it as it turned its back on her (Healy 2017, pp. 281, 288, 294). What originally flowed through her turned rigid in bodily pain from arthritis, increased smoking, bitterness and sorrow. They continued a weekly visit but not the closeness, it seems. Her remarkable intuition re the psyche continued yet many who knew and cherished her thought she died before her time of a broken heart (personal communication). Concretization entraps us. We are destroyed by a reified solution that does not materialize into living.

A second danger, equally real and perilous is the opposite. We become absorbed by the archetypal dimension in the lure. Jung writes, "When an archetype is constellated, there is always the danger of assimilation into the archetype … those who come into such a situation usually don't realize it at all … We are dissolved from within … Consciousness is simply depotentiated" (Jung 2008, pp. 190- 191). We feel panic, or something uncanny, as if we are changed into something else, or we may catch ourselves as if coming to from a spell. Then we don't waft away into the lure. We stick to the text of the dream; Jung says for example, "I stay with the original image. I understand nothing of the dream ... I amplify an existing image until it becomes visible" (Jung 2008, p. 26). We stay with the specific focus of the lure in this time and place and with these consequences if indulged. We look into ourselves and re-member the understanding we have gained of the danger tempting us; we attach it again to our awareness. That rescues us from the lure just to be done with it, make it nothing, not get into a state about it, not recall our just yielding to the pull and slide over the chasm's edge, or, as if for a moment we went unconscious only to wake up with a jolt I have done it, pressed the wrong key on the computer, or swooped again into the bad boy's magnetism. We allow ourselves to reflect on what we know from experience. When we lose space and time, forget the wise advice to write the email but do not send it; look it over the next day. We recognize the seduction to go abstract as if we do not live on this earth, within the limits of finitude.

Another way to misstep is to get sentimental. Beneath sentimentality is always brutish power: I will be powerful, in charge and direct this show. We indulge the image of being really serious about dealing with the psyche but miss the shadow side of the image and forget the contagion of what we involve ourselves in. We overdo feelings we should be nice, open to nature and then get infected with its reality, at expense of our own. Jung gives a repelling example of a child's dream where the pigs get out of their boundary and sneak into her "little garden" from the back. The young dreamer joins the pigs – it would be nice in the garden but no, from the back it would become a pigsty as they would root up the flowers, trample the vegetables, make it all mucky. That's what pigs do! She distorts her feeling to befriend them, get cozy with them. Further, the pigs have lice and now she is infested; she has become a pig.

She was sentimentalizing she was one of them, forgetting the differentiation that consciousness brings. Jung says she made a virtue out of necessity, swooned over being one with the pigs and became a pig (Jung 2008, pp. 464-465).

Reading that I suddenly recalled a look of horror sweeping over an analysand's face, as if paralyzing her. She gasped the words, 'black satin sheets.' Remarkably beautiful, she described an exciting meeting up with a fascinating stranger in a glamorous club. Clicking with him, with the surroundings, she felt herself charismatic, fascinating. Then a time and space lapse, not an intermission but an interruption. She woke up in the black satin sheets the next morning. Sometimes we do not take the frog to our bed but hurl it against the wall! Only then does the transformation of frog to prince occur. We need aggression.

The opposite of the danger of wafting off into inflation with the archetypal is the opposite of getting dragged down into finitude: inertia. We are not dragged away from the personal but mired in its entanglements. We have no energy to do anything; we're stuck in the conflict forever and can do nothing to get liberated. We cannot make the doctor's appointment to get scheduled the chemotherapy we are due to take with the urging it could bring us through to more years of life and if too much delayed we are at risk. As if in slowed up time or walking through water up to our thighs we cannot step to it and take the chance of health, but wander as if in an unfocused dream. It is dangerous and can be literally destructive; the lure succeeds.

Such inertia may show in a quiet denial – not the noisy assertion that X does not exist, but rather a stepping away from awareness of a serious conflict by simply disappearing from it. No conversation with the person involved, no responding to their phone calls or efforts to find out what is going on. We simply are not there and act as if the conflict is also not there. I have seen a few instances where this being mired in stasis but erasing all consciousness of it goes on for a number of years.

On return to resume connection, the tendency is to act as if that erasure never actually happened. Hence returning to the persons involved it is never acknowledged nor the lapse in time when denial held sway. The erasure has been erased. If there is any knowledge of it, it is disincarnate knowledge. I know about it but as if I am describing a third party it happened to; I am not involved in it. This is a kind of dissociation. The price can be high. Jung writes, "You can never individuate if the process does not happen in reality … The individuation process cannot get in the right spot, the here and now. There is no escape from this fact" (Jung 2019, p. 333).

References

Healy, N.S. 2017. *Toni Wolfe & C. G. Jung A Collaboration.* Los Angeles: Tiberius Press.

Jung, C.G. 1916/1960. "The Transcendent Function" *The Structure and Dynamics of the Psyche Collected works 8.* Transl. R.F.C. Hull. Princeton N.J.: Princeton University Press, paras 131-193.

— 1953/1966. *Two Essays in Analytical Psychology Collective Works 7.* Trans. R.F.C. Hull. Princeton N.J.: Princeton University Press.

— *Memories, Dreams, Reflections.* 1963. Recorded and Edited by Aniela Jaffé, Trans. Richard and Clara Winston. New York: Pantheon Books Random House.

— 1975. *Letters.* Eds. Gerhard Adler and Aniela Jaffé. Trans. R.F.C. Hull. Princeton, N.J.: Princeton University Press, vol. 2.

— 2008. *Children's Dreams: Notes from the Seminar Given in 1936-1940.* Ed. Lorenz Jung and Maria Meyer-Grass. Trans. Ernst Falzeder with the collaboration of Tony Wolfson. The Philemon Series. Princeton N.J.: Princeton University Press.

— 2014. *Dream Interpretation, Ancient & Modern.* Eds. John Peck, Lorenz Jung, Maria Meyer-Gras. The Philemon Series. Princeton N.J.: Princeton University Press.

— 2019. *Dream Symbols of the Individuation Process: Notes of C.G. Jung's Seminars on Wolfgang Pauli's Dreams.* Ed. Suzanne Gieser. The Philemon Series. Princeton N.J.: Princeton University Press.

Kierkegaard, S. 1957. *The Concept of Dread.* Trans. Walter Lowrie. Princeton N.J.: Princeton University Press.

Raff, J. 2000. *Jung and the Alchemical Imagination.* Berwick Maine: Nicolas-Hayes Inc.

Rovelli, C. 2016. *Seven Brief Lessons on Physics.* Trans. Simon Carnell and Erica Segre. Penguin Random House UK.

Shamdasani, S. 2020. "Toward a visionary science: Jung's Notebooks of Transformation" *C.G. Jung's The Black Books, 1913-1932 Notebooks of Transformation,* volume 1. Ed. Sonu Shamdasani. Trans. Martin Liebscher, John Peck, and Sonu Shamdasani. Philemon Series In collaboration with the Foundation of the Works of C.G. Jung. New York: W.W. Norton & Company, pp. 11-113.

Stolorow, R.D. and Atwood, G.E. 2019. *The Power of Phenomenology.* London and New York: Routledge.

Tillich, P. 1957. *Systematic Theology Volume II, Existence and the Christ.* Chicago: The University of Chicago Press.

Ulanov, A. and Ulanov B. 1994. *Transforming Sexuality: The Archetypal World of Anima and Animus.* Boston: Shambhala.

Ulanov, A.B. 1971. *The Feminine in Jungian Psychology and in Christian Theology.* Evanston, Ill. Northwestern University Press.

— 1982. "Transference/Countertransference A Jungian perspective" Ed. Stein, M. *Jungian Analysis.* La Salle, Ill: Open Court, pp. 68-85.

— 1996. *The Functioning Transcendent.* Wilmette, Ill.: Chiron.

— 2001. *Attacked by Poison Ivy: A Psychological Understanding.* York Beach Maine: Nicolas-Hayes, Inc.

— 2007. "What is the Self engineering?" *The Unshuttered Heart: Opening to Aliveness and Deadness in the Self.* Nashville Tn.: Abingdon Press, pp. 187-206

— 2013. *Madness & Creativity.* College Station, Tx.: Texas A&M University Press

Chapter 3:

In Defense of Dissociation and of Its Undoing

If we remember the two projects of the psyche, our personal one of struggling to become who we are, including all the parts of us – individuating – and, as if to say, the psyche's project of furthering a "goal oriented, purposive nature" that draws on many conditions (physical, environmental, social, consciousness and spontaneous products of the unconscious), we can understand dissociation as a piece that goes missing in either or both projects or separates the two into conflict (Jung 2008, p. 4; Jung 2019, p. 226). The missing piece falls back into unconsciousness, or segregates from consciousness. We lose a vital personal detail and we lose the link to the archetypal source. In relation to the lure to destructiveness, the dissociation is what we get lured back into. Even though partially aware of its existence and its power over us, the lure fascinates. Entranced, we fall prey to it.

I. Dissociation

Work with analysands brings me to state two main ideas about dissociation: first to speak in defense of the defense of dissociation – how cleverly we construct protection to match threat of trauma that nearly killed us. The life instinct secures a riverbed to keep flowing despite serious obstacles of what would interrupt it or destroy it. With Jung's notion of the prospective function – looking to what the problem leads us to, not only from whence it comes – the life force drives us through the tiny crack left open in the door that nearly slammed us shut. Second, through the clamor of disabling symptoms, we feel pushed in our psyche to undo this defense of dissociation, to destroy it in order to house aliveness pressing our desire for something more.

Dissociation is first mentioned by Pierre Janet in an 1887 paper on systemized anesthesia. Jung and Morton Prince, emphasized the *dissociability* of consciousness (Jung 1934/1960, para 202). A review of dictionaries of psychoanalysis defines dissociation as "two or more mental processes co-exist without becoming integrated" (Rycroft 1968, pp. 35-36); It is a process "whereby … [a] group of psychological activities possessing a certain unity among themselves lose most of their relationship with the rest of the personality" (Hinsie and Campbell, p. 221); "An unconscious defense mechanism in which a group of mental processes are separated (or split) from the remainder of the person's activity … symptoms are fugue states … multiple personality … may also lead to conversion symptoms (Harre and Lamb, 1986, p. 74).

Harry Stack Sullivan says dissociations are expressed in dreams, phantasies, unobserved action, and can produce such anxiety the person fears "going to pieces" (Wyss 1966, pp. 282-283; see also Sullivan 1953, pp. 316-322; see also Sullivan 1972, pp. 74-75). That is because we thereby confront a 'not-me' aspect of ourselves – unrepresentable, unsymbolized and confined to exile that cannot be allowed to be experienced. Further, fragmentation may occur in each of these mental units. For views of contemporary theorists on dissociation,* it is pertinent to note that dissociation as a category was not discussed thoroughly until the later 20th century.

Jung describes dissociation throughout his works. For example, in a person whose personality seems to be falling apart, it may be that the various units were never developmentally "properly grown together" (Jung 2008, p. 71). If we cannot suture the elements together, dissociation can result, as compartmentalization, or "a schizoid personality ... which if everything goes wrong, may turn into schizophrenia. The personality will disintegrate into islands that no longer have relation with one another" (ibid, p. 73). "We always seek to discover" Jung avers, "a holistic idea, allowing us to live as a whole, and to create an optimum of possibilities in life" (ibid, p. 74). The same dissociation turns up in international relations. If one country is left out, then "everybody does as he pleases ... no longer held together by an idea" let alone a greater unity, as today, in the idea of the United Nations. Jung does not see the personality as initially a unity, but rather disparate parts that grow toward greater wholeness. I think of it as a unity of diverse parts.

The dissociated part, separated from the community of elements that make up the personality may "make itself felt very unpleasantly." Jung says, "organ representatives can separate from one another and begin to march on their own." Strange attacks can happen. Jung cites examples: "The heart behaves like a lunatic no longer under control [tachycardia]; digestive problems or some paralyses may occur as well. The functions become independent of one another" (ibid). If we become unmoored from our body itself, inflation and dissociation occur, floating off into unconsciousness not secured in time and space here and now. For example, it is important, I suggest, when in profound grief, not to engage it nor do the work of

* See p. 98 for a selected views of contemporary theorists on dissociation.

mourning when crossing a busy street or when driving. The grief shrouds us away from immediate reality. Accidents may happen.

Another example of leaving our body base is when a strong archetype constellates. It is as if we split away from who we are and the reality situation right then. Without a flesh and blood body reality grounding us, "there is always the danger of an assimilation into the archetype ... Consciousness is simply depotentiated ... If you realize this just in time, you are already protected against it" (ibid, pp. 190, 191). But if we don't, we may lose a sense of time and place, of control in what we are speaking to others, for example, so we transgress the time limits and then feel shamed and discounted when our excess is pointed out. An example happened to me when in India. I felt bus sick and vertigo traveling with the group the first day to villages outside New Delhi. When we stopped by the road and I stepped down from the bus and stood on the ground, I suddenly saw every reference point I had ever had to orient myself was useless. The otherness of India had tremendous impact on me. With that conscious perception, nausea and vertigo vanished. The body did not have to enact my disorientation. I could suffer it consciously.

Because the psyche is not a given unity, dissociation is not a pathological condition necessarily. Jung's states: "The play and counterplay between personalities No. 1 and No. 2, which has run through my whole life, has nothing to do with a 'split' or dissociation in the ordinary medical sense. On the contrary, it is played out in every individual" (Jung 1963, p. 45). Encounter, negotiation, dialogue lead to balance between these two personalities as both make up the whole. Saban provides helpful information of the context Jung drew upon to form his own idea of the role of dissociation in the psyche. William James, Theodor Flournoy, Pierre Janet and especially Frederick Myers were influential to Jung (Saban 2019, pp. 36ff). Going further back in attending seances of his young cousin Helene Preiswerk whose performances Jung used for material in his doctoral thesis, he averred that the various figures she evoked were split-off subpersonalities of her psyche. Janet understood such phenomena as pathological as he saw the psyche as unitary. Jung did not.

Complex

Jung observed the unconscious has a nature of its own, including autonomy, both creative and intrusive, and in compensatory relation to consciousness but also capable of independent action. Indeed, Jung's Word Association Test gives evidence of such sub-personalities in the persons taking the test. Jung notes their hesitation to respond and their physiological reactions (e.g. rise in blood pressure, sweating) to the stimulating word as indicating a dissociation appearing or as developing further into a more coherent unit as a 'complex' appearing (Jung 1973, paras 7, 198 and passim). Such complexes compose a normal makeup of the personal unconscious and are not pathological, but could become so if their power overwhelms the ego. If the element remains unconscious, too long, it can constellate a dissociation that shows in anxiety, bad temper, not feeling at home with oneself (Jung 2008, p. 396). Or its anxiety may provoke the person simply to run away, to escape the situation, fearing it to be impossible (Jung 2019, p. 226). If the anxiety consolidates into an obsessional neurosis, "it can mean a complete split of the personality" which Jung thought to be a serious dissociation as it may harbor a hidden psychosis (Jung 2008, pp. 338, 343).

Jung's notion of complex describes the independence of dissociated contents from the reign of consciousness:

> "Complexes are psychic fragments that have split off owing to traumatic influences or certain incompatible tendencies. As association experiments prove, complexes interfere with the intentions of the will and disturb conscious performance; they produce disturbances of memory and blockages in the flow of associations; they appear and disappear according to their own laws; they can temporarily obsess consciousness, or influence speech and action in an unconscious way … they behave like independent beings, a fact especially evident in abnormal state of mind. In the voices heard by the insane they even take on a personal ego-character" (Jung 1937/1960, para 253; see also Jung; 1948/1960, paras 200, 202; see also Jung and Riklin 1906/1973, para 198).

Dissociated bits, then, can range from fragments to whole complexes. I focus here on dissociation of grave suffering that we register as threatening our survival. It may appear in bits and pieces that trip us up like slipping on hidden slivers of ice. Or it may gather into a coherent complex that threatens like a pit into which we fall, out of control (see Jung 1921, paras 344-345). My aim is to explore the double thrust of dissociation in our psyches – to instantiate it and to disassemble it, to construct it for protection to support aliveness and to destroy it to make space for more aliveness. We do both unconsciously and with some consciousness. Work in analysis makes both vectors much more conscious.

Doing the Defense

We discover dissociation is a remarkably helpful defense and that it presses to be undone when we are forced to look into its badgering, harassing symptoms that intensify if left uninvestigated.

The defense of dissociation mounts a bulwark against what would kill us or interrupt our going on being and leaving a gap in its wake (Winnicott 1963/1965, p. 86 and cited in Ulanov 2001, p. 160). A lot of hard work with one analysand brought us to see that when sleepiness overcame her in the midst of an activity that was very important to her – writing her memoir, or chanting prayers to her guru – it meant she was drawing near to precisely that vacuum where no space of location was, to that interval where no moment of time was. The thread of her living was as if broken off and then resumed on the other side of the fracture. Eventually, instead of attacks of shame for nodding off and of disrespect of the honesty of her intention to write or to pray, a flash of insight appeared between us. Sleepiness raised a flag! Precisely here is where she went missing and was going missing now. This brought excitement. The attacks of shame and dishonesty seemed to dissolve, especially in the efforts to find words for what this missing piece was and might be now. It felt like a lost piece of herself, the center, the core. And the loss of it implicated someone else, some relationship where something happened that should not have, or nothing happened where something should have.

Over the years working with people this theme emerges, of words found and created to name this treasured core piece – soul, me-ness, essence, heart, the sorrow, the gold, to cite the names given by a few patients. These words of specific persons are personal to them and universal to all of us, like our particular choice among the thousand names for Allah. In response, the tone of such work softens. We grow aware we have fashioned something that protects us. We are moved to tender gratitude for our psyche's inventive capacity to defend us against someone else erasing us.

Dissociating puts the threat of being annihilated into another space, not entirely cut off, but also not integrated, nor even on speaking terms with our going on being. It segregates what could wound us again. Seen in what Jung calls its prospective function – where the defense is heading and what it is communicating – dissociation holds an unconscious part of us that aims to be included in consciousness, rounding us up to a fuller sense of self, and to feeling it matters to do so – to us and to the world. I emphasize the huge pain that results in such dissociating remaining neglected.

Literally, dissociation saves our lives. Without it, we turn our face to the wall, and let the threatening annihilation take us out. Or, we more or less function, but at half-mast; one man phrased it, "with the volume turned down." Or, we may achieve high functioning but with a bigger gap between our beingness and other parts of us living in the realm of nonbeing (words that have come to mind when listening to patients' stories of feeling cut off). Our dissociation carries the burden of this sequestered self in symptoms of past and ongoing trauma (acute and cumulative).

Examples

We defend against something stark and intolerable bundled into a particular presentation that fences off what could hurt us but which thereby reduces our agency too. Instead of being tossed up and down on a rollercoaster between feeling alive and dead, an intelligent man whose job demanded he increase his technological skills, suffers a blanking of his mind. He cannot acquire these new skills, nor can he remember instruction he took to learn them, nor retain the tricks the tutor he hired devised to anchor these techniques in his mind. Technology in its new forms is the monster he cannot defeat. This blanking, we discovered, linked to the pain of feeling flung upward from being seen by those he loved as a child and then downward because no, he is only in the other's attention because of his skill to do for them. The pain of this emotional alive-dead tossing is dissociated and projected into technological machines that he had mastered and now cannot. Despite feeling his mind deleted and of the threat of losing his job if he cannot crack this problem, the dissociation of his technological skills functions to protect him from the emotional rollercoaster of fragmenting and his helplessness before it.

For another person, by looking into the symptom of losing precious or important objects like an office folder or beloved jewelry, we discover the problem is she cannot safeguard what she cherishes. It vanishes as if it was never there; her loving proves impotent. Even deeper she discovers it was not as if she had been cherished and then lost it due to death or war, etc. Rather, it was that she had never been found. She was on her own from the very beginning and assumed this was reality, no one to blame, just the way things were and she had to cope with it. She took on herself sole responsibility for dealing with the trauma of not being acknowledged as existing in the first place. But she is protected from that pain by worrying instead about the symptom of losing things: how that could happen? Where did the jewelry go? Not about never having existed in the other's eyes, as if falling through to no-place, no-thing, just as the man was worrying about the monster technology defeating him and his job, not about his mind breaking up that tossed him onto a roller coaster of feeling aliveness and then deadness.

The symptom that carries our dissociated content and affect both presents and blocks recognition of where the hurt really is. The symptom shifts into something else that we can bear to suffer that will not snuff us out. We unconsciously project into the loss of our technological skills or into losing valued objects the power to destroy us. We see here the intertwining of what we usually define and classify separately – dissociation, displacement, projection. In fact, these mental mechanisms are variations on the same theme of music, separate parts of the same melody that sings what we cannot yet bear to hear. We are thereby protected against the full blast of pain of being devoured by a monster, or by the loss of being a never-found subject. The dissociating symptom offers refuge for the pain, shelters it somewhere else, unconscious or half unconscious.

Sometimes it is positive talents or capacities that have been separated into dissociation. Gifts belong to the person, may even manifest and develop, but are not claimed consciously as belonging to oneself. They are not dead or deleted, only left disowned. We may know about them if someone points them out, but a gap exists that is never crossed. If claimed, we expect destructive attack from another like an envious mother, or we dread our destructiveness to another if our gift when owned makes this other feel inferior. Better not to own it then.

Promptings to Undo the Defense

The prompting and conflict about undoing this defense of dissociation begins by feeling worn down by the weight and chaff of the symptoms of this shut off part of us. The resilience of our psyche, its life force, presses us to cross the gap caused by cloistering part of us in the unconscious. We feel urged to wake up, come alive, get to the bottom of what the vexing symptom signals. Symptom may transform into symbol. People often seek analysis at such a time, saying they are here in my office not only to get over something but to get to onto or into something.

The symptoms of dissociated affects and ideas that repetitively interrupt our going on being also communicate that this split off stuff is alive and seeks admission into daily living. A woman dreamt of huge excavation begun just beyond a specific corner of her house outside the precise window over her desk where she does her work. A week later comes a dream of a huge wave scooping out earth under the sea. A digging up of her, she felt.

A big temptation to avoid such digging can be to disappear into symptoms of body pains, food and substance disorders, sexual and rageful actings out. Our body wants liberation while there is still time to make space between body and psyche to hear the communication of deep soul hunger or need for peace, or to channel sex and aggression. These elements signal from the body: here, look, attend, do something, relieve me, find the right places for these urges; live, do not disappear into them and lose your life; do not lose your chance.

Flooding

But our psyches are not neatly ordered nor scheduled according to what we will consciously. The undoing of dissociation is followed by flooding in of all that the symptoms kept out. We cannot underestimate the sheer force of what was cut out of awareness and remains in undifferentiated mix-up as seen from our conscious perspective. Instinctive impulses, outsized affects, destructive urges, lavish loving flood our ego. A rush of stimulating thoughts, creative ideas, new perceptions also crowd in, overwhelms. Feeling utterly vulnerable, helpless to organize this fast current, dimly aware this torrent of chaos is also plenty, all the unlived life surges. Ignorant of what to do and how to do it, let alone just keeping in mind all this undifferentiated life/death material, we feel like a piece of driftwood tossed back and forth on waves. Terror, sorrow, shock, pain alternate. Those emotional flashbacks bring to consciousness just how bad the trauma was/is.

Terror submerges us of being hurt by hands that interfered with our bodily self as if it was not our own but at the whim of the hands. Fear inundates, paralyzing the breath seeing that one was not seen as a subject in the other's eyes. They reflected back nothing and that defines us in our own eyes as nothing, left to exist in a vast nothingness, as if a small lone survivor in a demolished village. Sorrow drenches us for the pleasures of loving and being loved we never experienced; we missed them.

Shock – how could this be happening – jerks us as if from behind, shoved into awareness it *is* happening and cannot be comprehended. Impulses crowd in, to put hands on the red-hot stove, fall down steps splat, be hit by a car crossing the street. Such fantasies jolt us and are themselves a red-hot self-attack. We are pushed to recognize the trauma that happened to us that we tried to oust into dissociation, that it really was that bad. We have no escape, saying well, others have had it much worse, as if we have no right to our own suffering. Such suffering is not to be dismissed in comparison to victims of war, of rape camps, concentration camps, forced starvation, random street violence in one's neighborhood, intentional sadism to rub out a child's or a spouse's or an elder's confidence in their body and mind.

Our own suffering in all its details was really bad and all the shame of suffering compounds it. One person said it made sense why when a schoolboy he sought out horrific plights of prisoners, slaves, imposed because of color or creed, for money or sex, or simply because the other person could do it and they did. It feels as if right then in the present, the person understood for the first time he was seeking community, others who knew about abject suffering and went on living nonetheless. Such emotional horrors engage analysand and analyst in his or her reign of terror. A poem of Paul Celan's always comes to my mind then:

Once
I heard him,
He was washing the world,
Unseen, nightlong,

Real.

One and Infinity,
Dieing.
Were I'ing

Light was. Salvation.
(Celan, P. 1971, p. 253)

And another translation:
Once,
I heard him,
He was washing the world.
Unseen and nightlong.
really.

One and Infinite.
Annihilated.
They I'ed.

Light was Salvation.

John Felstiner writes of Celan's struggle "how to name a God who so washed the world … after 'annihilated (*vernichtet*) Celan's next verb *ichen* could be part of *Licht* ('light') or opposite to *nicht* or a past tense of *ichen* 'to I'" (Felstiner 2001, pp. 226-227).

Dangers

Once the wall of dissociation comes down, a deluge of terror, helplessness, sorrow threatens our ego now shorn of its protection by locating the danger elsewhere in dissociation. Trying too hard to get a conscious fix on all this volatile material too soon can lead to concretization of unconscious affects, overwhelming impulses and barely formed powerful thoughts. Through forcing that unlived accumulation into concrete forms may appear to be building up an observing ego. In fact, all this raw material is still unconscious and therefore subject to automatic projection onto an 'other' or an 'other' group.

Our inability to house our psychic stuff infects our society. By improving, correcting this 'other' whom we fill with the repudiated stash of our own, we define them as lesser, to be segregated. They carry what we have yet to assimilate. Failing to do that assimilating leads to walling off the other from familial and social community. This breeds terrible strife, unsolvable because past and present, personal and other, individual and collective fuse into a mass and we lack sufficient perspective to engage in Freud's wonderful phrase "the procrastinating function of thought." Differentiation gets mixed up with repudiation. Pseudo-consciousness replaces space to reflect slowly and gradually include chunks of ourselves that have been denied by dissociation. Undoing that defense means all that was not lived comes gushing in to be adapted into living experience of it.

A second grave danger is simply overwhelm. Our ego gets submerged by unconscious material, has no nexus points to deal with it yet. There is not yet a medium by which to begin step by step incarnating what belongs to us and relating to what is different from us. We each have such a task and an idiosyncratic vision and capacity to do it. If that gets swamped, the personal particular half of the meeting between conscious and unconscious, individual and social, gets lost. We get conscripted into mania because we fall into identification with all the energy of the unconscious raw material now coming into our awareness. Instinct takes over; a specific image takes over. Or we become deflated to extreme degree, persecuted by what we cannot house in smaller proportions. We do not make available this new energy to our community but, falling into identification with the energy, we feel moved to proclaim it or dictate actions from it.

A third danger comes from still less distinction between ordinary and extraordinary dimensions. When something gets dissociated into the unconscious, it frequents company with all sorts of things – archetypal images, primordial forces, intimations of the beyond, collective currents deep in the present society and from historical ones too. The limited, finite, conscious me and the broad expanse of the other than me, including a glimpse of eternal or infinite is now affecting me, touching me. But a meeting point is not yet emerged or developed. So we may be saturated and then left high and dry. Steadier encounter has to grow.

We can get endangered, even our sanity, and the social group's sanity can be threatened through the portal of an individual, especially a powerfully placed one, a leader of some sort, where the collective energies are seeping into their ego consciousness and not yet related to and hence exerting violent effects on self and others.

Again, as individuals we could fall into identification with this extra surplus of potent energy, images of the divine or the mana-imbued place or political option. Even the neurotic strategies of an individual influenced by a long deceased parent whose either/or mafia style or winner/loser credo infects the individual. If this individual is the leader, they infect the family, the company, the political party, the country. What makes them powerful is the unconscious sway that comes with their views, the whiff of the extraordinary as if their view is *the view,* or at least put forth to the public that way. We fall for it because gripped by its incitement and its utter denial of any optional view. Here we find flagrant, or worse, secret fanatics, identified with their views, lacking reflection, lacking consultation with others. Their identification insists we too immerse in state of identity with the view. They wield a certainty that can roll over any opposition with an urge to destroy anyone who disagrees with it or with its holder as the superior one amongst us.

Because their identification with the collective unconscious conducts its power into our smaller ego, it overpowers us. They must be right! Everyone says so, feels so, goes along with the tide. Now we are not only persuaded to join the collective current but intimidated not to do so. In the worst case, the view is identified by its holder with God's view, the ultimate view, the absolutely best value, without doubt. Thus now it is our holy duty, our religious obedience to conform, and enforce this view and to shun or even kill those who refuse to identify with this view. We saw this in the perpetrators of 9/11, and we see it recently in leaders of various nations. (Jung 1954/1960, para 372; see also Ulanov 2001/2004, p. 316).

II. Undoing the Defense

Symptom to Symbol

The undoing of dissociation proceeds, I suggest, as a series of small *coniunctios,* bits of unconscious and consciousness meeting and discovering their interpenetration. Images appear or something in the formless begins to form – a whiff of scent, a sound barely heard, even a texture emphasized in a dream. It can be positive or negative, but it is a something, small, insignificant until engaged. Then it grows like a magic potion as the ego invests energy of attention in it and we meet it with conscious reactions and responses. Just as the symptom is idiosyncratic to the individual, so is a proto symbol, something on the way to becoming rich and multivalent, but begins simply, singly. Engaging with it, talking with it, waiting on it, as did Jung in *The Red Book* encounters, it seems to lead nowhere. He often complains of ignorance, fear, even nausea. This process is not wand-waving all stress into cure. Jung puts it well – one gropes from stone to stone (Jung 2009, p. 246; see also Ulanov 2001c, pp. 55, 59).

The process that develops a nexus point Jung later formulates as the method of active imagination (Jung 1916/1960, paras 131-193). We stay alert to what animal appears from the edge of the forest, so to speak, and we respond in vibrating attentiveness, listening with intent to hear, smell, even taste what the other side, the unknown side, the foreign side presents.

The man who deleted his mind in protection against the monster of technology hit upon what became symbol: a wall. He saw that as a small boy he had walled out what nearly killed him, that roller coaster speed of emotional up and down – being loved, being used. His wall functioned as protection by providing steadiness, reliability in the face of the tantalizing other, looking as if they recognize and cherish him, only to discount him when of no use to them. The other seems to be there and then vanishes, hence setting off an inner ego inconstancy between excited loving and loss of hope. Hence, he too seems to go 'poof' out of existence (Fairbairn 1944/1954, pp. 89-90).

Our present work in analysis functioned as the steadiness of a wall, not to wall out but to reliably validate his experience. Our work and I too was a first witness to his narrative. Dependence on the work and on me in the work was possible. Near the end of a period of several months of what became his active imagination he told me coming out from behind his wall, "I love my wall; I couldn't have survived those constant ups and downs without it." The psyche, so to speak, is the second witness in creating or finding this image of the wall (Ulanov 2017, pp. 44-47). I joined his wonder and gratitude that somehow the image of the wall appeared and he could make use of it and take the chance to move out from behind it.

In addition to its protective function, the wall also made space on its other side that kept alive what he had rejected. It acted as a refuge for his pain, sheltering it until it could be admitted into consciousness. In the beginning the process seemed to him impossible: How can you talk to a wall? It is not person or an animal even, but impersonal. But he stuck to the task and the wall unfolded and changed, moving from proto-symbol status to become a full symbol with its many meanings and effects, as if disclosing a life of its own. He conducted meetings with the wall outside in warm months of the season.

The wall assumed a tone of pale gold color and stood in wave-like contours that undulated in response to his words and began to radiate a golden light. He felt its friendliness. His words fell away as he yielded to moving his body back and forth. He spoke in body gestures to the wall. This connecting felt satisfying to him, as if they stood and made a space together. The wall was alive and other than himself and near. He said it felt like "compressed energy." Later, it became "compressed light," though he was unsure what he meant. This went on for a number of weeks; there were intervals of experiencing each change for an extended time. Eventually, a second wall appeared, same height and wavy contours, this one colored, he said, "like air with flickerings of blue" and was "compressed air, an intensity of energy." Then a third wall of similar appearance and undulating presence appeared of "gorgeous black, compressed darkness."

Many weeks later the three walls formed a protecting crescent encompassing him but not closing the circle. It lay open as the crescent faced him like half a circle, leaving space where he stood and also behind him. A bit later the three walls drew near to one another forming a dome over his head but retaining the open crescent of space. A childhood memory popped up of standing behind the floor length living room curtains of his original family's house, safe and successfully hidden. In contrast, the walls made a space within their drawing together for him to move in body gestures and to stretch out his arms in greetings to them. We have not translated these images and experiences into words, except descriptive ones;

no interpretations. The body experience is dense with thick, positive, lively, graceful feelings. It was only then he stepped forth from behind the walls and said he loved them.

Personifications, Dreams

Another source of help in undoing the defense of dissociation can come from dreams and imaginative work with personifications of dream figures. The woman who lost precious objects and had to discover she was never found as a subject in her own right, suffered the gap between living in a family whose persona was wonderful – normal, intact, privileged, and, in great contrast, she attuned to submerged suffering in most of the family members. Looking back, she saw she 'lent' her family to her best friend who came from a dysfunctional family with a 'bad' persona. Her mother tried to thwart the friendship for those reasons – its unsuitability – but she persisted and her best friend became a happy addition, accepted and genuinely liked by her parent. Her friend profited from this borrowing and felt sustained by the girl's family. She never breathed a word of her own unhappy experience of the gap and confusion of living in a 'normal' family and feeling utterly alone. She felt she could at any moment, in her words, go 'poof' out of existence. She lived on the edge of being and nonbeing, and, like her family's persona, was seen to be 'normal' and fortunate. When, as adult she sought analysis, in response to my saying, what brings you here, she said "I could go crazy at any moment."

In our work, her losing precious things got worse. In those plaguing losses she bundled the sorrow of never having been found, unable to take for granted and feel secure in the value of her own existing. I was struck by the big gap between her functioning life in the world with her substantive accomplishments and her cluelessness about her own worth. At that time there was much in the news about citizens in Syria, Yemen, sub-continent Africa fleeing war, persecution, abject poverty. She felt horror and devastating empathy for hordes of refugees with no home anywhere now risking their lives and their children already cheated of health, education, play, to find a home across miles and oceans.

One dream poleaxed her. She was a refugee in a huge warehouse, a holding station for hundreds and hundreds of refugees – lost souls. Crowded, stuff all over, children yelling, whimpering, lying sick, adults squashed together in no space of their own, trying to find food, space to lie down on the cement floor, to fight dirt, find rest. Noise. Horrible. Sobbing, dazed by this abject misery, she rushes outside onto a country road. A car stops and she gets in. Driving away she suddenly comes to her senses. What was she doing getting into a strange man's car! Still sobbing, she cries, "I must get out now! I must go back!" The driver is Chinese; she is white; he says nothing, drives on. "Stop! I made a mistake; I must go back. You are driving farther and farther away; I will never get back!" He says nothing. Eventually they arrive at another huge warehouse which he runs, with many workers, creating out of wood. The dream ends with her assigned to a space to create a wooden creche for the infant Christ and two parents.

She engaged this middle-aged quiet collected Chinese man in active imagination, repeating there 'I have to go back!' He is silent, looks at her and finally speaks: 'You do not have to go back.' She understands his meaning: she does not have to go back to living as a refugee – not found, not claimed, not recognized as worth existing. She must create a holding in wood for arrival of an infant that changed the world, the new coming into being. She kept in mind this man was Chinese; it seemed to her the epitome of foreignness. As a kid she would play 'digging to China' as the farthest depth and other side of the earth on which she stood. He was completely other to her.

She also felt she was prejudiced about the Chinese encountered in tourist groups when she was traveling. The young women just pushed you out of their way to the Ladies Room, she said, or in a Chinese city the Chinese masses just pushed you off the street to make their own way thus showing off an aggressive entitledness to their wishes. They had no doubt they existed and a right to assert it!

At the same time she was mulling the Chinese man, her losing of important things persisted, culminating in loss of her car keys in an inexplicable way that bordered on the mysterious. It was the undoing of her defense of dissociation. Alert to her symptom of losing important things, she had learned to take care, even keep lists of where things should be placed to secure their continued existence in her world. She was moving the old car out of the garage attached to her house, in order to put into the garage the new car she drove up at night from the city. Conscious of the two different sets of keys in her hand, she is saying out loud to herself, where shall I put the old car's keys, having moved it out of the garage, so I do not lose them while I move the new car into the garage? She finishes with both cars and goes to put both sets of keys into the drawer she chose to safeguard them. Shock! She holds only one set of keys, not both. Where did the set of keys for the old car go missing? It happened just when she questions out loud, Where shall I put the keys to safeguard against losing them? We went over this sequence and this question in painstaking detail and repetition.

She said it was like an electric shock through her body. The old keys vanished, 'poof' as if they had never existed, and all in the small space between the garage and her indoor house, so they must be here somewhere, but they were nowhere. She searched the garage, the outdoors where the cars had been parked, the indoors, the drawer as the safe place for the keys, the pathway to and from the drawer. She felt she went 'crazy' as she feared she could and had sought analysis to prevent. The disappearance, the gone-ness hit her on every level of herself, enacting the disappearance of her own being, despite all her careful procedures to guard against herself going 'poof' out of existence. This terror of 'going crazy' as her blanking utterly on where the keys went and of going out of existence was enacted through the keys disappearing.

Much time and repeatedly over days, she searched the driveway in the dark, in the daylight; she searched coming into the house, in the drawer, the cars, the garage, the furniture. No keys. She gave up, feeling 'crazy,' feeling 'gone.' It is hard to convey the lostness emerging from not being found. It was deeply unsettling: although sitting near her in my office it felt possible as if we too could pass out of sight, leave no trace, cease to exist, be lost to view, go 'poof'; everything and anything could be gone.

A dream made an announcement: A slim Chinese girl of mid-teen years shows she stole the car keys. Much imaginative dialogue ensued between my patient and this girl. In contrast to how hard my analysand secured her existence in many activities first in schools and then in jobs and relationships in the world, this Chinese girl had cut off all attachments, crawled into a dark place and lay there, maintaining indifference as a way of coping with flooding sorrow for being forgotten, never sought, missing all the closeness.

What stood out, and surprised me and then my patient who suffered a lot of annihilation anxiety, was that yes, the Chinese girl knew about going 'poof' out of existence and she knew about nonbeing. Yet she was not annihilated. She was *alive* even if abandoned. Nor was my analysand annihilated, for she suffered all these ins and outs and observed them enough to find words for them. So who was annihilated? That kind of anxiety was strong and chronic in my patient. Yet she was alive. The Chinese girl was alive lying in the dark space, and eventually wandering in a wasteland. And eventually she made a discovery: she discovered a not-being-human-realm of being that existed and of which we humans were a tiny part in the whole of the cosmos (see chapter 7, subhead 'Ontology').* This Chinese girl part of her was secluded until now but was alive, not annihilated. So who or what was annihilated? That requires another paper. It took time to unearth and amounted to her connection to the world: it was annihilated. She cut off expecting anything from others.

Undoing this defense of dissociation – of loss of validation of her subjective self symbolized in losing things – is not easy and does not succeed right away. But it makes its mark and destroys the defense of our putting elsewhere what was so painful. It closes the gap of dissociation that had allowed a splitting off of the painful trauma. Now pain comes rushing in as does the terrible confusion how this painful erasing of us could happen even though the sequence of symptom to symbol begins to get clearer.

The symptom was ever losing some precious object, realistically important and with serious consequences to do so. Losing brought tremendous anxiety too and feelings of craziness and feeling uncorrectable because it kept happening and got worse as the analysis proceeded. A first marker was insight through a living experience that *she* was the lost item displaced onto a precious object. "It's not the object, it's me! I am lost, not seen, not noticed, not recognized as existing!" She had to discover, to 'find' that she had been lost. The insight was overwhelming and terrible, but possible because it brought relief from dreadful confusion, always a sign of trauma, as if losing one's mind, one's ability to perceive and to register how can this be happening?

* The not-human-centered-being realm is different from what Harold Searles describes in his excellent book *The Nonhuman Environment* that describes our person-centered world of relating to e.g. dogs, plants, rocks, landscapes, beaches, water, etc. The realm I am pointing to is outer space, the vastness of multiple galaxies and universes.

It looks as if I am lucky to be in this intact functioning well-off family. How can I be feeling I am in a camp, prison, exile, left as the one small survivor in a village burned to the ground?

The next marker was the symptom became a communication: when she lost another valuable object, she was experiencing in a living way her subjectness, that she was not a lost item but finding her capacity to be a subject in her own right: "I am alive, not annihilated, I see me." Not only was the lost object valuable, meaning her subjective self that it symbolized was valuable, but she was not annihilated. She was there suffering the loss consciously, deeply; she was there existing and in pain.

The third insight was that her loss was never in being found. She had to achieve recognition that she was a lost object or subject in someone else's eyes. The problem was not hers so much as it belonged to others not noticing or holding her in their mind. These gleanings were accompanied by pain now felt consciously and hence feeling worse than ever before, but actually the worst had already happened. It felt worse because she was there to experience its flooding into her consciousness. (see Winnicott 1963?1989, pp. 87-96).

Then came the keys so mysteriously disappearing. In active imagination she gave warm attentiveness to this thin forgotten Chinese girl who announced in a dream she had taken the car keys. My analysand felt she got the Chinese girl in place of the keys, knowing that this was a symbolic transaction of the meaning of her symptom of losing things. She cared for this part of herself in imaginatively bringing her tea and hot sweet milk, even singing to her, sitting with her in her dark place.

She saw she too had abandoned this part of her that the Chinese girl personified. When she recognized she was not found of interest to any in her family, not noticed to exist, she saw she had jumped into the busyness of a small girl's life, then an older girl's and on up to being a busy functioning adult. She too had never noticed this hurt as if dead part; she also left it behind in the dark. She did to it what she experienced done to her, too busy to notice the livingness of this part of her. It filled her with remorse.

Dissociated parts of us do not just spring back into adult life at an adult age. They have to grow, develop, depend on being in touch with our conscious ego in the world. That brought the insight that what got annihilated was her connection to the world of others as dependable and wanting to be there with her.

Returning to my main point, my patient came to understand and experience in active imagination with the Chinese girl that she lost the keys to get the Chinese girl, this missing dissociated part of herself. And it was *car* keys – the ignition needed to get going to be about in the world. She got the missing connection to the world through getting the missing part of herself. I was amazed and she was too, that the psyche witnesses to such a profound trauma and to its beginning healing through such a mundane symbol of car keys. It is as if psyche, like a second witness, creates the move out of dissociation with the car keys and with a teenager of a culture so foreign it not only has different alphabet but an alphabet of images, not letters.

But Undoing Gets Undone

Now to focus on the undoing that made its presence felt by not getting undone because she could not remember the crucial step. Her mind 'blanked', like the other patient above not remembering what he tried to learn technologically. She could not fill in the steps of what had been made to go away. We cannot think it through. We must live it through on a level of arational apprehension meeting our efforts to compose a reasoning sequence. Here, this patient was able to experience the missing link. She held in mind the blanking, the link that went missing, the gap between intention and action. But it was absent; she held present to her mind the absence of the gap.

Her intended action – to secure the keys safely from being lost – was erased from her memory as if it never had existed. She had to accept this hard fact because it was symbolized by the keys gone for three plus years. She never found them. They were discovered by chance by her cleaning woman being extra thorough under a cushion. The keys fell out, lay exposed on the couch surface. When shown this discovery, my analysand thought, oh, I see now how that happened; there was no big revelation or excitement. The accent had long shifted to another emphasis – experiencing the missing link consciously and carrying that gap around.

I was amazed how her psyche worked, how our psyche works, even here to show when it did not work, when something went out of consciousness and stayed there for several years. When the keys were found three years later, it caused little commotion because by now she had accepted the defense of dissociation and her intent to undo it by not losing the keys. *But she dissociated her undoing of dissociation.* She lost any idea of where she had in fact put the keys.

She dissociated her rational plan to undo dissociation by safeguarding the keys. She intended to use her capacity to destroy dissociation by undoing it. But, her intent to destroy dissociation instead got destroyed from her consciousness and dissociation was reestablished. However, she now held in awareness both the defense of dissociation and her missing element of how to undo it, both together, one and then the other, and then the one again. The absence of the keys was held in her conscious awareness; the absence was the point now. She held consciously the gap in her awareness as she intended to close it.

She accepted the arational outcome that she got the Chinese girl part of her in place of the lost item of the keys. She felt moved into a ritual of willingly sacrificing her need to understand each step and the cause and effect of losing the keys which symbolized her never found self. Now she held all this in awareness along with the addition of a part new to her – the Chinese girl who accepted being dissociated and suffered being never found and found herself also discovering another realm of being that included us humans but did not center on us. She did not get rid of the gap but held it in awareness of what had happened to her not being held in mind by others she loved and depended upon.

We could not find any memory of where she placed the keys to safeguard her trying to undo the defense of dissociation by *not* losing the keys. She intended not to lose the keys. But dissociation was enacted anyway, getting rid of pain and confusion of her never being noticed as existing by ousting them onto the keys which vanished. But this time the pain and confusion were held onto consciously and suffered there, the terrible gap of going poof, goneness.

Nonetheless, this time she experienced the keys as a real symbol that ushered her into awareness of her defense of dissociation, her intent to undo it, it happening anyway. She got aware of that missing step that was 'blanked' from her mind. The keys as symbol ushered her into the experience of holding in her awareness her mind blanking and also representing her dreadful feeling she too was blanked out of existence. It was as if she bracketed the experience of where she put the keys to protect them. But now it was the keys that went poof, not she herself. She held in consciousness the missing link, what wasn't there; it was the emblem of her not being there in another's eyes.

Our work together in analysis and my part of it was the validating first witness to the narrative of going out of existence. The psyche dreaming up the Chinese girl and the mystery of keys that vanished was the psyche's second witness that gave her and me too, opportunity of holding that we can be gone out of existence and simultaneously witness to it, exist now. We house the annihilation and go on being.

We make space for the gap in the narrative and go on housing nonbeing in our being without going out of existence. It was the seeing and living this over time with different versions that undid the defense of dissociation.

The losings slowly decreased and now were always accompanied by awareness of the gap, the missing link, the item in safekeeping that could not be found, just as she had experienced not being found in her family, with no safe place for her held in their minds. Her awareness of playing an active part in the losings, that she eradicated the object and herself, oddly gave her a small but valuable sense of empowerment that lessened the dreadful helplessness she felt. This was not a comet that struck her without meaning; this was a meaningfulness that she helped engineer that she was getting more sense of with each losing. This was an achievement of holding absence in her present mind, without enacting it.

Transference/Countertransference Field

She dreamt now of forgetting her appointments with me for analysis. At times she felt I did not hold her in mind and we went over them again. At times she felt I did not fully understand her struggle to express the rubbing out of her effort to undo dissociating in order to build a bridge across that gap. She was right. I saw it and had my own trouble verbalizing this process to myself and with her. In those times I was not quite with her because it was so hard to express this elusive rubbing out. I thus received the transference of the one who did not get it, thus re-presenting, making palpable the impact of family members who did not notice her. I also received the transference of the unknowing one in her who was still trying to reason her way through something that could only be lived through ritually – exchanging the Chinese girl for the keys. I received as well transference of the part of her that yielded to this unknowing or a different way of knowing. In that role I personified the hope this could be done, and that was sufficiently true so I could bear when it surfaced her negative affect without undue objections.

Deep gratitude for analysis and for me too would erupt that we together created a space and time to move into and remove that deranging confusion that trauma inflicts. She felt such a disarray, a shambles, a tumult so complicated to explain the madness to anyone, that the analysis bore the full weight of the word 'temenos.' Here we entered the bedlam and found along with it (and hence the plenty of the psychoid level of psyche) a way through it. We were doing the work and felt its significance of contributing to all of us, as if putting into collective atmosphere we all inhabit, beams of clarity, of meaning, of wonder at the capacity of us humans to love the whole that included gaps and live it in the here and now.

She was letting go of her rationalizing in aid of entering more fully a symbolic level of mind. I carried the blank, the hole of the missing step, as well as the key to the missing keys: that she was undoing her old defense of dissociation. She was making space to hold the missing element in that undoing, seeing now how the undoing of her dissociation was itself being destroyed because she dissociated where she kept the keys secure. Instead of getting the keys safe she got the safety of carrying that gap, that missing step in her mind. Carrying that gap in mind, she got the sheer brunt of having gone missing so many times over the years of her life. She was present now to the absence that plagued her.

We were holding in mind the undoing that did not work and thus did get undone. When I could not hold it, she did, and vice versa. So together, a different kind of transference/countertransference played between us, added to the ones listed above. Here, in constellating the psychoid level being, we are also two human beings, our roles as analyst and analysand persist but in the background. In the foreground, the two of us as the human beings we are, getting to this point by our own routes (not for the analyst by induced countertransference), facing together forces of creative aliveness and destructiveness that are also together in the work we are doing and enduring.

We dwelt together in confused uncovering, not me an expert that knew for sure what was happening, but me also struggling to get this sleight of hand that erased the erasing factor, so the undoing could not complete itself, but was undone. The losings repeated themselves as she was trying to let them be undone, and she would lose the undoing of them. The destroying of the defense allowed seeing and housing its nullifying her mind while her mind is not nullified. She and I held 'blanking' of mind in our ongoing consciousness.

A Discovery

An unexpected effect of this housing what was not there, accepting its absence in an ongoing awareness, was the Chinese girl not being reduced to and defined by nearly being snuffed by abandonment to the dark. She stayed there, to speak symbolically, and did not fight her unnoticed state; she suffered it, let it happen. What slowly emerged was dim and then sharper perceptions of the dark. She looked around, consulted what she felt. I noticed a shift of interest in the Chinese girl and this, to repeat, was the time in the treatment when the pivotal question was asked, who did get annihilated because it was not the Chinese girl; she was alive and so was the patient. We discovered retrospectively that what got annihilated was the patient's contact with the world with others, a subject for another paper. But we also discovered prospectively a different dimension of nonbeing. We shifted our attention to what was this Chinese girl doing now alive in the dark?

The shift meant the dark unnoticed place could not be reduced to abandonment. Something else was there too. My analysand imagined, and I did too, the Chinese girl was exploring nonbeing: she knew about it as part of existence she had inhabited. She had news to tell of it. It could not be reduced to trauma of nonbeing as the going poof out of existence that had threatened all her life. She was feeling out a vastly bigger realm of nonbeing, as if recognizing its existence rather than its threat to eradicate her.

This grew and my patient went along with its unfolding by beginning to read Chinese masters like Laotzu. I began reading physics.* I formed in my mind a realm of nonbeing as non-human-centered-being. It was huge and cosmic; we humans had a place in it but a small one in relation to the wholeness of reality. That entirety included being and nonbeing that trauma threatened, and nonbeing as not-human-centered-being, the vast completeness in which our planet dwelt. It was outer space, void, but not empty. A coincidence occurred at that precise time of insight.

My analysand reported she read in the newspaper an arresting headline: "Scientists Blast Antimatter Atoms With Laser For the First Time." At the particle physics laboratory in Cern Switzerland that studies antimatter, they know at a subatomic level, antimatter is pretty much the complete opposite of regular matter. The matter particles that are classed as positive have electrons that have negative charge. Antimatter particles classed as negative, have electrons that have a positive charge. When antimatter particles come into contact with matter particles,

* "In quantum mechanics no object has a definite position, except when colliding headlong with something else." (Rovelli 2014, pp. 15-16). "The equations of quantum mechanics ... are used daily in widely varying fields ... yet they remain mysteries ... What does this mean?...Or, does it mean, as it seems to me, that we must accept the idea that reality is only interaction?" (ibid, p. 18; see also Randall 2013, pp. 20-21; see also Greene, 2005, pp. 115, 122, 171, 194, 200-216).

"touching the walls of its container they both disappear in a flash of light ... Because if his team makes antimatter and then it touches the walls of the container ... then poof! It's gone." Even the word 'poof' occurred!

The Big Bang theory of the origin of the universe (i.e. of being) where matter and antimatter collide in that flash of light, supposes that there should be nothing left, that both matter and antimatter would be 'annihilated.' But somehow some matter survives and we don't know why. To trap and study antimatter as a particle of antihydrogen atom allows measurement and comparison with matter of hydrogen atom, and as well, study of sense of the light as positrons in the atoms returned to lower energy levels. In effect, the annihilation resulting from the collision of matter and antimatter atoms results in release of energy, and in the possibility of studying in greater detail what makes up atoms. These results have already led to applications to cancer research medically, to research of fuel resources, to research in constructing new weapons.

An application for analysis might be this. Matter and antimatter particles collide and go poof into annihilation. This gets reframed as interaction not eradication. Life, aliveness, and antilife, destructiveness interact, go together and the empty space that persists in annihilation is not empty. Trauma psychologically is a huge 'antimatter' image with impact of destructiveness. But even the threat of 'poof' out of existence is not killing of aliveness. We must then discover that and experience its ongoingness and its nonhuman dimension of the felt void of this non-human centered nonbeing realm. This kind of nonbeing is not nonbeing of extinction but of belonging in a larger totality that includes the human as a small part but not the center. One may be blasted into this entirety if we can trust the example of the Chinese girl who let the psychic event happen and then explore what was happening. That antimatter on a personal level felt as nonbeing, is partner to, in partnership with the other half of beingness in matter particles, just as the Chinese girl left in the dark belongs with the busy girl active in seeking life. Only seeing the two together allows glimpses of a larger reality of which the human is one part, not the center.

That experience allows a kind of healing of destructive trauma, the collision where both in that oppositional form go out of existence replaced by going on being of interaction and discovery we are part of a larger totality. Further, we catch a glimpse and hold in consciousness that the missing element is not missing in fact. The enacted absence becomes present, held in awareness which leads to perception of being (matter) going on, persisting, surviving that can lead to aliveness and to sensing one's particular place in the large completeness of the whole of reality. Such a glimpse sustains faith in life. And its source.

This discovery heralded in science impressed us both as showing that as bad as the trauma of her early neglect through which she fell into nonbeing, nonbeing also exists as a different realm, as a subject in its own right, (not reduced only to the negative of trauma that threatens to replace beingness with nonbeing, explored through part of my analysand through the figuration of the Chinese girl).

Most of us eschew this realm of nonbeing in favor of the realm of being. We usually fall into nonbeing through trauma that knocks us out of simple happiness in being, some of us forever. We want to recover from feeling erased as a subject. The imaginative discovery of the psyche's witness through the invention of the image of the Chinese girl conveyed to this analysand both her desperate suffering walled off behind indifference, and her capacity to survive that worst experience of being left and forgotten, not emotionally held in mind or heart by a loving other in a family community. But that part of her personified as the Chinese girl had survived and had news to tell of this other realm that may not be reduced to being caused by damaging lack. Could we in our analytical work simultaneously hold in awareness these opposites: being, nonbeing as erasure, nonbeing as other than human being, all existing simultaneously? And when opposites collide they do so in a flash of light and go poof and something else gets discerned and gradually discovered.

In conclusion, we see integrating is hard work and painful and it is an amazing accomplishment to include the capacity to house the frightening possibility of being emotionally erased and not be killed by it. Nonetheless, psyche presses to undo this threat, an accomplishment we feel impelled to seek. Our working with psyche sustains such glimpses of meaning and such courage and contributes both to our culture.

This chapter was written and presented at the Journal of Analytical Psychology Conference on Dissociation New York City, 2018.

Addendum

The following are selected views of contemporary theorists on dissociation.
Philip Bromberg writes, "Dissociation ... is a healthy, adaptive function of the human mind. ... a basic process that allows individual self-states to function optimally ... when full immersion in a single reality, a single strong affect, and a suspension of one's self-reflective capacity is exactly what is called for or wished for." "When the illusion of unity is too dangerous to be maintained there is then a return to ... dissociation as a proactive, defensive response to the potential repetition of trauma." (Bromberg 1998, p. 273)
"Dissociated experience thus tends to remain unsymbolized by thought and language, exists as a separate reality outside of self-expression, and is cut off from authentic human relatedness and deadened to full participation in the life of the rest of the personality." (ibid, p. 133)
"The essence of dissociation is that the mind is disconnected from the psyche-soma to protect one's illusion of unitary selfhood from the potential threat of traumatically impinging experience it cannot process cognitively."(ibid, p. 232)

"Remedy involves allowing ourselves to stand in the spaces between self states and also allow them to link up with each other." (see ibid, pp. 182, 186)

M.L. Hainer presents Ferenczi's theory of the dissociative model of the mind as a creative response to pain and terror of trauma, and also how Ferenczi's contribution was dissociated from psychoanalytic tradition and only noticed, discussed and celebrated in the last half of the 20th century (Hainer 2016, pp. 58, 67, 69 in E. F. Howells and S. Itzkowitz 2016, pp. 57-71).

E.F. Howell and S. Itzkowitz write "Dissociative processes function to prevent the person from knowing the past, i.e. to obstruct knowledge of the past and to prevent it from breaking into consciousness and threatening to overwhelm the damaged, fragmented self and its tenuous hold on reality" (2016a, p. 16, E.F. Howell and S. Itzkowitz, 2016). "When dissociative barriers begin to break down and the need to not know diminishes, there is likely to be an initial period of emotional uncertainty, anxiety and disorientation ... as previously dissociated parts of the self are located or relocated." (ibid in Howell and Itzkowitz op.cit, p. 17)

The same authors continue, "The capacity for dissociation is an inherent aspect of the human mind and dissociative phenomena have played an important part in the human life since earliest time ... intrinsic to religious ceremonies ... as a response to life's problems" (2016b, in Howell and Itzkowitz 2016 op. cit. p. 20). "Dissociation protects the mind from the unthinkable, the unimaginable, and the unbearable helplessness to stop events that trigger feelings of terror, annihilation, and nonbeing." (ibid, p. 30)

The same authors continue "The dissociative unconsciousness then is characterized by gaps in our conscious experience. Yet the 'unconscious' experiences in these gaps continue to exist as living experience in that self-state." (2016c, in Howell and Itzkowitz 2016, op. cit. p. 9)

These three articles (2016a, 2016b and 2016c) all appear in E.F. Howell and S. Itzkowitz 2016. Eds. *The Dissociative Mind in Psychoanalysis, Understanding and Working with Trauma.* London and New York: Routledge.

J. Leighton writes that for self psychologists dissociation can leave "sustaining ties intact" so one's sense of self goes on split off from the trauma that can be dissociated, whereas in psychoses, says George Atwood, trauma "annihilates and subverts connections to fundamental levels of selfhood." (Leighton 2016. Eds. Howell and Itzkowitz, op.cit. pp. 128-129)

J. Newirth, a Kleinian, describes dissociation: "Because these experiences were not contained and therefore could not be thought about and elaborated, they remain concrete, unthinkable experiences, which are dissociated and repeatedly enacted and reexperienced in new relationships as new events, perceptions, and facts in the external world." A clue that dissociation is happening in the patient in a session is the analyst gets sleepy, bored, as does even the supervisor hearing about the case, twice removed (Newirth 2016. Eds. Howell and Itzkowitz 2016. op.cit. pp. 107-117).

D. Stern writes dissociation is a defense against identity: "to avoid the creation of a certain kind of a *state of being* or *self-state.*" It constricts freedom of thought, feeling and imagination. (Stern 2020, pp. 13, 64).
B. Van der Kolk writes "Dissociation is the essence of trauma. ... split off and fragmented, so the emotions, sounds images, thoughts, and physical sensations related to the trauma take on a life of their own." (Van Der Kolk 2014, p. 66)
Winnicott left notes on dissociation to be given, had he lived, to the Vienna Congress some months away. He sees dissociation as both a normal capacity, even playful as in an artist's work, and as a response to trauma. He hazards in his notes that analyses may fail because dominated by the mechanism of repression and a failure to see the dissociated states hiding in the material related to repression. It is essential to know the context in which dissociation is used. Similar to Jung's emphasis on the importance of a person telling his story to another who is an interested and devoted listener, Winnicott emphasizes the importance of the person being seen from outside themselves by another person. A sense of wholeness of personality is only possible by another seeing all the parts that go to make up the individual. (Winnicott quoted in Abram, J. 2012, pp. 312-313 and also in Goldman 2016, in Howell and Itzkowitz, Eds. op. cit. p. 97; see also Jung 1928/1954, paras 266-267, 269-271, 275)

References

Abram, J. 2012 "D.D.W. Notes on the Vienna congress 1971: A consideration of Winnicott's theory of aggression and its clinical implications" Abram, J. 2012. Ed. *Donald Winnicott Today.* London: Routledge, pp. 302-33.

Bromberg, P. 1998. *Standing in the Spaces.* Hillsdale, N. J.: The Analytic Press.

Celan, P. 1971. *Speech-Grille.* Translator Ajoachim Neugroschel. New York: E.P. Dutton.

Fairbairn, R. 1944/1954. "Endopsychic structure considered in terms of object relationships" Fairbairn, R. *An Object-Relations Theory of Personality.* New York: Basic Books, 1954.

Felstiner, J. 2001. *Paul Celan Poet, Jew, Survivor.* New Haven: Yale University Press.

Goldman. D. 2016 "'A queer kind of truth': Winnicott and the uses of dissociation" Eds. Elizabeth F. Howell and Sheldon Itzkowitz *The Dissociative Mind in Psychoanalysis.* 2016. London and New York: Routledge, pp. 97-106.

Greene, B. 2004. *The Fabric of the Cosmos.* New York: Vintage Books.

Harre, R. and Lamb, R. 1986. Eds. *The Dictionary of Physiological and Clinical Psychology.* Cambridge, Mass: MIT Press.

Howell, E.F. and Itzkowitz, S, 2016. Eds. *The Dissociative Mind in Psychoanalysis.* London and New York: Routledge.

Hainer, M.L. 2016. "The Ferenczi paradox: his importance in understanding dissociation and the dissociation of his importance in psychoanalysis" Eds. E. F. Howell and S. Itzkowitz, op.cit. pp. 57-69.

Hinsie, L. E. and Campbell, R. J. 1974. *Psychoanalytic Dictionary.* New York: Oxford University Press, p. 221.

E.F. Howell and S. Itzkowitz, 2016a. "Is trauma-analysis psychoanalysis?" op.cit. pp. 7-19.

— _ and ____ — 2016b. "From trauma-analysis to psycho-analysis and back again" op.cit., pp. 20-33.

— _ and ____ — 2016c. "The everywhereness of trauma and the dissociative structuring of the mind", op.cit. pp. 33-44.

Jung, C.G. and Riklin, F. 1906/1973. "The associations of normal subjects" *Collected Works* 2 *Experimental Researches Including the Studies in Word Association.* Trans. Leopold Stein in collaboration with Diana Riviere. Princeton N.J.: Princeton University Press.

Jung, C.G. 1907/1960. "The psychogenesis of Dementia Praecox" *Collected Works* 3 *The Psychogenesis of Mental Disease.* Trans. R.F.C. Hull. Princeton, N.J.: Princeton University Press, paras

— 1916/1960. "The transcendent function" *Collected Works* 8 *The Structure and Dynamics of the Psyche.* Trans. R.F.C, Hull. Princeton, N.J.: Princeton University Press, paras 131-191.

— 1921/1928. "The therapeutic value of abreaction" *Collected Works* 16 *The Practice of Psychotherapy,* paras 255-293.

— 1921. *Psychological Types, Collected Works* 6. Trans. R.F.C. Hull. Princeton N.J.: Princeton University Press.

1935/1976. *The Tavistock Lectures, Lecture V Collected Works* 18 *The Symbolic Life.* Trans. R.F.C. Hull. Princeton, N.J. and Oxford: Princeton University Press, paras 304-415.

— 1937/1960. "Psychological factors determining human behavior" *CW* 8, paras 232-262.

— 1939/1960. "On the psychogenesis of schizophrenia" *CW* 3, paras 504-541.

— 1948/1960 "A review of the complex theory" *CW* 8, paras 194-219.

— 1956/1960. "Recent Thoughts on Schizophrenia" *CW* 3, paras 542-552.

— 1957. "On simulated Insanity" *Collected Works* 1 *Psychiatric Studies.* Trans. R.F.C. Hull. Princeton, N.J.: Princeton University Press, paras 301-355.

— 1963. *Memories, Dreams, Reflections.* Recorded and edited by Aniela Jaffé. Trans. Richard and Clara Winston. New York: Random House.

— 2008. *Children's Dreams, Notes from the Seminar* Given in 1936-1940. Eds. Lorenz Jung and Maria Meyer-Grass. Trans. Ernest Felzeder with collaboration of Tony Wolfson. Philemon Series. Princeton, N.J. and Oxford: Princeton University Press.

— 2009. *The Red Book, Liber Novus.* Ed. Sonu Shamdasani. Trans. Mark Kyburz, John Peck, Sonu Shamdasani. New York: W.W. Norton.

— 2019. *Dream Symbols in the Individuation Process, Notes on C.G. Jung's Seminar on Wolfgang Pauli's Dreams.* Ed. Suzanne Geiser. Princeton N.J.: and Oxford: Princeton University Press.

Leighton, J. 2016. "Precarious places: intersubjectivity in traumatized states" Eds. E. F. Howell and S. Itzkowitz op. cit., pp. 127-137.

Newirth, J. 2016. "A Kleinian perspective on dissociation and trauma: miscarriages in symbolization" E.F. Howell and S. Itzkowitz, op. cit. pp 107-117.

Randall, L. 2013. *Higgs Discovery, The Power of Empty Space.* New York: Harper Collins.

Rovelli, C. 2016. *Seven Brief Lessons on Physics.* Trans. Simon Carnell and Erica Segre. New York: Penguin.

Saban, M. 2019. *Two Souls Alas Jung's Two Personalities and the Making of Analytical Psychology.* Ashville, North Carolina: Chiron.

Searles, H. 1960. *The Nonhuman Environment.* New York: International Universities Press.

Stern, D.B. 2020. *Partners in Thought, Working with Unformulated Experience, Dissociation, and Enactment.* New York and London: Routledge.

Sullivan, H. S. 1953. *The Interpersonal Theory of Psychiatry.* New York: W.W. Norton.

— 1972. *Personal Psychopathology, Early Formulations.* New York: W. W. Norton.

Ulanov, A.B. 2001a. *Finding Space: Winnicott, God and Psychic Reality.* Louisville, Ky.: Westminster John Knox Press.

— 2001b/2004. "When religion prompts terrorism" in Ulanov, A.B. *Spiritual Aspects of Clinical Work"* Einsiedeln, Switzerland: Daimon, pp. 313- 318.

— 2001c. "Encountering Jung 's Encounters in *The Red Book. Jung Journal, Culture & Psyche* vol 5, No. 3, pp. 54-63.

— 2017. *The Psychoid, Soul and Psyche: Piercing Space-Time Barriers.* Einsiedeln, Switzerland: Daimon.

Van Der Hart O. 2016. "Pierre Janet, Sigmund Freud, and dissociation of the personality: the first codification of a psychodynamic depth psychology. Eds. "E. F. Howell and S. Itzkowitz op.cit. pp. 44-57.

Van Der Kolk, B. 2014. *The Body Keeps the Score.* New York: Penguin.

Winnicott, D.W. 1963/1965. "From dependence toward independence in the development of the individual" Winnicott, D.W. *The Maturational Processes and the Facilitating Environment.* New York: International Universities Press.

— 1963?/1989. "Fear of Breakdown" Eds. Clare Winnicott, Ray Shepherd, Madeleine Davis, *Psycho-analytic Explorations.* London: Karnac, pp. 85-93.

Wyss, D, 1966. *Depth Psychology, A Critical History.* Trans. Gerald Onn. New York; W.W. Norton.

Chapter 4:

Holes, Helplessness, Incapacity, and Limits

Holes

Defensive dissociations that do not get undone leave us feeling there are holes in us. It may be a pothole. We sort of see it coming as we make our way and steer around it but then hit another we failed to notice. Our way is pockmarked by first this threat, then that one. Will it look trivial or will it break an axle? No way is unobstructed.

More grave, an analysand may say he or she is damaged by some experience; it left a hole in them. Something happened that should not have happened, an intentional cruelty of someone more powerful whom we could not avoid who inflicted on us emotional or physical pain. Or, a hard knock of fate happened, a loved parent suddenly dying, not ever there again. Whether personally caused or impersonally happening like the parent's illness, a big hole, a gulf inhabits our being from then on.

Other analysands might use the word deficit to describe the hole. They say here exists a lack in them, something that should be there is not there. It did not grow in them and they do not have it; they feel flawed, defined by defect. Or, the larger collective force of present society and this historical time effects a breach in something taken for granted, relied upon like the earth under our feet. A hole lurks there instead.

Sending our children off to school is broken off by danger of pandemic virus (2020-2021 and 2022) and with no certain end to its threat. Education is broken into. When will classes in person resume? Are they broken away forever? Will this hiatus go on indefinitely? Is the relationship with the person teaching replaced by relationship to one's computer and the illusion through zoom that self and person are in contact? It looks as if so, but is it? No texture of the space between them exists, no touch in body gesture of greeting or farewell from the taste and scent of the shared space. How many of us, for example, can return right there to school cafeteria lunches when the smell of overcooked vegetables assaults our noses. Zoom is an illusion of person to person relationship, not the real thing. We are each looking at a camera, not at each other, even though it looks as if we are seeing each other.

Is the new frame for the intimacy of discovering the sound of a word, the finding of a new word, the mystery of equation describing the meeting of mass and energy, of lines and angles of geometric forms, the puff of smoke of chemical experiment now between me and my machine and the invisible ether as the means of conducting our congress? Have the children in lockdown mode in their homes to protect their physical health had a chunk of learning broken away from them now and for the future? Will we not need it any more just as we once used horses to draw carriages instead of using a key to start our vehicles? Not only have we lost the emotional ritual of graduating and celebrating fulfilment of a degree and phase of life, but also deep experience of meeting with others through acquiring skills of thinking, measuring, calculating, finding words in themselves and in books and conversations with others around specific materials. Imagination bloomed as if out of nowhere to describe a continent we maybe knew before, but now behold as vast. Has all that disappeared into a hole so vast we think it is the new landscape?

Lures to destruction are so fascinating and frightening that even our conscious will to resist can panic. We do not want to fall into that hole of entrancement again, but we might! We could! By one little error or sip or gesture or by failing to stand up and object we could instantiate entrapment down at the hole's bottom. Or, we might fall into this hole simply to release the tension of teetering on its edge.

One of the dangers I emphasized about such fascination is we overconcretize what the lure lures us to or what it reminds us we lack. We bemoan loss and then define ourselves by the hole it has left. The person, for example, knows in their bones the inhibition, misdirection, evasive detouring around contamination with parents' problems and how that dislodged their footing. They slipped into that pit and judgment resounds from its walls. They have failed to find their ownmost life; they should have tried harder, worked longer, took the little goods they had and not given over in compliance to others telling them who they should be.

In a hole where nothing grows or guides, we can get so lured by the narrative of destruction that it feels impossible to step outside the hole. Instead, inside it the narrative replicates and sticks them fast as if they never can get out of that cavity, only elaborate it and mourn the life never found to be lived. Or another person felt keenly the loss of sexuality with the death of her partner, and then defined herself by its absence – she is becoming a juiceless wrinkled prune, dying before she was dead; a living death now, rather than the real death then.

A hole in us affects others around us, as well as the reverse: we can fall into what is a gap in them. Jung addresses this in the transference/countertransference,

> "A 'hole is something unconscious. We do not notice it ... the blind spot ... When patients fall into the dark 'hole' of the doctor, they are the victims. At the same time, however, they have power over the doctor. They are always standing where he cannot see them, and can then exercise their magic – but not as they want, but as it happens to them ... We ourselves create effects we do not like, because we do not see ourselves there. Such a hole is missing consciousness." (Jung 2008, p. 76)

Elie Humbert notes that successful analysis indicates that the wound of the analyst and the wound of the analysand touch each other as does their transformation. As Davoine and Gaudilliere put it, the abandoned child in the analyst goes to the aid of the abandoned child in the patient, especially in relation to social neglect and persecutions (Humbert 1984, pp. 67-71, 81; see also, Davoine and Gaudilliere 2004, pp. 140ff). We must know the differences between the two as well, lest they fall into a hole as a folie à deux.

Related to these near and far aspects is differentiation of archetype and person, of the mother as the vitally important person who anchors our psyche in our body and fosters the growing of our ego in relationship with her and with others. There is also the mother residing in the unconscious in a deep place, presiding over the passage to consciousness (or its destructive aspect, mother as witch sucking consciousness into the unconscious). Such are known as the mothers of the deepest creative life force. Jung notes that a singular mother, for example in a dream, means someone's mother with a specific personality. To describe the plural Mothers of transformation (or its defeat), Jung cites Goethe where Mephistopheles says to Faust,

> "You're in the last deep, deepest there might be.
> By its light you'll see the Mothers,

Some sit about, as they wish, the others
Stand and move. Formation, Transformation,
Eternal minds in eternal recreation." (Goethe 6285 cited in Jung 2008, pp. 76, 87)

Does this suggest to us that the Mothers represent the primordial life force in each and all of us, regardless of whether we have had a good or a bad mother? Does it mean the hole we feel as what is missing in our consciousness and is negative – a shortage, a defect – may in its deepest layer give access to the creative and transformative powers of the life force of the Mothers? (See Jung 1930/1966, para 159; see also Jung 1956, para 459; see also Humbert 1984, p. 122). Mother in this sense represents returning as the brooding spirit on the waters of creation, on the waters of our unconscious, as a remnant of aliveness lying hidden in the heap of trauma and sorrow if we can stand to get through to it there.

Two views pertain, mix and differentiate: the vicissitudes of personal relation to one's mother and all she represents, and the journey, as Jung puts it, "after the peregrinations of a long life full of confusion and error, to become the *filius regius,* son of the supreme mother" carrying the burden and precious value of the infinite lived in the unique finite, the hero in the fool, the blazing feminine in the ordinary woman (Jung 1946/1954, para 407). They meet, mix, interpenetrate, interdepend. They do not identify but rather relate one to the other and other to the one. Who would think a hole that trips us up would convey a blessing?

Helplessness and Holes

The worst thing about holes is that they render us splat on our face, flat on our backs, buried between soft caving walls, or held fast in rigid sides, too deep to crawl out and who will remember we are in there and come to find us. One analysand tells in beginning our work, he would play hide and seek as small boy and hide so well he could not be found. The other children would give up and go home. Winnicott notes the opposite danger: it is fun to hide and disaster if found, referring to our incommunicado core that must never be violated. That would be worse than rape or losing an eye or cannibalism (Winnicott 1968, p. 187; see also pp. 179, 185-186, 190). So we have hole, good and bad, refuge and what Steiner calls a psychic retreat from which we must be rescued to emerge into a fuller life. We must not make a permanent hole out of an initial defense against trauma (Steiner 1993, pp. 1ff.).

Holes plunge us into helplessness. We hit bottom and there is nowhere to go. All efforts to vie, improve, call up former successful strategies amount to nothing. Here are patients' dream snippets and their mixing in with external events and collective upheavals that make our helplessness feel outer as well as inner. A woman dreamt of crowded narrow street. She looks for evidence of blood flowing in the street and then underground below the gutters, a second blood flowing. She is alone, no one with her 'in myself, managing myself.' I thought of her early trauma as the first blood flowing, and the second blooding in the present analysis where all this suffering was coming up to consciousness. She associated to hordes of people amassing on southwest borders of America. They were fleeing in grave fear from the wreckage of their countries being taken over by poverty and crime and many Americans were frightened of an invasion of their country. She felt both fears. She knew if she lived in a country of poverty, of no jobs, no safety, no school for her children, "I would be in the caravan too" despite the loss of her homeland. She didn't know how to solve their plight of being unable to solve their country's messes, nor understand her fear of them as if invaders of her safety. She felt outer collective problems crossed into her personal wreckages and efforts to help herself but her efforts had not succeeded. She could not clean up her messes any better than asylum seekers could fix their countries' plights.

She barely escaped an outer disaster by suddenly remembering that 'missing piece of consciousness' (a hole) and running flat out on the street many blocks to her city apartment to whip off the stove the small pot she left boiling an egg. She knew the water would have run out and it could set the kitchen on fire and endanger her neighbors on the same floor and the floors above and below if fire broke out in her kitchen. She arrived just in time, seeing the egg had exploded but the flame still had not burned through the pot. The pot was so hot that when she lifted it with double mittens and put it on a breadboard, it burned an indelible black circle into the wood. Cleaning up the egg scraps, even on the kitchen ceiling, scouring the pot, she gushed thanks that her inner 'missing consciousness' did not endanger herself or her neighbors. Only fate, luck, chance, allowed her to get back in time and heave the egg and ego mess and inflamed pot into cold water. But she knew her psychic 'hole' crossed over into outer reality with potentially terrible consequences. Was it the same with the countries the caravaners were fleeing? Their psychic and social 'holes' spread wreckage to their citizens and to neighboring countries?

Sometime a patient's dream shows a great danger threatening, but escaped by consciousness of it. The driver of the car sees just there ahead at ground level, barely visible, the circle of the rims of two giant cylindrical containers with shiny steel edges, razor sharp, as if buried in the ground but not covered up. The cylinders are empty and open. The driver realizes if he had driven over them the car's tires would be sliced open., or the wheels could have fallen into the open vat. The scene menaced him. But he had not driven over them. The cylinders were completely empty. What could they be, these two vats of emptiness? Did they house all the losses of his life, the broken pieces, the moments of feeling he was a discard? Had the work of analysis been to empty these cylinders?

Another analysand when reading in a book I had written felt something jerk him and he fell into a hole. Was he just another of my analysands, one example of a collective psychic problem? This thought-feeling abolished his sense of the intimacy of our connection where he felt found and seen, valued as a unique person. The hole embodied helplessness he felt now to recover that connection and feel worthy and genuine. This hole in our relationship revived the helpless disorientation of his early life that not only was he lost to himself as a small boy with no one to hold onto but also that he and his mother lost the closeness they might have shared. They missed it. It never happened. He felt his helplessness to fix it then and now felt helpless to recover with me our connection where he felt validated.

But the shift out of the hole happened, perhaps by seeing at once the present and past invalidation of himself in contrast to the intimate connections we shared. Going back and forth between those opposites nudged a shift from him feeling the cause of his not being valid; he was no longer defined by a lack in himself. Instead of taking himself as the author of that loss and the lack of closeness with his mother and then defining himself as that lack, he saw his helplessness. He and his mother shared the same helplessness. Something went missing between them and its causes had multiple roots. He and I were not helpless like that. We could explore it and hold it between us and let it mend. We could explore the collision of seeing himself as part of a collective human problem and a unique valuable person, maybe even contributing to all of us learning how to heal such a problem, not losing our connection to a reduction to an abstract category of lack.

In a similar but not identical way, the woman horrified at what she felt was her prejudice against the caravan people invading her country, got nudged to see her prejudice was fear-based. When she stood in their shoes, she felt the same fear and helplessness they felt to repair the wreckage in the country they were abandoning. And it was a similar helplessness she felt to redeem the wreckage from her early life. She and they were similar, the same in fear. They were caravaning to find in the new country security and satisfaction, the basic need/desire His Holiness the Dalai Lama says belongs to all of us. But helplessness to install an ego solution makes room to see something else. Helplessness when acknowledged and owned surprises. It makes space for something outside self to be seen.

What we see first is helplessness that we have fallen in a hole and cannot get out of it. We reach admitting it. We cannot manage it nor effect a plan that succeeds. Falling in a hole makes us aware we are not in control and that we are dependent, contingent, not in charge, at best a sous-chef or assistant to the greater power. We call that the gods, or You, the God, or fate, or cosmic rhythms, or more vaguely, the beyond.

Whatever our name for that something more, recognition of its thereness changes experience of the hole from trap to door. Acceptance of helplessness makes space for something more to emerge. No longer fighting our helpless state our dependence on something more comes to the fore, letting it be such as it is; that allows us to perceive the something more in one of its many varieties, the one that shows itself to us.

Wolfgang Pauli, Noble Prize laureate, whom Jung describes as "a man with a great mind, so he observed accurately" (Jung 2019, p. 174), was grounded in science yet also full of big dreams about something more. He has a shocking experience when he accepts there is a something more that his dreams point to, that he has not made it up, but consented to in lavish terms. He dreams he talks to a friend who turns up often with helpful advice for the terrible conflict Pauli is suffering. But in this dream Pauli himself gives the necessary advice. He confesses he must surrender to the other side. In the dream he says to his friend, "I must endure this situation, in front of the bleeding Christ, and I must work at it (namely, at my redemption)" (Jung 2019, p. 309).

Jung notes that often we must go back to words we outgrew to express the soul's reality and needs in the present time. Jung writes of Pauli, "that scientist talks in such a style! It is almost hieratical or a biblical style. He is forced to go back to such language in order to formulate the attitude which is really needed, and from that you can see how serious his conflict is and how terrible it is to him to submit to the other side" (ibid, p. 309). Pauli's conflict is between the validity of his intellect grounded in science of the time and the sacred pointed to in his dreams. When the something more shows itself to us, perhaps inflected by a different conflict but nonetheless ruthless, "you doubt your sanity and then you are forced to an extraordinary attitude … of complete submission … to your suffering" (ibid).

Accepting helplessness is not lying about eating chocolates and leaving to others to do what is our job. The shift includes going on doing our personal work whatever that may be and the action it inspires in the world. The shift is toward what Jung means, I suggest, when he says, let psychic events happen. Quiet the interfering ego that is planning, plotting, managing, with one's effortfulness taking up all the oxygen. Or as a patient dreamt, "stems of flowers that hold their seeds of future growth are now almost depleted and tunnel brown, so I can pull them out, but if too soon, will miss the future growth promised." Prematurely trying to arrive at something (even a good something) instead must go along in its own time; don't yank it up according to your plan. Another woman who reached this acceptance, expressed it: "I am incompetent" meaning unable to do all things she planned to master. She gave up that achieving. The sentence was a triumph and a renunciation, both. It involved not stealing the space for her daughter to fight for her own goals, to not rush in to fund a degree to get a job. This had never worked before. This time she accepted her helplessness and the reality of needing money urged the daughter to make her own effort; and she did.

The Collective and Holes

Acknowledging helplessness makes space for a door to open, something new to emerge because the overactive take-charge ego is knocked out. But that chance can be snuffed if we lack curiosity to spy what emerges. The problems remain sealed. We fail to look into what we repudiate as the bad in us, our shadow. Jung writes, "He has to descend in order to find his shadow. He has to turn around once to look at himself from the other side" (Jung 2008, p. 19). This is serious, I suggest, because not looking leaves a hole in the ego and then the collective unconscious stuff in which we dwell – in our families, our groups, our societies – seeps in. It is as if the psyche seeks a holistic direction or aim as discussed in chapter 1 as the psyche's project which anchors our personal project on a basis broader than our individual conflicts and aims. Even our most personal problems mirror the social milieu in which we dwell; they reflect the spirit as atmosphere we inhabit with its violences as well as its openings to wider deeper movements.

Dreams, for example, not only show an archetypal dominant in the midst of our personal situation. For we also dream "out of our environment and take up problems. Themes from all around flow in though no word is spoken" (ibid, p. 86). We need to see the general human issue in our personal problem and find our personal application of the general human difficulty (ibid, p. 59). Dreams bring the collective: "This is the secret of dreams. We are the object of the dream, not its maker … The dream is dreamed to us. We are the objects. We simply find ourselves in a situation." (ibid, p. 159).

To be penetrated by the collective unconscious is to lose our feet on the ground. "We lost touch with reality, are governed by the unconscious, no longer feel our weight, and lose our orientation in space … feelings of dizziness, or outright symptoms of seasickness … lifted into the air by the wind" (ibid, p 71). Where there is a hole in the ego, collective energies will seep in or stream. Then we are in personal trouble. We cannot assimilate what we do not understand nor what is common, not personal (ibid, p. 147). "The collective unconscious is not oneself – it is collective. That is a fact, that is not a projection, it is not an opinion … it does not belong exactly in my own psyche, despite the fact that it influences my psyche" (Jung 2019, p. 174).

The collective unconscious houses archetypal images like tectonic templates, like deep underground structures that support the buildings in which we live, like primordial images that describe the course of humankind. Energies coming from there can swamp our small egos, inflate us into fantasy we can be 'the winner!' not a loser! We have caught hold of the truth! We sense ourselves to be above common law. We can learn to integrate personal shadow material and, to some degree, aspects of our societal and cultural shadow. But we cannot integrate collective structures nor archetypal primordial images; they are impersonal, like a tidal wave, a pandemic, a revolution, or a new paradigm of knowing. But that does not mean we dare ignore such structures or movements or primordial images. We learn to relate to them, not act as if they are part of our personal property, nor treat them as if they have nothing to do with us.

That grievous mistake we learn and learn again in the poor parent who thinks God told him to burn the devil out of his child, or the Charles Manson who has a genuine religious experience of transcending the opposites of good and evil but utterly lacks ego strength to know what to do with such a blasting experience. He acts out literally the sameness (not the reconciliation) of the opposites in mass murder, or it acts itself out through the hole in his passive nonrelated ego (Zaehner 1974). Worse still, the seepage into the hole in many peoples' egos of the collective energies, and their lack of curiosity to deal with these shadow bits landing within themselves where they are permeable to the collective unconscious as if in a trance, can result in their voting into powerful office of a country's leadership the man caught in identification with archetypal powers. He woos their votes with the promise they will become the *Übermensch*. With one caveat: they must pledge loyalty to him. And if they do not, they must be shunned, humiliated, not thought of as equal citizens, called horrible names, segregated in torture camps, and killed.

Jung also shows his dependence upon something more appearing in clinical work. He recognizes his value lies not in what he does or even says. What matters is that he is there with the analysand, in it, the two together in the face of the unconscious:

> "Most of the therapeutic effect depends … upon invisible things. I often say to my patients, 'It does not matter *what* I say; it is important that I say *something*, that I am there, that I am on the spot with you. That is the thing that really counts' … some plan as to how to cure the patient … would be a big mistake because it would be arbitrary and calculated … We have to follow the lead of the unconscious. Usually when there is a conscious purpose we are defeated because that has nothing to do with the unconscious. We are really up against something which is not identical with our conscious." (Jung 2019, pp. 93-94)

It is also the actual relationship that matters and conveys that its two participants matter.

Further still, we are not, finally, alone:

> "one is never quite alone because there is something in the invisible space behind consciousness. You receive all the time from that source; there is not one thought in your head which has not been received. You do not make thoughts; they come to you … It can make you forget things … It fills you with emotions you haven't made, and things happen to you which you have not chosen … Who is the maker of your thoughts?" (ibid, p. 132)

If we can understand these things in the space behind consciousness because we have given up we are author of all that happens to us, our helplessness collapses our schemes, defenses and absolute plans for our future.

If we understand this sort of fact, then we can integrate it and not succumb to feeling crazy. Instead, a door opens and we can speak our story to another – that valuable first witness again – our fumbling for the way, the truth, the good, our failures to effect them. Again, clinically, the saving thing is the other who wants to listen and hear because they know there is something behind what terrifies us. Jung states "as long as man has the desire to explain himself, he is not crazy." But if no one understands, then we are

> "just over the border … Repeatedly, such patients have told me things I simply could not swallow … I felt aversion … but something in me had an instinctive feeling: 'There is something back of that talk, no matter how absurd it seems to me; something is back of it, something I can't grasp.' That was sufficient. They saw that flash in my eye, and that was enough for them." (ibid, p. 148)

For any of us, if we go down far enough through layers of conscious and unconscious, from personal powerful figures of father mother, sister, brother, child, friend, enemy, into cultural images of power, service, mentor, victim, into primordial images of different archetypal figures of the wise one, the radiating center, the philosopher's stone, down to primitive forms like shapes of square, circle, depth, and animals, like lion, lamb, wolf, serpent, spider, and lower still to creative and destructive forces, we follow where the hole's door leads. Would this justify the presence of the hole, the rent in our ego? No, probably not. It came by suffering and pain is pain. Would knowing that through those holes we get ushered to what is beyond them and redeem holes from only negative connotations? Yes. Probably so, knowing through them we get ushered into what is beyond them. We find ourselves with tasks we never dreamed or only dreamed of and we learn our way of facing, balancing, working with these forces all the way upward through the same layers to arrive at the personal work of our individuation. People say it to themselves: I knew I was to be a chef; I was where I belong working as teacher of the voice; It was car mechanics that I fell in love with as a small boy; It was dance; it was caring for the uncareable; it was to repair hurt beyond repair; it was to paint the joyous moments of life; it was to secure a place of safety to live; it was to survive, to kick the habit, to make a difference, to give back.

Holes and the 4th: Incapacity

The hole becomes a door and, as Jung puts it, we say, yes of course "how nice, how beautiful!" But when it is our hole, our helplessness, "when it comes to you in such a nakedness, just so and nothing else, and with all the weight of a most important experience, well, then, naturally, you doubt your sanity" (Jung 2019, p. 309). For then we too, like Pauli, are forced to consent, submit, let happen. For Pauli it was sacrificing his extraordinary intellect, "to overcome his most cherished function." For us with different superior functions – feeling or intuition or sensation – it is the same degree of sacrifice. What we share in common is submission to the something more, achieving, however briefly as did Pauli and as did Jung himself in *The Red Book*, identification with the movement of "Christ who simply surrenders to his suffering" (ibid, p. 309).

The something more, the unconscious as the other side, as the maker of our thoughts or emotions or conflicts and forgetting things, is found through what is undeveloped and left inferior in us. Jung initially in *The Red Book*, called it our 'incapacity' meaning literally where we are unable, resourceless, have no idea how to do or even be. We function on an inferior level. But there we are. Further, we do not like this ill-equipped part of us, but scorn it, call it stupid, wrong. Pauli did not know how to accept this other side that his dreams presented as an unknown woman sending him a letter about a pain in her womb that suggested a pregnancy and "a possible birth" that made its way in a serpentine manner. Then he had to go through a jungle full of monkeys that pointed back to a previous dream of his having to reconstruct the gibbon which associates to the instinctual man. This seemed to Pauli incomprehensible, ridiculous; it should not exist (Jung 2019, pp. 302-304).

Whatever our incapacity is, we feel there unevolved, childish, mediocre, enfeebled, even paralyzed, made powerless. It happens to us, in dreams or in life events. We are taken there. The experience is humiliating yet also enlivening, even exhilarating in liberating us to the resources of the unconscious. Energy rushes in. This is not to anthropomorphize the unconscious. It does not say you ought to but just shows you what is from its point of view.

The inferior function is slow, clumsy, never firmly in hand and puts us in touch with the fountainhead of the unconscious. An example of this happened to me with rust and the insistent necessity to replace the boiler in my house, a task I had evaded for six years. The boiler man prevailed. By sheer luck or the beneficence of the boiler gods, when the men came to chop up the boiler because it was 61 years old and its model too large to exit the house whole, they just caught it in time from collapsing into an entirely rusted-out bottom that could flood the boiler room off the kitchen, the kitchen, the dining and living areas with water dyed red from the rust. Despite the workmen's valiant efforts to clean up the boiler room, its floor looked like a murder had been committed on its concrete base, now stained blood red. Tiny particles of fine soot and cement dusted every shelf and counter in the boiler room and nearby kitchen.

By synchronistic chance I was reading Murray Stein's excellent article (Stein 2017, pp. 161-162, 277) on the place of failure in individuation at the same time I was full of resentment at this sensate task thrust upon me that took so much time!! A new boiler required finding and meeting with the proper workmen as the radiant heating valves were old, numerous, and required a special skill. Then scheduling the day, a big expense, and hours to get this chore done were required. I felt outraged and robbed of my life. When inhospitable to such necessary tasks, they turn persecutory; we feel assaulted by them. I was full up with that captious, complaining, indignant attitude. And I knew my fault too, that my attitude was wrong. But a complex bit its teeth into my neck and shook me. I felt put upon by my incapacity, and delivered even, as Jung says frighteningly in *The Red Book*, to "evil looking at me coldly" (Jung 2009, p. 300, n 204). What we cannot accept, we repudiate. We would kill it if we could. And in projected form onto our neighbor or the next group, we fantasize such killing. Hence my horror and my laughing in naming the boiler location the 'murder room,' covered in rust-blood.

Jung has a huge reference library in him of myths, legends, ancient rituals and esoteric and exoteric disciplines to draw upon as analogous to unconscious process. Most of us do not have that library within. But we do have our own contexts and traditions and it is those that float up into consciousness when our conscious words cannot explain the ingress of the unconscious inferior function. An odd association swims by and makes sense of what is happening. Murder room: my love of mystery stories where the villain gets caught and punished, good persisting in the company of evil, and the insight that resentment against sensate tasks with its odd entitled attitude that I should not have to do this chore. It is not my responsibility!

It has all the marks of projection with its agitation and leads to the question: when did you assume sole responsibility for something an adult in your life should have carried but did not notice? Maybe this is the first time you have connected with anger about taking on a job too big for you as a small child, as if it *was* your sole responsibility? Is this the first time you said No! and sought something in the relationship that was missing, not there and that should have been? Is this what all the resentment is about?

Where is the ordinary good parent, the other who does these tasks silently and generously for her children without expecting a thank you note. Billy Collins' poem "A Mother's Day Gift: The Lanyard" sums up the view of the child who can and does depend on the parent, with all its entitlement to depend, at least for a short time. Mom loves to scrub the kitchen floor from the mud I tracked in; Mom endured a perilous birth for me and I made her a lanyard for Mother's Day (Collins May 8, 2015). Our incapacity when faced, brings up the wounds under whose weight we soldiered on without compassion or understanding, just feeling stupid about it and pathological. We enact in entitled outrage at the present task the anger we failed to register and communicate to the other when a small child.

Facing the inferior function in us means facing our utterly rejecting attitude toward this that belongs to us and will not yield to our usual ways to work out adaptation or compromise. Jung hypothesizes, which is clarifying, that this function is not like the other three. They are detached from the unconscious and become developed parts of conscious life and adapted to reality. The most developed hence superior one we rely on as our habitual mode of approach to understanding ourselves and others and the world. The second function, also pretty well developed and the third, a less but still identifiable capacity, act as auxiliary to the superior developed one. But the one at the bottom, in the hole, left undeveloped and in fact inferior is not even registered as a function. We say of it – Oh I never could do numbers; oh all that emotional stuff always put me off; oh that cold logician's thinking I detest, so unrelated; oh I hate those horrible chores that invade your life and gobble up all your energy. We disown the inferior function and dismiss it if we can get away with it.

Unlike the other functions, the inferior incapacity is embedded in the unconscious hence has been contaminated by all the unconscious stuff both personal and collective residing there. When we try to lift up this inferior function into conscious development it brings the whole unconscious with it. We regress to being a child once again. That accounts for the exhilarating and liberating effect: so much energy and excitement flows into us, feeling like a rebirth – falling in love again, drawn in a deep way to a whole new area of sport or history or the country or music's new fashion. Life is flowing again! The treasure of the inferior function is aliveness: we feel vibrant and real here and now and open to livingness whole heartedly.

A whole change of attitude is necessary. Stein's article led me back to Jung on rust! In alchemy rust was metal's leprosy, pathology, failure, and simultaneously its greenness on the bronze metal that was the basis for its transformation into the treasure of gold: "In the alchemical view rust, like verdigris, is the metal's sickness. But at the same time leprosy is the *vera prima materia,* the basis for the preparation of the philosophical gold." Jung cites an older view of Thales "'Tis rust alone that gives the coin its worth!" Rust is the inferior of the inferior and the basis of transformation to the highest aim: "life calls not for perfection but for completeness: and for this the 'thorn in the flesh' is needed, the suffering of defects without which there is no progress and no ascent (Jung 1953, paras 206-208 also cited in Stein 2017, pp. 161-162).

The simultaneity of humiliating suffering and gratitude ensued. I was literally brought low to my hands and knees by the necessary chore imposed on me by rust. For hours on two successive days for two successive weekends I was scrubbing the stains of the murder room. Yet gratitude gushed forth. Outrage and submission together. I felt something hard to name and slow to come working a change in me. Not 'it could have been worse' though that was true. But rather, I was wrong; I am lucky escaping disaster here; I need to be on my hands and knees scrubbing my way down to my failure and to others' failure in my life and my newly felt anger toward them and to whatever this new animal is, making its way with me. The staining rust and the work it required held meaning of some new attitude I needed but I could not invent it, nor will it into being. Kneeling, scrubbing, sweating, was a living experience, not an idea, not even a clear logical plan, but a necessity. Accepting it, I was submitting to where I belonged. An odd pleasure surprised me that although greatly improved, the blood rust stain could not be entirely lifted from the floor; its design and color remained in fainter hues. Its color marked this event.

Encounter with our inferior function calls up the problem of the 3 uniting with 4, attributed to Maria Prophetessa, "called the Jewess sister of Moses, or the Copt" who cried without restraint "One becomes two, two becomes three, and out of the third comes the One as the fourth" (Jung 1953, paras 206-208; see also Jung 1952/1960, para 962; See also Ulanov, 2007a, 2007b). How to reach a unified sense of personality when, as Goethe wrote about his own inferior thinking function:

"The three we brought with us
But the fourth would not come.
He was the right one, he said,
Who thought for them all." (Faust I and II, 309, par. 8200, cited in Jung 2019 p. 256)

Jung said thinking was his superior function and feeling the inferior. One plot of the Red Book can be seen as the upending of this order. He recognizes that for him as thinker and like Pauli also, feeling which "is a function of values" "has descended into the unconscious because it wasn't tolerated in the conscious" (Jung 2019, p. 257) for "only those values are allowed to exist that fit in with preconceived intellectual statements … anything independent … autonomous, will not be tolerated but will be wiped out" (ibid, p. 257). Access to the totality of the four functions is reaching for the totality of the personality, a never ending process.

When the inferior function comes up everything archaic, historical, in collective memory in the unconscious is interwoven with our incapacity which is also in the unconscious. So, as Jung says, "You pull up a world; the whole world shakes when you try to pull it up, and that is why the fourth won't come up, and therefore you have to bow down to him" (ibid, p. 258) Jung cites Goethe, "The fourth, that is the real thing! That is the God! That is the one that functions for all!" It is the stone the builders rejected that becomes the corner stone, the philosopher's stone, "the light greater than all light means a new manifestation of the deity almost … identified with Christ … the Redeemer (ibid, p. 264).

To feel the wonder and the horror, the fear of the whole system changing, just think of your own inferior function. We find that directly by going "where you are most afraid. Follow your fear to find your destiny and there you will find your fourth function … real life … an attractive reality, and so, quite often, it is most advisable *not* to seek it" (ibid). For it requires a great risk for bringing it up.

We can imagine the grandeur, the pivotal nature of the fourth when it is one of the psychological functions we admire. But it is not. It is what each of us would scorn: the pig, filthy and greedy, yet also the fructifying feminine. It is tremendous aggressiveness in the murder room of rust staining into the floor, yet also the greenness bestowing energy and new light (ibid, pp. 277-278). It is the toad that Nietzsche could not swallow, and it swallowed his sanity. It hides in what lures us. It is the lowly one with no place to be born who drew the high and the lowly to his manger with animals that we celebrate in Christmas ritual but too often not feeling the revolution changing our own heart.

Limits and Holes

Addressing holes, helplessness and inferior parts of us means facing limits. We cannot be seeking the unconscious every minute. We need to leave it to lie fallow like the land between harvesting and planting. In analysis there needs, I believe, to be time off during the year. (I remember laughing and feeling abashed to learn my analysands all improved from such a recess of our sessions.) Jung writes, "If you observe carefully what happens within, you will see that you cannot do more than your ability permits you to do" (Jung 2019, p. 311). The unconscious is nature within us, as well as around us.

Facing our incapacity shows us limits. The intuitive superior function meets up with brute sensation that says, here, now, this earth, in this space and time is where you take root. Or a feeling type feels found when achieving emotional clarity about the values heretofore hidden in a besetting and confusing turmoil. At such a point the person may dream in geometrical forms like a rectangle, a square that delineates what matters. Jung points out how for a thinker the feeling value of an idea or image has to plant us before it becomes real to us, and further, for insight to cross into ethical action depends on feeling its truth. For the sensate superior function the options intuition sees grant a lightness and lifting of weightedness to give even in the body a sense of soaring, dancing, imagining beyond the fence.

The intimacy of limits makes us feel anchored, with a definite shape, moored to a foundation, within boundaries that may even allow their transgression because they are clear. In the clinical relationship the limits of time and place and fee and what the work is contrasts with more open possibility of exploring a personal relationship and entering into sexual, or financial or legal commitments. In clinical work a bond is forged by living through together a profound experience of a past wound or an immediate one, or a happy blooming, a bond that may last long after the work has ended. It is a kind of love, passing back and forth between the two and love of the work and love of the psyche, indeed of the soul that grounds the work.

Yet the limits of intimacy also free the work. For we are together for this work, not to be social friends, or lovers, or editors or activists together, or, or. We may be imagined to be any or many of those things but our purpose is to see through them the personal project the analysand came to do and the psyche's project to find our space and time in the wholeness of the whole, and what our contribution is to it.

In this way an aspect of healing includes depersonalizing the mess I find myself in when seeking analysis. Not only do I have to enunciate and get clear about the major complex besetting me; I have to explore in detail each side of the oppositions that are idiosyncratically my own. Examples from analysands show the oppositions between expert controlling and learning to follow what prompts; going up into the stratosphere to escape pain of childhood loss and coming down to earth in ordinary, lively even strenuous living with other people. Each of us has her or his own peculiar strife of opposites of conscious and unconscious aims, personal and collective ambitions and hopes. We need to detect their secret handshake, each side oddly mirroring the other as part of a larger purpose and meaning trying to get lived.

The superior function that gets dislodged, does not disappear; it still exists and can function and be used; it does not dominate anymore. We gain a bigger vocabulary of functions. The unconscious from its side, so to speak, tries this and then that approach. We see it in a series of dreams around the same hurt or problem or breakthrough. If this does not work through to conscious realization, then let's try that approach in the next dream, or next transference role cast upon the analyst. The very personal way of putting things gets relativized, not depotentiated nor scorned, but set in a larger bowl.

Here is where psyche's project may dish up symbols that seem impersonal but actually hit the mark. Jung writes of the immortal part in him and the image that brings that close is not just the circle but becomes mandala that enlarges in meaning to become "a cosmic mandala" (Jung 2019, pp. 279, 277-281). That conveys a mirroring of physical and psychological, material and spiritual, of inside and outside, of me and you, of all of us and all of them, of space making place for time both fleeting and eternal, and time making space accessible in the here and now and the forever. We may stumble upon the greater experience of the stone both adamant and lasting in us, yet linked to the perishable and mortal. Its presence mirrors the God who mirrors us; we are feeding the God who feeds us.

This chapter was written during the pandemic 2020 for this book.

References

Collins, B. May 8, 2015. "A Mother's Day Gift: The Lanyard" Wikipedia.

Davoine, F. and Gaudilliere, J-M. 2004. *History Beyond Trauma.* Trans. Susan Fairfield New York: Other Press.

Humbert, E. 1984. *C.G. Jung The Fundamentals of Theory and Practice.* Trans. Ronald G. Jalbert. Wilmette, Ill: Chiron.

Jung, C.G. 1930/1966. "Psychology and Literature" *The Spirit in Man, Art, and Literature Collected Works* vol. 5. Trans. R. F. Hull. Princeton N.J.: Princeton University Press. paras 133-162.

— 1946/1954. "The psychology of the transference" *The Practice of Psychotherapy Collected Works* 16. Trans. R.F.C. Hull. Princeton N.J.: Princeton University Press, paras 353-537.

— 1952/1960. "Synchronicity: acausal connecting principle" *Collected Works* 8 *The Structure and Dynamics of The Psyche.* Trans. R.F.C. Hull. Princeton, N. J.: Princeton University Press, paras 816-997.

— 1953. *Psychology and Alchemy Collected Works* vol. 12. Trans. R.F.C. Hull. Princeton N. J. and Oxford: Princeton University Press.

— 1956. *Symbols of Transformation Collected Works* 5. Trans. R.F.C. Hull. Princeton, N. J.: Princeton University Press.

— 2008. *Children's Dreams. Notes from the seminar Given in 1936-1940.* Eds. Lorenz Jung and Maria Meyer-Grass. Philemon Series. Princeton and Oxford: Princeton University Press.

— 2009.*The Red Book: Liber Novus,* Ed. Sonu Shamdasani. Trans. John Peck, Mark Kyburz, Sonu Shamdasani. New York: W. W. Norton.

— 2019 *Dream Symbols of the Individuation Process Notes of C.G. Jung Seminars on Wolfgang Pauli's Dreams.* Ed. Suzanne Gieser. Philemon Series. Princeton and Oxford: Princeton University Press.

Stein, M. 2017. "Failure in the crucible of individuation" in *Inside, Outside, and All Around.* Asheville N. C.: Chiron, pp. 151-171.

Steiner, J. 1993. *Psychic Retreats Pathological Organizations in Psychotic, Neurotic and Borderline Patients.* London and New York: Routledge.

Ulanov, A.B. 2007a. "The third in the shadow of the fourth" *Journal of Analytical Psychology* vol. 52 no. 5 pp. 585-605; and an earlier version, 2007b. *The Unshuttered Heart Opening to Aliveness and Deadness in the Self. Nashville Tn.:* Abingdon Press, chapter 7 pp. 157-186.

Ulanov, A.B. 2014/2020. "The Inferior Function" *Knots and Their Untying, Essays on Psychological Dilemmas.* Einsiedeln, Switzerland: Daimon, pp. 87-102.

Winnicott, D.W. 1963. "Communicating and not communicating leading to a study of certain opposites" *The Maturational Processes and the Facilitating Environment.* New York: International Universities Press, pp. 179-192.

Zaehner, R.C. 1974. *Our Savage God.* New York: Sheed and Ward.

Chapter 5:

The Agony of Integration and the Blessings of Finitude

Introduction

Jung's work is permeated with the goal of integration as the positive ideal of individuation: becoming all of who we are. This process gathers the parts of us to live from their taproot in our unconscious into relationships with others and societies in which we live. But this ideal leaves out the agony of facing madness that has been eclipsed from our living. Contrary to the utopian ideal of composing all our puzzle pieces into a unified picture of who we are, integration is more like Cézanne's unfinished blue painting of a woman writing at her desk with big swatches of unpainted white canvas right down the core of her body, imaging a process never completed, including unknown spaces to be lived (Cézanne 2016).

Cézanne, Portrait of a Woman 1902-1906

Further, integration as the engine of individuation is a natural, instinctive process that drives us, whether we consent or not, toward psyche centred in Self, not ego, and thus will press to include our traumas, mistakes, unlived parts (Jung 1966, para 186). It is a mark of health to reach for madness in us. For now we suffer consciously, whereas what happened then was not experienced by our too young, too little organized ego, as Winnicott explores on a developmental level, nor could we assimilate the event into Self living, as Jung explores on an archetypal level (Winnicott 1963/1989; Jung1959a, paras 1-14, 149-155, 187-190). An analysand approaching near to madness, dreamt, "Something terrible happened but I pretended it didn't."

But reaching for our madness means agony. For now we suffer consciously the pain that was consigned to our unconscious that provoked us to split off, dissociate, displace or project it to defend against intolerable anxiety. And thank God we erected those defenses for they allowed us to survive, but with the flag at half-mast. One man dreamt of bodies in the freezer he must take out to be thawed back into living. So now we feel fragmented or abysmally confused, erupting with rage or cut off from body, abandoned by soul or buried alive in sadness.

The worst has already happened in the event of madness. But we feel it is worse now because we are consciously feeling the anxiety and the emotions madness inflicted. An analysand with aggressiveness imploding into consciousness was shocked she identified with 9/11 terrorists flying planes into office buildings to kill as many citizens as possible. We are alive to intolerable affects that we had shut off so they would not kill us. Now we can afford to feel them and struggle to find representation for the unbearable. It is agony.

Why would we undertake this painful, never completed integrating process? Why not just ignore those swaths of white unpainted canvas in Cézanne's painting? Or ingest a substance to benumb pain? We can see why a collective defense against agonizing work of integrating is to minimize psyche as only a subset of the brain, or to objectivise it as a commodity to be fixed in so many sessions and markers of progress dictated by the insurance company. That impingement contrasts with letting something grow from within, ignoring Jung's insight,

"Only what is really oneself has the power to heal" (Jung 1966, para 258).

Something more presses us to take down our wall of defense, to discover where our soul has been hiding, to see others as they are, freed from the cloak of our projections. Jung writes this is "a force as real as hunger and fear of death" (ibid, para 403). Or a life-crisis convinces us we do not want to die before we escape this half-life; we want to get all of us back, to receive all we are given to be. Or, we see the cost of pushing so much out of consciousness falls into our body that, like a faithful dog, carries our burdens for us and gets sick. Or, we discover our neglect of dealing with our anxiety complex hurts our children whom we love. For them we take on our task of integrating. Or, a positive event of falling in love happens, or with a new idea or an original possibility coming into view that we dare to accept. Attempting intimacy of any kind requires every bit of strength from every part of us. In short, life forces us to face up, though we still are free to say yea or nay. Even if we fear we have no courage to do so, life presses us to find the courage to do so.

To our amazement, our struggles to integrate what belongs to us, includes new life that floods in - chaos as plenty, multi-perspectives in place of one 'ruling principle,' and our 'incapacity,' that Jung later calls our inferior function, brings with it 'the fountainhead of the unconscious' (ibid. para 366; see also Jung 1954a para 408). New perceptions surprise us - of ideas, connections, possibilities we want to develop. We see how challenges from the upending of archetypal foundations of our culture in our 21st century upend ways we think, patterns of feeling we took for granted. In America for example, we suffer cultural anxiety that structures of our democracy are being undone. Does this upending go forward to new equalities? Or to anchor back to their honoured beginnings? Not knowing makes us feel shaky, but also, unexpectedly, liberated from the way things should be, as if doors are flung open to new ways to think, new imaginings of how to devise our government. But can we stand the ingress of multi-possibilities, not sure which, if any, are best?

Jung counsels: "psychic wholeness will never be attained empirically, as consciousness is too narrow and too one-sided to comprehend the full inventory of the psyche. Always we shall have to begin again from the beginning ... the work does not prosper without the greatest simplicity. But the simple things are always the most difficult" (Jung 1977, p. 145). Can we stand it? Whom do we thank? Praise? Integration thus includes becoming aware what we believe in and what we experience as the largest reality believing in us; we matter. We have something to contribute. Jung writes, "The man at peace with himself, who accepts himself, contributes an infinitesimal amount to the good of the universe. Attend to your private and personal conflicts and you will be reducing by one millionth of a millionth the world conflict" (ibid).

And if we do not participate in the process of integration, we miss the boat: "To the extent that a man is untrue to the law of his being and does not rise to personality, he has failed to realize his life's meaning" (Jung 1954b, paras 314, 315).

Jung described his process of integration as being 'smelted anew' feeling unbearable emotions that now grow together afresh in a different form that demands giving our blood (Jung 2009, pp. 229, 247, & 345).

Extinction Points

I want to focus on a hardest thing to integrate that causes us agony. I have come to name it an 'extinction point'–a moment of madness where we feel extinguished, dropped out of existence, eradicated for seconds, engulfed in anxiety of psychotic proportion. We quickly surround that injury by defenses in order to survive, to give scope to the primordial life impulse to recover our living. I focus on this great danger of integration, the one that threatens us at any moment with going 'poof' right out of existence, gone from living. Individuation drives to include all the parts of us. If we tackle a 'presenting problem' and see it through, it can take us down to its deepest meaning to introduce us to forces of creativeness and destructiveness operating in us. For those of us who suffer trauma, the extinction point appears usually through that door. But for any of us, it is an impulse of health to reach for the X of madness. It shows itself idiosyncratically as if custom-made in each of us, and requiring the first witness, usually an analyst, as a necessary other who validates our forming and communicating its narrative.

We fear reaching this X of madness and project it into some terrible future, as a patient said: "I fear I will not show up for the rest of my life." Jung used images from alchemy to express this danger of confronting these forces: "The integration of contents that were always unconscious and projected involves a serious lesion in the ego. Alchemy expressed this through the symbols of death, mutilation, or poisoning" (Jung 1954a, para 472). Jung's journey soon leads to descent into his particular hell (Jung 2009, pp. 237 ff). He later elaborates: "The scope of integration is suggested by the '*descensus ad infernos.*' The descent of Christ's soul to hell, whose work of redemption also encompasses the dead. The psychological equivalent of this forms the integration of the collective unconscious which represents an essential part of the individuation process" (Jung 1959b, para 72). Our individual effort to assimilate bits of ourselves is collective too and contributes to all of us. An example is the Lynching Memorial in Montgomery, Alabama. It calls us to become more aware of our wound as a people, an acknowledgement that leads toward healing. One blessing of finitude is to gain a sturdy ego, here as 'a collective consciousness' that knows of danger and protects against it (Jung 1963a, para 756).

Epistemology, Inferior Function

Still further, we must face that the whole way of communicating with what presses for integration requires a different epistemology. As Jung emphasizes, the Self perspective surrounds the ego on all sides, above and below, as if seeing the whole of our reality and our placement in reality as a whole. Whatever is pressing does not present itself in terms to which we are accustomed – reasoning, reflection, position papers. The psyche dramatizes itself and shows what is from its point of view. The psyche itself is the second witness to our individuation process. For example, beginning with what feels like a lesser threat than extinction – our 'incapacity' that Jung later calls our inferior function that has lain neglected and undeveloped in us – now requires redemption. Jung said his 'incapacity' was his feeling function (Jung 2009, p. 240). But those intellectual words come way after his shock discovering a beheaded, violated little girl left in the bushes, and the command to ingest part of her liver! (ibid, p. 290). Jung's revulsion, and initial refusal, displays how we register something inferior in us as a destructive horror. This murdered child is not a matter for reasonable discussion, nor weighing up pros and cons about the command to cut a piece of her liver and eat it. This discarded small girl pictures Jung's mangled feeling function. The command to atone with this healing act by partaking of her flesh surely forms a challenge of the creative.

An analysand dreams of sitting in her living room – her room of living what was a full life with husband, child, job – when a commando guy busts in. Standing before her in his soldier fatigues, he unstraps a tiny baby that has been fastened to his thigh, even in battle. He hands the infant over to her and departs. She must care for it now. This helpless baby says with intensity: 'more milk!' On waking this woman feels fear – caring for this infant will upend her life! And what about her past life when this tiny part could only survive if strapped to a soldiering commando, even in fighting battles? Yes: destruction and creativeness. What will come of their linking?

My point is the new, left out, unguessed part arrives. And it confounds in its style: it appears, does not explain; it demands, does not reason. We cannot think our way through it, nor prove its scientific verifiability. It is such as it is. Now what? It does not present logic, nor persuasive argument, but dramatizes its point of view (Jung 1960, para 421). We must take its impact, admit it to consciousness, make something of it making something of us. Only then might we translate it into conscious terms, without substituting our version for its animal life. The danger comes from ignoring it or falling into identification with it or feeling persecuted by it. It really is inferior, slow, clumsy (See Ulanov 2013, pp. 87-102). The surprise is, it brings the wealth of the unconscious with it – the 'fountainhead' (See Jung 1954a, paras 408-409).

Madness, and Blessings of Finitude

But, much more vexing, are frank examples of madness that terrorize us. If engulfed in psychosis, we split off emotional and reality testing reactions to divorce ourselves from madness, while becoming engulfed in it. Jung feared psychosis happening to him – utter destruction. Yet in the midst of that danger he made a discovery that changed his work (Jung 1963b, pp. 176 & 188, 192, 196, & 199). He saw that these threatening psychic elements and patterns belong to all of us, thus previewing Bion's later statement that we all have psychotic and nonpsychotic parts of our personality. I have found this so in my clinical work too. If a person's presenting problem entering analysis persists in seeking full resolution, those psychotic parts will surface. Further, the reigning metaphor is not container/contained, important as that is, but, I suggest, interpenetration between those parts (Ulanov 2017, pp. 58-61).

The difference between psychosis that falls on us like lava of uncontrollable fantasies from an irrupting unconscious, and our voluntary intention to integrate missing chunks of ourselves, is the ego. Here are found blessings of finitude. The fantasy material is the same in both cases but "the insane person falls victim because he cannot integrate it but is swallowed up in it" Jung 1963a, para 756). With a finite ego, equipped with willingness and effort to understand, we aim to assimilate what we can of compensatory unconscious images, affects, impulses, not only for our own personality, but also in relation to "the collective situation of consciousness." We thus contribute into our social atmosphere our individual experience of what is denied collectively. The ego has limits. We do what we can and sometimes a dream helps. A man dreamt he was shown a room full of dead bodies to be dug up, but over there in the corner is one not to be dug up, one to leave buried. Having a finite ego makes possible a decision to do what we can; and let go what we cannot "and thereby produce a whole meaning which alone makes life worth living and, for not a few people, possible at all" (Jung 1963b, para 756).

The fact that integration is an unending process, never complete, can add to our dread. What if no form ever takes shape to emerge out of the formlessness of the specific madness besetting us? This arouses intolerable anxiety and renders us helpless. We are utterly without resource. That helplessness is an extinction point, I suggest, found in us when reaching for the unknown 'X' of the specific madness we suffer. Helplessness, I suggest, is an extinction point in any of the varieties of madness that result in splitting off an experience of going out of existence that was not registered. We vary in what we split off – for some, it is relation to the world, so that we prematurely adjust to expecting nothing from others as protection against being utterly let down, dropped. For others, it is our body which is eclipsed and that leads to psycho-somatic distress. For some, it is unlived aggression that arouses the intolerable anxiety and can lead to outbursts of rage. Still others harbour a small child who never found and formed her or his true voice, and its lack impairs any sense of self-worth and self-authority. In all varieties of craziness we must look into the anxiety, take it apart and track it down or it will 'blot out' the taproot of our psychic energy (Rodman 2003, p. 347).

Whatever the specific unregistered part, I suggest, we land in utter helplessness. We reach the end of the road of self-effort, the bottom of the barrel to make things better. We hit a dead-end and fear we will be ending dead. Yet we dimly sense a familiarity; we have been here before and finally now land fully. Bad as it is, we may feel some relief now to have hit bottom. Here I stay: I do not know what to do, feel, hope, nor how to find sense in the non-sense, meaning in meaninglessness, orientation in the no-where space, some companionship in this no-one space. But I have no idea how to do any of that. Helplessness pervades instead.

As analysts we, too, are helpless, and in the transference the patient tells us so. We do not come up with the constructive word, let alone effective interpretation. We are told we are useless, not helping. The limits of finitude press hard. Analysis as a profession comes into question too. What good is it when nothing can be offered to this descent into helplessness? Theory and technique do not hit the mark. The analyst who knows this, accepts arriving as another human living together with the analysand through experience of the end of the road, having no effective word. A danger is that, as analyst, we succumb to panic, or hidden narcissism, or omnipotence, trying to remedy what is going on, yank the patient out of facing destructiveness of everything that has been built to counteract the madness event that happened. Then the analysand misses the chance to reach the X. Non-sense meets sense here, meaninglessness meets meaningfulness, futility with hope. Forces of destructiveness and creativeness coincide.

What is left is analyst and analysand together living an experience of this Nothing space. We each retain our roles but in addition are present as simply two human beings facing the extinction point where primal absence faces us. Further, as analyst, we arrive there by the route of our own experiences of primordial life force and destructive death-dealing entanglements, not by what the analysand sketches out for us in subjective-object transferences. We are thus simultaneously both the object of transference roles and a fellow human being facing life and death forces, a sister companion in face of creative and destructive elements. We are not in charge of the bad nor can we banish it.

The philosopher Iris Murdoch's words come to mind: what is goodness good for? She writes, "The only genuine way to be good is to be good 'for nothing' ... the experienced correlate to the invisibility ... of the idea of Good" (Murdoch 1969, p. 254). It still makes me laugh with its truth that, oddly, points to something more there outside our finite powers. A blessing of finitude is that we see our limits and may glimpse what exceeds them. That relieves us of overconscientiousness as if the outcome of analysis is entirely up to us. No. Can we yield to dependence on that something more? Like Winnicott's "discovery of spontaneous, accidental beauty in the ordinary," or Bion's counsel to reach for O, the ultimate reality, the godhead, the infinite, in each session? (Rodman 2003, p. 272; Bion 1970, pp. 26 & 69).

Symptoms mark the descent into the X of madness. If analysis is working well, the analysand's symptoms will not only increase but magnify the desperate sense of loss, meaninglessness, refusal, no words. It helps to remember it is an impulse of health to reach toward the X of one's madness, that individuation is driving to include a pivotal experience that did not register in the past and is now making its way toward consciousness. Like a mythic descent into hell, we are stripped of what worked in the past – one effective defense undone after another until we face our utter helplessness. We cannot make it better. Nor can the analyst. We arrive at the No-thing space, No-where, No-one (Ulanov 2013, pp. 218-219). We live now in the present what happened in the past that we could not experience fully then because our ego was too undeveloped and because there was no supportive setting nor holding of us to experience it so our defenses quickly organized against the unthinkable anxiety. The unendurable anxiety around what has been exiled needs to be explored, taken apart, rescued into life. For that anxiety covers the taproot of psychic energy that has dwelt in us waiting for us to retrieve and integrate it with living.

Hence, when analysands reach this deserted space, they also feel immense relief and even gladness. Examples circle around the creative happening right next to the destructive. A blessing of finitude is incarnation into this body of mine here, now, able to house this living moment instead of disappearing into 'the black hole of formless infinity' as Lombardi describes when emotions intensify endlessly to overwhelm the ego in psychosis (Lombardi 2016, p. 43; Lombardi 2017, p. 147 ff.).

Heidegger describes *Dasein*, our mortal, finite being, "as a clearing, like an open place in a forest where the light gets through" (Heidegger 1962, p. 171; Macquarrie 1968, p. 20). We glimpse this space in getting near to "the split second in which the threat of madness was experienced," which arouses unbearable anxiety so defenses against registering madness are immediately organized (Winnicott 1965/1989; see Rodman *op.cit.* p. 299). It is a relief to gain the place of clearing, where we can perceive and assimilate and spontaneously recover from what could kill us.

A blessing of finitude is conscious capacity to approach what happened with understanding. Winnicott has faith in the person showing the point of distress and feeling the relief that the worst they feared has already happened. Experiencing that, they can make spontaneous recovery, or at least blunt the edge of the past breakdown. Jung trusts the self-regulation of the psyche: let psychic events happen and the animal will come forth from the forest thicket. With dependence on the first witness of the analyst, and on the second witness of the psyche, we reach the extinction point and check its destruction by creating a larger whole, with room in our sanity for madness. Jung writes:

> assimilation of contents of the unconscious contents leads us back to ourselves as an actual living something, poised between two world-pictures and their darkly discerned potencies. This 'something' is strange to us and yet so near, wholly ourselves and yet unknowable, a virtual centre of so mysterious a constitution that it can claim … kinship with beasts and gods … I have called this centre the *self.* Intellectually the self is no more than a psychological concept … that transcends our powers of comprehension. It might equally be called the 'God within us.' The beginning of our whole psychic life seems to be inextricably rooted in this point, and all our highest and ultimate purposes seem to be striving towards it. This paradox seems to be unavoidable … when we try to define something beyond our … understanding. (Jung 1966, paras 398, 399)

Clinical Example

One analysand, when connecting with the X of her madness, said 'there is nothing to say at all.' She felt utterly shorn; stripped of defences to keep herself alive – of protecting vulnerability behind a wall of dissociation, of splitting into parts, overdoing, as if pedalling her bike faster and faster to do work, chores, appointments, activities to keep herself in being. In her long analysis, we uncovered she had not been lost by her family, but rather never found, held in mind, with loving interest in her. Because this lack happened from birth, she accepted it as 'the way it was – reality.' Thus it was her job to cope with not being held in another's loving mind, and with cumulative trauma of living in a family and feeling utterly alone. Confusion reigned. A primal absence was her lot. Her reaching out spontaneously was met by the other replacing it with their need and expectation of her compliance. She saw very young she could not make the other want to be interested in her, nor, as she grew up, make the environment in word or recognition validate the beauty of her being alive. This loss of not being found lived in her but bypassed consciousness. What she was conscious of was compelling necessity to be busy keeping herself in life, while coping with a background threnody that at any time she could go 'poof out of existence', or into craziness.

The worst was going to happen. The worst did happen. She prized above all else learning to and becoming a poet. There she felt alive and real and connected with reality. But then, her recording of her work went out of existence in manuscript and machine. It had been deleted and she felt deleted with it. Silence fell upon her as if she lay shorn of life. She knew in her bones she had no idea how to get her corpus of poems back, nor, given the particular circumstances, whom to call with expertise to recover it. It was gone. Poof, out of existence!

She knew right away this loss was a surrogate of her being gone. Simultaneously, she was reliving her extinction point of earliest life of feeling erased with her original family in the past. Now in the present explicit event, not just a flashback memory, she was living through the loss of the corpus of her poems, erasure of her vital connection with being alive and real in the world. Toward both past and present she felt helpless to erase the erasure. Everything she knew from experience to help herself was no longer viable, effective. She lived the feeling of going out of existence. I, too, as the analyst lived it with her. There was nothing to say, to remedy, to offer as encouragement. We dwelt in silence of our helplessness to undo the space of never being found.

The connection she forged to stay alive through becoming a poet was severed. And she felt complicit through her mistake in handling the technology of securing copies of all her poems. She somehow erased the corpus that did exist, as if enacting on herself the erasure she had suffered from not being held in the mind of family members, as if she was of no account, hence no accounting was given of this behaviour, or perhaps even noticed. She remembered then a series of dreams from the previous year portraying this danger: 'hands grasp my throat from behind, choking'; 'a sharpest blade severs my foot from my ankle'; 'a woman drips poison into my ear to kill any creative endeavour'; 'a feral animal sinks its claws into my back'–all variations of threat to existence.

We stayed in this field of not knowing what to do to help, rather, to let be what is. As sometimes happens, something unexpected occurs that both analysand and analyst know they did not invent. It came from somewhere else. In the poet's case it came through a dream the night after the disaster of loss and falling silent and shorn. The dream made her burst out laughing. Weirdly, the dream introduced into her helplessness a firm realization: yes, it was true. We are dependent. Whatever made her think we have a shred of control, or it was in our power to give life. She dreams her soulmate, lover, spouse, long deceased, coming to her (pun intended), not from or in a distance, as characteristic of her dreams of him since he died, which she thought was because he was dead and she alive. In this short dream he was standing up close, near her, right there in his loving vibrancy. "He ejaculated semen all over my body, seeds and seeds of life," she said, "in big blobby whiteness, all over my body! Of course," she exclaimed, "Not until I reached the place of helplessness beneath all the things I did to keep myself alive in the world, did I grasp that I do not author my life and life could be given all over me, in big clumps of blobby whiteness, seeds of life from my dear one, all over me!" Here, I felt, was an explosion of creativeness in the midst of destructive erasure and despair, both primordial forces together at once.

Ten days later she dreamt of him again near up, close to her and saying he was tired of masturbating and wanted intercourse with her. She felt the dream annulling the line of death from life, rejoining their closeness. The two dreams led to a tremendous surplus of symbolism of this man whom she knew intimately from their life together, but who also, in himself, portrayed terrific life force, he so very alive with interest in so many things. He symbolised part of her as well and giving her seeds she could not create in her own body; and in the second dream saying in effect, open your body to this penetration, seeds of life to go inside you, within you now. It made me think of the *logos spermatikos* – the inseminating word crossing the divide of even life and death.

Like other clinical examples, this one presents a blessing of finitude: it is not all up to us. Our limits may make us notice what exists beyond them. Something comes from outside us, like the coincidence of shorn-silent-helplessness and being covered by inseminating seeds (*logos spermatikos*) and from a loving confirming partner. Further, this part of her that he represents does not want to carry this boon all by itself – to go on self-stimulating – but to put the inseminating word inside her, to plant it there as hers, to gestate and grow.

The improbability of both dreams arriving as if in response to her landing in desperate unmitigated helplessness, was what made her laugh. She knew perfectly well one did not cause the other. I thought of synchronistic connection with its powerful spontaneous impact of meaningfulness. Only by reaching the madness of loss of vital connection to life, by living through the going out of life symbolized by the loss of her poetry, was life conferred, or should we say spurted, gushed, fountained all over her body. It was her talent for and discipline in learning to write poetry that was her connection to life. It was what she developed in response to suffering the breakdown to primal absence that was not experienced. She now experienced consciously the agony of a dependence not met and hence life-threatening. Only then did something more break through, portrayed by one she trusted and depended upon, who also symbolized a part of herself that did keep her in mind and represented something beyond death that kept her in mind still.

The limits of the analyst also made room for something given that neither of the analytic pair constructed. The analyst lived through the experience with her, as the first witness, and did not have an answer or interpretation that brought any relief. Nor did the analysis. I embodied both the transference piece of the parent not holding her in mind in the past, and in the present embodied my limits and the limits of analysis. The failure of both to help make space to glimpse something more we could depend on beyond our limits and the limits of our beloved profession. Its appearance also suggested that our trauma over destructiveness may also be finite, limited, not endless. Glimpsing the something more announced itself in laughter.

Synchronistic experience is not manufactured by us; it happens to us and leads associatively to a network of symbolism. The seeds of this analysand's dream made me think of the signal image in Christian Trinity of God as Creator, distinguished from Son as redeemer, and Spirit as invisible enlivener of soul in the world (Ulanov 1996, pp. 96 ff). The psyche, as second witness to our individuation process, tossed up this fecund image. Creator begets a beginning that goes on all through eternity as the *creatio continua*. It happens now and exemplifies our dwelling in its creative moment up until death and beyond. Jung writes that synchronistic events not governed by causality must be regarded as "*creative acts* ... continuous creation of a pattern that exists from all eternity, repeats itself sporadically, and is not derivable from any known antecedents" (Jung 1960, para. 967, n. 17).

Jung found his own place in the wholeness of the whole, and his service to God through conscious work on his conflicts of the yea and nay, the destructive and creative (Jung 1963b, pp. 311, 334, 338, & 345). Unlike the 'doctor animals' who are the best servants of God because they do what they are supposed to do because ruled by instinct, we humans have a hyphen, a hiatus, a space where we must add our consent, freely add our yea or nay. Instead of reaching conclusive definition, Jung's full-hearted embrace of the givenness of his finite life, with all its blessings as well as trials, leave him at the end of his life, a wondrous mystery to himself (Jung ibid, para. p. 358; see Ulanov 2017, pp. 106-108).

For the poet, the richness of Creator symbolism aided her looking into her anxiety of going out of existence. The anxiousness was still awful, yet now simultaneously in company with the givenness of her life created from another Source through receiving life-seeds. Here the infinite enters the finite and there is mutual exchange of blessings, so to speak. A sense of the whole picture represented by the word infinite says, in effect, trauma is finite too. Though we bear scars, trauma is pressed by the limits of finitude to be located, named, reflected upon, related to, no longer overwhelming conscious, finite life by limitless unconscious affect. This bigger expanse becomes incarnated in our embodied understanding and that demotes trauma from defining us forever. Madness can be checked by the limits of finitude, just as finitude, with its liability to be stuck in one place, is loosened from stuckness by the multi-perspectives the infinite inspires.

Jung sees we have access to infinite and finite if each is allowed its scope. You know this quotation:

> The decisive question for man is: Is he related to something infinite or not? That is the telling question of his life. Only if we know that the thing which truly matters is the infinite can we avoid fixing our interest upon … goals which are not of real importance … If we understand and feel that here in this life we already have a link with the infinite … we count for something only because of the essential we embody, and if we do not embody that, life is wasted. In our relationships with other men, too, the crucial question is whether an element of boundlessness is expressed in the relationship.
> The feeling for the infinite, however, can be attained only if we are bounded to the utmost … 'I am only that!' Only consciousness of our narrow confinement in the self forms the link to the limitlessness of the unconscious. In such awareness we experience ourselves concurrently as limited and eternal, as both one and the other. In knowing ourselves to be unique in our personal combination – that is, ultimately limited – we possess also the capacity for becoming conscious of the infinite. But only then! (Jung 1963b, p. 325)

This chapter was given at the IAAP Congress in Vienna, Austria, August 2019, and again at the Psychology and Otherness Conference at Boston College Cambridge, Massachusetts, October 2019.

References

Bion, W.R. 1970. *Attention and Interpretation.* London: Tavistock.

Cézanne, P. 2016. "Portrait Of A Woman" Metropolitan Breuer Museum, March 9.

Heidegger, M. 1962. *Being and Time.* Trans. J. Macquarrie and E. S. Robinson London: CSM; New York: Harper.

Jung, C.G. 1954a. *The Practice of Psychotherapy. Collected Works* 16. Trans. R.F.C. Hull. Princeton N.J.: Princeton University press.

— 1954b. *The Development of the Personality. Collected Works* 17. Trans. R.F.C. Hull. Princeton N.J.: Princeton University Press.

— 1959a. *The Archetypes and the Collective Unconscious Collected Works* 9:1. Trans. R.F.C. Hull. Princeton N.J.: Princeton University Press.

— 1959b. *Aion. Collected Works 9:2.* Trans. R.F.C. Hull. Princeton N.J.: Princeton University Press.

— 1960. *The Structure and Dynamics of the Psyche. Collected Works* 8. Trans. R. F. C. Hull. Princeton, N.J.: Princeton University Press.

— 1963a. *Mysterium Coniunctionis. Collected Works* 14. Trans. R.F.C. Hull. Princeton N.J.: Princeton University Press.

— 1963b. *Memories, Dreams, Reflections.* Recorded and Edited by Aniel Jaffé. Trans. Richard and Clara Winston. New York: Pantheon.

— 1966. *Two Essays in Analytical Psychology Collected Works* 7. New York: Pantheon Books.

— 1977. *C.G. Jung Speaking.* Ed. Willliam McGuire. London: Picador.

— 2009. *The Red Book Liber Novus.* Ed. S. Shamdasani. Trans. John Peck, Mark Kyburz, Sonu Shamdasani. New York: W.W. Norton.

Lombardi, R. 2016. *Formless Infinity, Clinical Explorations of Matte Blanco and W.R. Bion.* London and New York: Routledge.

— 2017. *Body-Mind Dissociation in Psychoanalysis After Bion.* London and New York: Routledge.

Lynching Memorial for Peace and Justice, Montgomery Alabama. Founder of Equal Justice Initiative: Bryan Stevenson.

Macquarrie, J. 1968. *Martin Heidegger* Richmond, Va: John Knox Press.

Murdoch, I. 1969. 'On 'God' and the 'Good"; in: *The Anatomy of Knowledge.* Ed. Marjorie Greene. Amherst, Mass: The University of Massachusetts Press, 233-259.

Rodman, F.R. 2003. *Winnicott's Life and Work.* Cambridge, Ma: Da Capo Press Books of Perseus Books Group.

Ulanov, A.B. 1996 *The Functioning Transcendent.* Wilmette, Il: Chiron.

— 2007. *The Unshuttered Heart*. Nashville, Tn: Abingdon Press.

— 2011. 'Encountering Jung Being Encountered'. *Jung Journal of Culture and Psyche* 2011. 513, 54-63

— 2013. *Madness & Creativity*. Collegeville, Tx: Texas A&M Press.

— 2014. *Knots and Their Untying*. New Orleans, La: Spring Journal Books.

— 2017. *The Psychoid, Soul and Psyche: Piercing Space/Time Barriers*. Einsiedeln, Switzerland: Daimon.

Winnicott, D.W. (1963/1989). 'Fear of Breakdown'. *Psycho-Analytic Explorations*. London: Karnac. Originally printed in 1974, *International Review of Psycho-Analysis, 1*: 103-107.

— 1965/1989. 'Psycho-analysis of Madness'. *Psycho-Analytic Explorations* London: Karnac.

— 1988. *Human Nature*. London: Free Association Books.

Chapter 6:

Projection

We might begin with the unexpected statement: in Praise of Projection, or at least In Defense of Projection. It is a normal and inevitable happening in our psyches, both individually and together. We do not outgrow it, though becoming conscious of this pattern, and in particular what we ourselves project onto others, can change our relation to it. We become curious what contents and affects we put onto others – why these contents and why onto those specific others. We become merciful, refraining from harsh judgments against ourselves and others for dumping into the common atmosphere what we avoid in ourselves. We become patient and invest time and effort not to pollute our surroundings with our undigested rage and lamentation.

The psychodynamic rhythm of introjection and projection is like breathing – taking in and putting out. We accept this basic process of being human. Jung's insight is immensely helpful here: projection happens when an emotion, thought, impulse is on its way to consciousness, the first stop is projection.* Projec-

* "The prima materia/lapis philosophorum is … to be discovered in man himself. But … the content can never be found and integrated directly, but only by the circuitous route of projection. For as a rule the unconscious first appears in projected form." (Jung 1946/1954, para 383)

tion, if we notice it, furthers consciousness. Instead of getting rid of projection we need to look into it.

Yet in our present turbulent times, hurling our inward affects and thoughts onto other people and other groups increases divisions among us, and saps energy from within us. We fear the violence that issues from unnoticed projections – at all levels. From letting our projection run loose on our neighbor's lawn instead of housing it on our own, to feeling aghast when discovering what we put onto our own dear daughter or son, to being kidnapped by horror at the television image of beheading a man because he does not ascribe to the god this group esteems, projection becomes an enemy to peace, justice, getting along well with each other in enriching ways. We fear projections run amok, and rightly so: totalitarian 'us-them' mentality results.

We go back to basics, to six different meanings of projection and how it functions in us and between us whether we know it or not. I want also to relate these meanings to destructiveness and its place in society, how we cannot deal with projection in isolation but only in relation to each other, in relation to social and collective life, and to the something more which can be thought of as your image of God, or of what you value ultimately, what you love best, beyond and through all things.

Projection as Defense

A usual definition of projection views it as a defense, a protective mechanism "employed by the unconscious part of the ego, through which internal impulses, feelings that are unacceptable to the total personality are attributed to the external object, and then enter consciousness as a disguised perception of the external world" (Eidelberg 1968, p. 331). What we do not like and find painful in ourselves we deny as an internal perception and allocate to someone else. We throw out onto the other affects or impulses that belong to ourselves and thus give objective reality to what is subjective. This anger belongs to you, not to me. It is that other group, not our group who is destructive (Hinsie and Campbell 1974, p. 593). Projection is preceded by denial. Literally it is "throwing in front of oneself ... viewing a mental image as objective reality, a "process by which specific wishes, impulses, aspects of the self ... are imagined to be located in some object external to oneself" (Rycroft 1968, p. 125). Freud asserts, "with any internal excitations which produce too great an increase of unpleasure ... there is a tendency to treat them as though they were acting, not from the inside, but from the outside ... to bring a shield against stimuli ... as a ... defence against them. This is the origin of *projection*" (Freud 1920/1973, p. 29; see also Freud 1911/1973, p. 66; see also Ricoeur 1970, p. 287 n8).

We can become aware that we are projecting by three repeated signs of its disturbance. When our projection is operating – to do with another's fault or talent – we feel *agitated.* We cannot let the topic or incident alone but are *compelled* to respond in what amounts to sterile repeated patterns. It is as if we are caught a *state of identity* with the projected content and with the person on whom we are projecting (Ulanov and Ulanov 1975, pp. 222-223; see also Ulanov 2001, pp. 97ff.).

All schools of depth psychology see projection as normal psychodynamic process. Jung states, "Projection is never made; it happens; it is simply there" (Jung 1953, para 346). Jung emphasizes that projection happens as a first step on the way to consciousness; we throw it out onto an other on the way to seeing it, with luck and effort, as belonging to ourselves. Projection is protective, defending against pain by locating the content outside ourselves.

Melanie Klein emphasizes that the processes of introjection – taking in – and projection – throwing outside ourselves, both function to begin differentiation between bad-unpleasurable-painful from good-pleasurable-enriching. Morality starts at birth practically – we sort out good from bad and use them in extreme degrees to grasp the difference of good from bad and build up pictures inside ourselves and outside ourselves attributed to others and to locations, ideas, beliefs, spirits and gods as good or bad. In addition, projection furthers the beginnings of empathy. Projecting our feelings and impulses onto another person promotes an identification with that person and we begin to understand them, stand in their shoes. (Klein 1952/1975, pp. 68-69; 252-253; see also Klein 1959/1975, pp. 247-264).

We can remember being a child and see in children now their fierce insistence this is good and that is bad! A sharp distinction to get it right! When we approach something new and are much like a beginning child, we may feel again this decisive separation in order to gain clarity. Destructiveness thus turns up in our wanting to embrace the good and eschew the bad. If we languish in that initial exaggerated position, we are compelled to discriminate against anyone and anything that differs from our definitions of these primal elements. The defense of projection thus transmogrifies into a prosecution of our view of the good as *the* view, the only view to hold, lest one is seen as a malign object with bad motives who should be exiled.

Yet we can see that failing to take up the task of differentiating good from bad but instead staying in a state of identity with an authoritative figure like a parent or an institution we treat as parent can lead to disastrous social strife. We do not develop our own point of view but stay simply projecting out the bad and identifying with the good as dictated from without. We are marooned in a world that does not yet feel real, existing external to us. Nor do we perceive the otherness of the other person but see them only through our projections. We remain equated with our point of view without acknowledgement that other points of view exist, conflict, may even be valid. A direct line from our psyche to the world can be drawn: unconscious state of identity with our own view, to prejudice manifest in familial and social discrimination; then to acts of segregation financially, politically (redlining districts to exclude loans, restrictive laws for voting by groups we disdain), even to persecution, and, God help us, to genocide. Psychological development, or its lack, makes a political difference.

What gets halted is our intrapsychic aliveness, our sense of other person as real, not just a "bundle of our projections" (Winnicott 1967/1989, p. 221). What gets halted is reaching to spiritual perception that whatever we call God, is there, a thing in itself, not because we projected it there. Aliveness means that the other, the object, is real, exists external to us, a subject in itself, not existing as our projection. If we do not reach this in analysis, for example, we are doing self-analysis in consultation with the analyst, not experiencing the analyst as a real resource outside ourselves. In religion the Christian creed expresses belief in "the true god from the true God, "begotten not made"; Judaism asserts the otherness of the Holy, Muslim faith accentuates the otherness of Allah by forbidding any likeness in human or animal symbols for the divine.

In grasping the real as existing in itself, not because we projected it there, Winnicott helps by showing that destructiveness just turns up and is not initially imbued with anger or hate, Destructiveness at this earliest state lives in the baby as muscle movement, not as a reaction to the reality principle that may restrict us. Instead the baby has a living experience with the mothering one that includes destructiveness as movement that establishes the realness of external reality. The feeding mothering one is there to be found and created by the infant in a living experience. The object does not exist "for the subject because of the operation of the subject's projective mechanisms" but exists outside the area of projection (ibid 1989, pp. 223-225). This beginning differentiation of inner state and outer object introduces the symbolic mode of experience and thought – the object is there to be found and the infant creates the object that is found. I found it and I created it: the baby contributes to the shared moment of recognition of each one as existing in its own right, so to speak, its own and the object's.

An example I heard years ago always comes to mind. A three-month-old baby bit his mother's nipple when nursing. The mother said she yelled Ouch!! A sharp piercing occurred. What was this?! Looking into her baby's mouth she saw a thin line of white on his lower gum. Teeth! she said she exclaimed. You have teeth coming! She said her son's eyes beamed at her as if recognizing she recognized his communication. They shared a congratulatory moment. She exclaimed, oh wonderful but please do not repeat it; it hurts; the baby, she said, smiled. And she was never bitten again, she told me, even in ten months of nursing. The baby runs into something there that he did not create but found and communicated his experience of through biting.

Biting represented an experience of something new and of a new communication between them. He found his teeth and he found he could hurt the nipple and he found he could communicate this discovery. His mother received the communication and talked back. Both acknowledged the symbolic value of the discovery of emerging teeth and of the communication and the objective reality of each of them. A space opened in which the traffic of projections and receptions between them happened. This is destructiveness in living finding its place, adding zest, excitement, an intensely vital quality of being alive. Creating a social space between the two, engendering symbolic thinking in the space constructed between baby and mother also represents realities of the living moment and a joy of each contributing to thrill of aliveness.

Projective Identification

Projective identification, a term begun by Melanie Klein and taken up by others since, is "a forceful entry into the object and control of the object by parts of the self" (Klein 1955/1975, p. 154). Like projection, projective identification happens unconsciously, but with added differences. Projection happens when a state of unconscious identity with an item in myself is breaking up. Projection is the first indication to myself, the first hint of moving toward consciousness of this item that I am putting on you. I see it first displayed on you. In projective identification, I am still unconscious of the item and of my projection of it into you. We could say I am more unconscious of it than in projection. My state of identity with it is unknown to me, deeply unconscious. I don't register the three signs of projection going on (p. 2) Further, I identify the item as yours; it belongs to you, is in you. I also identify you with the part I unconsciously put into you.

Those parts may be felt to be bad unacceptable parts of the self that are repudiated and now located in the object. Or the projector may put a good part into the receiver to keep it safe from the rest of the destructive elements in the projector's own personality that would attack the good part and damage it. But conflict and distress arise in every case because I feel you have parts of me inside you and hence exert control over me. Yet you feel I control you via the parts I put into you and I pressure you to comply with the role those parts of me now in you dictate. I want to control you through my parts now identified with you, and I fear you could control me because parts of me now lodge in you instead of me; they are yours, not mine.

Betty Joseph describes aspects of these projective identifications. They are spit-off parts we try to get rid of because they cause anxiety or pain. They are concrete and function to avoid awareness of being separate from the object onto whom we project. We escape awareness of dependence because we are in the object and it has us in it. We aim to dominate the object, getting the other person to take over these capacities in our stead. We also aim to attack and destroy the other's mind through the 'spies' we have placed within the other who can give us knowledge to use against the other. Yet, on the positive side, projective identification is a form of unconscious communication if the receiver can notice it and reflect on it (Joseph 2012 pp. 99-101, 104, 107).

A particularly troubling interpersonal example is when a man puts into a woman a soul animating part of himself (Jung's notion of anima) that offers a connecting bridge between his experiences of ego and Self. The woman feels made use of to enliven him; he feels enraged if she refuses this function, especially if it includes assigned sexual behavior and he may erupt in violent words if not actions toward her, because he feels cut off from an essential connection within himself, as if she robbed him of his soul. The intercession of consciousness is needed, which is not accomplished in words or even images; it demands a living experience of the receiver registering this live thing put into her, her responses to it and out of that a modification of it which as if sends a message to the projector of the return of the projection in less toxic form which the man may be able to receive as energy coming back to him and more consciously owning a valued part of himself.

But it is a difficult experience filled with fear of being manipulated, with anxiety that I have lost parts of myself. Even if I lodged it in you to protect it from being destroyed by other parts remaining inside me that could destroy it, I fear I may be in your power. I may idealize you, putting good things in you for safe keeping. The relation of spiritual advisors, gurus, may perform this role if the receiver can consciously carry it, by proxy so to speak. Robert Johnson describes this as the willingness to carry for another the gold of the personality, even the god, which cannot yet be carried by the person to whom it belongs; it is too heavy, too scary, But the receiver returns it eventually.

Dangers lurk everywhere. The split-off projected parts may be too many so I feel I am left empty and fearful I cannot get them back. In analysis a mother felt like an empty shell. Her daughter went off to college far away and took all the good parts that the mother had projected into and identified with the daughter. The mother now felt like a discarded banana peel. How to get the lost parts back?

This is a theological problem too and a social one. Reading the book of Baruch in the Knox translation of the Hebrew Bible, I was struck by the text imputing all blame for the devastation of the exile on the people who disobeyed God's commands. It was their fault and this ruin and catastrophe, spelled out in excruciating detail, was their punishment; they deserved it. How different is that God-Image from the one Job wrestled with as he insisted on praying to a just and faithful God in the midst of terrible suffering whom his friends told him happened because he sinned and this was God's punishment. Job wrestled with two conflicting images of God, and he is the only one in the book who continues to pray to God. In the end Job receives a whole new vision of God who speaks to him directly. He performs a leap to a new God-image beyond the Law which God had conferred.

In this new living experience Job gives up his narcissism, his need to see in human ethical terms a cause-and-effect explanation of suffering and for its meaning. He embraces the wholeness God shows him – including destructiveness, the Leviathan and the Behemoth – and the extraordinary fact that God speaks to him and shows him God's view, so to speak. This vision of God allows for human mourning for loss and faults while not elevating them to cosmic proportion. This vision allows for God-image of God who comes near speaking to Job of the wholeness of a whole reality that includes a meaning that surpasses what human ethics can explain. This vision beholds a God beyond even the Law given by God, now broken by God's behavior and Job's suffering. A noticeable detail stands out as well. When Job's fortunes and children are restored to him, his daughters receive in the text for the first time personal names and with rights to inherit. The feminine gains new recognition. Job is appointed by God as intercessor for his friends who condemned him under terms of the Law (see Ricoeur 1967, pp. 54-86; see also Ricoeur 1970, pp. 548-551; see also Houck-Loomis 2018; see also Ulanov 2007, chapter 6; see Ulanov and Ulanov 1975 chapter 11 on intercession).

The important point to grasp is that whatever the content projected – emotion, idea – it is not an abstract piece of information to be apprehended in a detached way. No. It is alive; we do not think it but live it. Jung calls it an imago, a carrier of images, of symbols (Jung 1948/1960, para 507). I cannot house this hot potato in myself so I put it in you. If you fall into identification with it, it is like a hand grenade force that pushes you around, entraps you.

Thomas Ogden offers good definition of projective identification: "one person makes use of another person to experience and contain an aspect of himself." On an unconscious fantasy level the projector is "getting rid of an unwanted or endangered part of himself … and of depositing that part in another person in a powerfully controlling way. The projected part of the self is felt to be partially lost and to be inhabiting the other person" (Ogden 1982, pp. 1-2). On an interpersonal level the projector pressures the receiver to comply with the feelings and thoughts put into the receiver and identified with him or her. On the positive side, if the receiver – be it parent, sibling, friend, spiritual director, analyst – can digest the projection and experience it in themselves which modifies the toxic nature of the content and hold it in readiness to return to the projector, then the projector may readmit the content into himself and be freed up from the fear of what had to be gotten rid of.

But this is hard work on the receiver's side – what does this make me feel about myself? How not to get entrapped? The task is somehow to contact in oneself the terrifying feeling and find their own different relation to the content and be able to hold that in mind while also carrying by proxy what the projector puts into them. If the receiver falls into identification with another's projective identification and with the imago at its center, then I lose my own sense of self, my identity in distinction from what has been put into me. For example, oppressed groups of people may succumb to negative projective identifications from dominant social groups and suffer feeling inferior because of corrosive prejudice against different religious belief, age, sexual orientation, race, class, economic level. Also on the negative side, if the receiver identifies with what is projected into him or fights against it, the receiver diverts his own energy to a problem that belongs to the projector.

Consciousness of what is going on, however, opens the receiver to a rich source of information about the projecting person and is invaluable in therapeutic work even if strenuous. In this sense projective identification is a communication of an experience, not in thought or words, but in enactment, which with a dose of consciousness can become a living experience between the two. If it cannot be registered at all as a communication then attacks on making such a link, as Bion describes it, happen and psychic degeneration follows where reality is attacked and the self is fragmented into parts for export.

On a social and on a political level we can see how dangerous this operation can be where depositing in the other all we fear leads to acts of repudiation, even killing. On the personal level, meaninglessness gives way to worse: to nonexperience. One has paralyzed one's ability "to think and to attach meaning to perception" (Ogden 1982, p. 8) hence one lives in shutdown mode.

Recovery of capacity for projective identification would begin again the process of coming alive (ibid, p. 9).

Let me return to intercession and its necessity and preventive effects. At the nub of what is projectively identified with another is what Jung calls an imago, a carrier of images that become powerful symbols. For example in one's feelings about one's mother is the image/symbol of the mother. I have my particular experience of my personal mother and my culture's images of the good and bad mother peculiar to the West. Further, my image of mother is not identical to the objective person who is my mother in herself but reflects my own subjective context and also the influence of a symbolic history of powerful images around mother – what Jung calls archetype – that exists at the center of my mother-image. The intermediate realm between my subjective picture of the object – mother – and the objective person I call mother also provides space to distinguish the personal image from the collective picture of mother in our societies and the inner collective archetypal images of mother (godmother, witch, earthmother). To make these distinctions expands my consciousness and makes it more flexible and more hospitable to my neighbor's reality and thus contributes to a spirit of more justice among us.

Recognizing the imago world amounts to the ability to develop an authentic symbolic life – differentiating the 'facts' from our representation of them. But dangers abound. If I entirely projectively identify the imago with the other into whom I place it, I lose contact with the other's actual objective existence and unconsciously try to force the other to identify with the imago I project onto them. White supremacy is a strong negative example of social coercion of a violent kind that annihilates the actual identities of people of different colors. I need to intercede with more consciousness from such bullying of the other.

If others fall into identification with the projective identification of an imago by another or by a different economic group, for example, they exert a violence against themselves, trying to comply with another's expectations at the cost of their own precious core self.

If we ourselves fall into identification with the imago, we can lose our actual identity and fall victim to restricting stereotypes that issue from an archetypal image. I declare I am such and such – the drug addict, not the woman struggling with affliction of drugs; I am inferior, not seeing the image of inferiority coming to consciousness pressing for differentiation. I am reduced to a label. If the imago concerns one's God-image, then religious inflation results with grave social consequences – rubbing out any differing God-images – religious persecution at its worst. The powerful imago rules me.

Tremendous energies constellate when we try to face our projections and our identifying them with others. We need the intercession of consciousness to make spaces between our sense of self and a powerful archetypal image that influences us, between our image for the other and the other as they are in themselves, between each of us and the influential images of our culture and society. Our world expands our curiosity about what belongs to whom and how these images meet, conflict, endow, transform. We learn to relate to them, not become them. This reduces destructiveness and impresses us how much we intertwine with each other and together come to see imagos of great energy circulating between us.

Projection as Noticing

A third basic function of projection is to make us notice things. We relate to objects through our projections As Jung says "All human relationships swarm with projections ... it is the natural and given thing for unconscious contents to be projected … the average person is not reflective and is bound to his environment by a whole system of projections" … they are "convenient bridges to the world" (Jung, 1948/1960, para 507). But as soon as libido strikes out from state of identity with the object, we come upon the difference of our projections from the object.

First, I notice you as a separate existing subject. The object's externality becomes noticed: you are different from what I thought. The other is an objective subject, not manufactured by my projecting. The world becomes peopled with people, not my projections. Here also is Jung's unique contribution. We stay linked with our projections. We do not 'lose' the content, change in the sense of it disappearing, opening a big gap between us and this part of ourselves. Instead, we change our stance with it, becoming slightly aware in a kind of proto knowing, that the content belongs to us as well as locating it, finding it in the other.

Second, we begin to notice when and what I project upon this 'object' – this person, this piece of art or furniture, this religious doctrine or special beach. I also notice the specific psychic content I am projecting – anger, admiration, awe, longing. Jung writes, it is "only by recognizing certain properties of the objects as projections that we are able to distinguish them from the real properties of the objects" (ibid). This affect or idea that I attribute to you becomes distinct.

Third, to see the object existing in its own right different from our projections upon it "can only take place when the imago that mirrored itself in the object is restored, together with its meaning, to the subject" (ibid). I notice the powerful imago nestled within the contents I project onto you. I notice my projection, with a powerful imago in it as a separate entity too. I notice this symbolic content that is issuing from me, attaching to you, but exists in its own right. This is the birth of symbolic thinking: psychic reality exists and we can notice it, feel and think about it.

For example, I see you different from my anger and I see my anger as my projection, that somehow latches onto you specifically hence having something to do with you, and I see the force of anger in itself that circulates between us. We notice ourselves, the other, and the symbolic imago. This is a fat consciousness! Hence, I can dream of you and ask what is my experience of you? Who are you in yourself? What do you symbolize in me? and in life? This kind of intercessory exploring is of great interest to artists, lovers and analysts, not many more. It is work. Apply it to God – our pictures of God which we think are real, who God is, and what imago gathers up a deep meaning of God drawn from ages of human experience.

Winnicott locates this shift to notice otherness, that the world exists outside us as objective resource, not just what I make of it, when destructiveness turns up when the baby's aliveness bumps into the mothering one who survives the baby's making use of her or him. The child begins "a fantasy of destruction which is different from reality …" noticing he or she destroyed the world yet "the world is still there" (Winnicott 1967/2013, p. 38). This noticing is possible because the mother identifies with the infant and survives "the baby's endless demands" which are often just feeling for a boundary, finding the object in the baby's unique style.

For example, a mother with a new baby worried that he seemed so slow at nursing, often interrupting it altogether, in contrast to his older sister who had pounced and fed lustily. What was wrong!? With me? With him? I asked what happened then, when he paused, and felt now I am the mothering one entering into identification with my worrying patient about her newborn. She says he stops nursing and looks around. I heard myself ask, is he pausing for conversation? I had an image appear of a dinner party of two, he pausing to say something or see something or communicate the need to stop eating and feel something. My patient received this imagining and played with it in her own elaborating way and returned later to say yes, he is different from his gobbling sister; he is busy doing some inner thing and I imagine we are talking back and forth; then the nursing continues. Her adaptation made space for the objective qualities of her son that subdued her projection of her own feared inadequacy as a nursing mother. Her baby used his mother to assert his style; she adapted and a beginning of a difference between them emerged. They together found and made a field between them to which each contributed. She notices him; he begins to notice her. They began to converse about a third thing between them. That is the beginning of symbolic mode of existing.

Projection thus leads us to notice the externality of the other; they are not the sum of our images of them; they are themselves also. We also notice the image they carry for us, an image that initially arose in us but which has a secret connection to the other and a life of its own, so to speak. Jung points out the "hook" of any projection found in the person or place on whom on which the projection lands: the object projected upon "must offer the content a 'hook' to hang on" (Jung 1946/1954, para 499).

Why of all the people in the room do I sense you are angry at me? Something there in you attracts my arising affect/image. Usually it is not an identical thing, that is, you may not be angry at me (until I insist and then you will be). But there is something analogous to my anger alive in you that acts like an attractor to my anger that then I attribute to you as originating there, not in me. You may be angry about something, or at the same sort of things I get mad at, but not at me – we dislike loudmouths, or you may need to be a louder mouth because you are too self-deprecating. Or you may fear I could kill you because some terrible life-threatening trauma long dissociated is making its way to your consciousness and attracts my anger. Your need to get angry about something done to you piggy-backs on my anger which is not of killing intensity; you may reach awareness that you are angry through me accusing you of being angry. It is not the exact same as what I project, but it is startlingly analogous to it. I aid in your consciousness as well as being a thorn in your side. You aid in my consciousness as I try to understand that the anger I project onto you is really mine.

Two new potential relationships open up: to the person on whom my projection landed, why this person and not that one, and to the content of what I project, the psychic stuff in me that I have tried only to export and now dimly recognize as coming from me. I may choose yea or nay to pursue each relationship. Whatever I choose I register an odd interdependence both with the other person who showed me I was really angry and with the psychic content brought to my attention. Projections promote kinship if worked with. I get a dim picture of this anger and may decide really to see what this angry stuff is. Jung's emphasis on the many layers of the imago helps – my personal anger, the influence of collective social customs permitting or forbidding show of anger, the particular archetypal image of this anger – fiery lightning strike by Zeus? Voodoo curse by witch? Anger delivered in warrior mode? Gnashing teeth mode? Passive sulking mode and grudge holding?

Projections can also infuse us with excess energy when directed at us. Unlived energy in the projector or in the projecting group can propel us into power, for good or ill. Some people thrive on this and learn how to elicit others' projections for their own gain and illusory appearance of being all powerful. In fact, however, theirs is a parasitic sucking of energy from others for their own inflation. An opposite example is people who give for the good of others and incite them to live their own talent or unique personality. This lends ignition to their unlived life, gets it going. A nursery school teacher, now a woman in her eighties, is still applauded by her nursery school children, now retired people, who felt she inaugurated them into the wonder of being alive and the wonder they had a self from which to live. They feel unending gratitude.

Projection as Cover

The fourth function of projection is to cover events with our projections (Ulanov 2001, pp. 99-102). We make meaning out of events we know we do not cause, linking them to our subjective needs and desires and spiritual reachings, as if the happenings corresponded outwardly to what we underwent inwardly. We might ask, for example, of all the people to come over the horizon into my life right now, what is the meaning of this person turning up? What does this bring me to see that I did not see before? Instead of feeling just assaulted, we also feel enlightened. The conjunction of outward and inward makes a two-way street where meaning traffics both ways: outer events confront us with something we need to face; inner events endow occurrences with significance of a meaningful encounter. Like a small synchronicity that feels big, the coincidence of outer and inner evokes an unexpected significance that makes something unbearable bearable because made meaningful, bringing a purpose to an otherwise awful event that makes us feel like a piece of flotsam in a random universe.

Or, the event may be amazingly positive, a synchronicity that we experience as a nudge of which way to go, or as a sign from the universe that our way is being found in a problem hitherto insoluble. Jung counsels outward events that happen to us must be made inward realizations where we find and create their meaningfulness. Otherwise, such events remain like thunderclaps that buffet or frighten us but have no significance nor give any support to our sense of agency in our lives. In *The*

Red Book he asserts meaningfulness is not found in the event nor in the individual but in the space between them. That is where God is found (Jung 2009, p. 239).

An example of projection functioning to cover a negative event is the meaning a woman made (before we began analysis) of a terrible event: the trauma of being raped. She covered it by seeing its connection to first claiming and then forsaking her own power. Just before the attack occurred, she gave her power away, she said, to the man in her life, when she knew better than to do so. She let him rant on again in complaints about his wife when she had already told him that behavior had to stop – he had to make up his mind in which direction he chose to go. She abandoned her resolve, she said, and let him use her once more as a sounding board for his confusion. The rape occurred on her way home from this meeting. She knew she in no way caused it; she was its victim. But she also viewed the rape as her rejected power assaulting her now from outside herself because she had abandoned her hold on it from inside herself. Such an interpretation did not deny her pain and rage from the violence inflicted on her body and psyche. But, she said, it did confer some meaning on the trauma and thus help her come to terms with it. She covered it in a net of coincident meaning that rescued her from feeling adrift in a frightening world where anything could happen at any time (Ulanov 2001, pp. 100-101). A symbolic meaning from "a neither exclusively conscious or an exclusively unconscious source" assembled "from the equal collaboration of both" and thus evoked a symbolic interpretation (Jung 1921/1976, para 821) that carries the weight of a synchronicity: "Synchronicity ... means the simultaneous occurrence of a certain psychic state with one or more external events which appear as meaningful parallels to the momentary subjective state" (Jung 1952/1960, para 850).

A positive example of covering with our projections an outer event we know we do not cause yet which we receive as a meaningful symbol in response to a dogged stuck place we are mired in is illustrated by a woman artist whose central distressing dilemma is expressed from "not knowing how to put myself in reality; I wasn't sure where to put myself to be in the right place for myself. This is how I feel about my life right now." Her accustomed approach, indeed ruling principle according to Jung's *Red Book* vocabulary, is to create harmonious happiness for others with a flair of fun, to make life pleasing for them adding gladness and joy. She lived her life this way for half of her middle-aged years. Crises caused her to find another path that connected especially to her painting as that was the one place that was her own, not given away to serving others. She said, "I sit in my studio and immediately come alive and am creative. I live here alive and myself." But painting all her life she could not find a way to show it in the world, to sell it and be seen as the artist she is. She remained an unknown artist, as if piling up hundreds of paintings crowding out the meaning of her work. Any ordinary ways of marketing her work she was paralyzed from doing or when risked, led nowhere.

The conflict between serving others' happiness versus finding her own path and the emotional truth in her art, came to a climactic conflict by a number of specific demands including helping increasingly ill parents, intense needs of her children in life-changing junctures and the birth of babies to whom heretofore she would be ready to go and devote her care. But now that old "requirement" conflicted greatly with her sharp conflicting sense of "going down with the parents, losing my life" symbolized by failing to find a way to bring her painting into the world.

Traveling across country to the child with the babies coming and all the demands that implied, she came upon, by "accident" (!) in a fancy clothing store that attracted her eye by the art on its walls a possible 'both-and' resolution instead of the usual 'either-or' response to her conflict. She asks about the possibility of displaying her art in the store. She is told to contact a certain person who is not in the store that day. She takes the name to call. She pauses when exiting to look at unusual colors of fabrics on display. Just then a woman comes in and spontaneously helps her with colors, recognizing her flair. Only after this enthusiastic meeting up between them does my analysand discover this is the person she hopes to meet about the possibility of showing her art in the store. Each woman is excited about an event so beneficial to both of them if her art is selected. For the store woman it would be an occasion the store hosts that would attract a whole new young adult clientele of my patient's child's age, soon to become parent to twins, hence producing profit for the store's bottom line which is the task of the store woman. For my patient it was as if a door opened through which she could walk to take up the task of putting her art into the world, not to give herself over to motherliness in a new form.

It felt like a sign from the universe: yes! look for your path and out of nowhere someone offers to consider showing your art to the public and maybe resulting with sales. Further, this happens when you came to help your child with new babies. Do not revert to being consumed by serving everyone's needs; pursue your reality, take your path. She knows she did not cause this event, and that it may not work out either; Yet it feels like an affirmation, a confirmation and she follows it. Winnicott notes "normal use of omnipotence … reinforces routine sublimatory activities, thus investing them with illusional potential that is both enriching and gratifying to the ego (Winnicott 1989, pp. 442; see also Ulanov 2001, p. 102).

Projection as Calling Goodness to Us

This fifth function of projection is an odd one to name. It might be called integrative projections. They function to make accessible a 'proper' amount of the good, a size we can assimilate into our ordinary personality and thus live in touch with its force, both individually and in shared existence with others. This idea takes us beyond 'noticing' and 'covering' which are important. This touches spiritual reality in addition to symbolic reality, to do with what we each imagine and have faith in as the real, the bigger reality encompassing all.

There are bits in theories related to taking in the good. Kleinian John Steiner says to heal from withdrawing into what he calls a "psychic retreat" that offers us respite from stress, conflict and even unbearable pain, but that also holds us hostage, we need to develop a feminine receptivity of the good. That includes a dependency on the good object and mutual give and take with it, to accept "a creative linking in which giving and receiving are complementary" (Steiner 2011, pp. 170-171). Steiner finds images of this creative linking in the baby-breast relation and later in the penis-vagina relation. These symbolize a mutual capacity to trust the good.

I understand this to recognize that goodness exists, to perceive it turning up, to open to it, lean our weight on its steadiness, confide our dependence to it. Like Jung, who recognizes a feminine mode of being, at least as I understand Jung and would refute the criticism this is a fixed content procedure called essentialism to be applied like set content to actual females, Steiner also recognizes a feminine mode that is a sturdy "receptive dependence" and aggressive in the sense of directing energy to the good in our dependency on it that can be accepted and endured.

Jung recounts a late dream where he could not let himself bow all the way to the ground in recognizing the 'highest presence.' That would stifle his freedom! He reserves a small space between his forehead and the stone floor in protest and in protection of his freedom. To go all the way down would be total capitulation and make him feel a "dumb fish' (Jung 1963,

p. 219). Dependency, I suggest, gets contaminated here with unwitting submission in a sense of meek handing over, passively yielding up the kernel of human authority symbolized by our tiny margin of freedom. I believe that is still a complexed area in Jung's psychology, not worked through fully (Ulanov 2017, pp. 106-107). However, I suggest, that Jung is not just protesting he is *not* a dumb fish. He is also asserting the inestimable value of human life, and its precious ego world of everyday life. He honors this personality #1, highlighted by personality #2 of the ages shining like a backlighting of our ordinary going forth in all the wonders of human relationships, thinking and feeling, responses to cosmos and nature (Jung 1963, pp. 218-222). This feminine mode which both Jung and Steiner recognize, is powerful acceptance of opening ourself to the good, that it exists, that we desire it, that it is already offered. We open out to it, to take it in, be glad: Praise is the thing, and thanks.

We touch here on soul issues, what sparks us alive from a deep place stirring us to venture, risk, register the other we touch and Otherness that touches us through all we experience. Our soul sparks us to fashion images of what matters most, what brings a sense of emotional purpose and meaningfulness in this life (Ulanov, 2017, pp. 8-13). Traditionally, the soul is often conjured with two feet, one in the here and now, embodied in the stuff of life, and the other in a realm transcending our ego needs, plots, purposes, pointing beyond them to another center Jung calls Self and, I suggest, to what lives beyond Self as its source. The Self points beyond itself to the something more the soul links us to. We make pictures; we see, smell, sometimes hear, taste of these two vectors and their meetings. Such pictures are God-images of what we find and fashion and believe or reject of a core of us meeting the core of reality. The examples are highly personal and varied. They turn up in what is so wonderful we call it miracle. They appear in dire circumstances of crisis, death. They reach toward healing of what besets and reduces us (see Ulanov 1996, chapters 9 and 10). God-images turn up in our humanity's most honored traditions.

What this means in terms of projection, remembering that it is a normal psychodynamic mechanism, is seen in adult forms of a baby hungering for the good feed, the good breast. We want it, we need it, we love it. From my long teaching career I remember the sheer fun of teaching students who call out this way for they are creatively ready to use what the material and what the teacher offers. From decades as analyst I applaud and enjoy analysands who want to make inventive use of what the psyche unfolds. Lovers gladly take the good offered by the beloved and offer it back, finding it there between them. New Testament Scripture salutes the one who weeps when it is time to mourn and dances when it is time for joy, never lukewarm, but who loves with all their heart, mind and soul.

This reaching out to the good, projecting images of it, is like a humming connection; we feel it for example when a dream answers a deep question we have been asking. These instances of a right fit arouse excitement, thanks, wonder. It feels like an energy that is already there interdependent among us, through us, around us, in events and animals and plants. In response, it is as if we send out our projections, our bridges to the good, like tiny tendrils to something very large, that could quell us if we did not create these personal connections to it. For a baby to achieve a good feed, its tiny gestures establish a mutuality between its small mouth and fingers and the largeness of the milk, the breast, the arms, the face. Similarly, our projections throughout our lives are our tiny gestures to the large goodness that is so big in comparison it scares us. It could squash us, blow us out to sea, as Jung says in the *Red Book* – that we have to get our self back from God lest God just overwhelm us wash us away: "unfathomable, powerful movement that sweeps the self away into the boundless" (Jung 2009, p. 338). Without our projected images of and to this energy, it burns us up. Without projecting this mysterious element of the creative in us – which is ours, inhabits us – creativity disperses.

In the gap between the good, big beyond measure, and our little goods live our projections of it, our pictures of what goodness is. I remember a student who worked with Children at Risk in New York City telling me of asking a boy of 11 who had tried to kill himself, what is your picture of something good? Silence happened. Then the boy said, 'My grandmother's smile to me.' Such pictures compose our spiritual life weaving back and forth across the gap there where we are found and create the central current of goodness already there, offered to us. Such a tiny image in face of suicidal thoughts has brute strength to rescue a boy from plunging into an abyss, not a cure-all, but a handhold.

Awareness that this big force could dissolve us, places destructiveness right in midst of a profound living experience, not outside it. We see in social life that goodness inhabits collective events or deep trends which I perceive going on now in this new century. This is not only a personal happening; it belongs to the whole of which the human family is one precious part. It pulls us into acknowledging the spirit in which we all dwell, that will push us to name the *what* in which we believe.

These images of the good are our God-images though we may reject them as of God. They embody in their names and symbols what we believe at the heart of reality and around which we revolve. In order for such a symbol to feel real to us we must project it and experience its reality external to us. Further, we need to pay attention to which image repeatedly calls to our attention – one of fear? Overwhelm? Peace? One woman said to me in analysis, I know God exists and loves me; I live from that. I need not to forget it, wander away from it, which she has done and must always find her way back despite big blows happening in her family of crippling, murder, addiction. To what image are we attracted? These images lasso life toward us, make it liveable for us, include destructiveness and love which is stronger (colder) than death (see Ulanov 2001, pp. 105-106).

To call these projections 'integrative' indicates two ways they partake of the collective. The first way is they are part of traditions through the ages (Jung's 'spirit of the depths') and also are part of structures of present society and cultural mores (Jung's 'spirit of the times'). Our God-images include bits of both, for example, like rituals from the past we do not understand but are moved by, and like influence in the present of personal mentors, authors, contemporary social movements that shape us and cannot be reduced to personal object-relations. These projections of God images put before us moving and powerful contents that we need to take in.

Yet the second way our projections partake of the collective dimension concerns the different way we deal with them. We cannot take in collective and archetypal contents the way we do personal ones and some aspects of the cultural ones. Collective contents are too large and the ego cannot assimilate them. Evidence of this are those who try and become inflated – they are *right* and brook no disagreement. They become dictators, tyrants, theological and psychological bullies persecuting, even killing, those who hold opposite views. They malign them and scorn them. Like the playground bully, they fall into identity with huge gusts of energy that they think are at their disposal, but in fact the reverse is the case: they are at the disposal of unconscious forces. Think of Hitler whom others idolized and feared. The manic state results or its opposite. Negative deflations result that invade the body as well as the mind in clinical depression, severe psycho-somatic splitting, or psychoses. Trying to integrate the collective unconscious rush of energy is like trying to integrate a tsunami wave. We need to relate to it rather than assimilate it as we do with personal projections.

With these 'integrative' projections, our visions of the good, or of justice or ethics or love that becomes our ultimate value, we need to put their mana outside us and relate to it there, to serve it, not house it as part of ourselves. Instead of gulping music *per se* or mathematics or motherhood, we must rest content with *my* music, the small part I listen to, or the few mathematical formulas for the essence of energy that I can comprehend, or the motherhood I experience with this child, not all music, all formulas for secret working of the cosmos, not mother to all peoples. We cannot house in our small personality the vast archetypal energy. We need outer structure to hold it. Jung gives the example of religions, mythologies, fairy tales, the anatomy of the body and of the psyche. They are impersonal. We relate to them, build bridges to the impersonal reality of the collective content, to its otherness that we build relationship to see it, and do not become it.

I remember an example of this in college that startled me. By luck or mistake (not musical talent) I was one of a small madrigal group under direction of Nadia Boulanger to perform French songs in the Gardner Museum in Boston. She drilled us mercilessly and I felt she was conveying a truth about life in addition to how to sing this piece properly. I experienced in trying to get right the song's entering note of F with the words 'Dieu qu'il a fait … ' I was learning how to enter all of music – through that one note F – its round sound, tone, pace, level of force, pronunciation, giving of breath to it. Through this small note we entered the entire world of music. Music was collective; we could connect to its riches by relating to it precisely through this single beginning note that was the door opening.

Negative examples are also of crucial importance. This insight came to me listening to Sam Kimbles giving a presentation to my local psychological group. This point he only referred to in passing but it struck sparks like flint on stone for me. He mentioned his idea of 'phantom narratives' (Kimbles 2014). What I understood about them was that the collective exerts profound impact on us in social prejudices, covered up acts of sadism, denials of intentional malice and that this impact remains unconscious. For me it is as if we wake up to the fact we have been walking around in crowded spaces, bumped, jostled by big hindrances, and discover, oh that is where this sharp cut, this big bruise comes from. That is why my analysand developed a chronic defense of holding her breath which though effective, also hindered her body's health. There was so much pressure compressing the supply of oxygen in the small collective of the family that she could not relax deeply into her own breathing rhythm.

In collective society pressures, some going on for generations, the effect of crowding out space to be and become is another source of people feeling 'there is something wrong with me.' Here is the collective piece of that complex that cannot be addressed without seeing it is not a personal problem or only such. The social ghost or phantom narrows, shortens, reduces the space in which we can live. These boulders, quicksand patches, searing winds have oppressed us. Waking up to these forces introduces a space between us and them.

To get conscious of such a collective force makes a big difference. We do not assimilate it. We build relation to it and thus change it to a degree, contribute to undoing its negative impact and redo its influence in a new form. The corpus of Jung's work Sonu Shamdasani avers (in zoom presentation on *The Black Books* 6/6/21), is Jung's response to the collective dismay of the dead confronting him in *The Red Book*. Their not having lived their lives fully results in confusion, unanswered questions and unrest when dead. Jung addresses their unlived life through Philemon who says they did not live their animal self, nor take responsibility for plundering the earth's oil and the velvet eye of the ox. This is Jung's social activism, I suggest, and is prescient, a hundred years before it became a cultural concern. He is opening a door (like that F note heard and sung exactly) to the root cause of what we now call climate change, the destruction of our precious island of blue and green in the cosmos.

Philemon also tells the dead they wasted Christ's message to love their neighbor, to love themselves and to love God above all, in their childish lazy demand Christ do all the work for them. They wandered away from Christ's love; they did not hear the F note and the door closes on them. Jung is providing through his work how to live one's life. This is the dead's problem of unlived life that Jung addresses in creating analytical psychology, not ours here on the life side of the door but the heartache and lostness on the other side of the door.

These images lasso life toward us, make it liveable for us, include destructiveness and love which is stronger (colder) that death (See Ulanov 2001, pp. 105-106).

Projection as a Gift from God

This last idea, even odder than our projections of the good, comes in relation to Saint Nicholas of Cusa of 15th century about whom Jung wrote. In my last book I wrote about Jung and Nicholas – their differences and similarities and implications of Nicholas' ideas for understanding Jung's complexes as described in *The Red Book* (Ulanov 2017, chapter 7). Nicolas' God-image sees God as "Posse Ipsum," "Can-Itself," "Can" as self-subsistent ..." Can "beyond, antecedent to, behind, and present in all that 'is' ... Whatness itself without which nothing at all can be" (Nicolas of Cusa 1453/1997, pp. 58, 339, 340; see also Ulanov 2017, pp. 94-95). For Nicolas, God is this "*Possest*, the center and author of reality." God is not any symbol. No name, no image, no imagining, no conceptualizing, no reasoning, no thinking, no beyond senses, no intellect, no inward self can define God. God is unthinkable, unknowable, beyond knowing and not knowing, beyond unity and otherness, beginnings and endings

... even being and nonbeing: God transcends all opposites" (ibid, p. 95).

I was struck forcibly by Nicholas' insight that in our trying to describe God – our forms for God, which I call here projections of our images for God, our God images – that our projections onto God (or whatever we put in place of God that we might understand as our highest value, what we love most) we think we are making God conform to our images of God. But no. In putting our pictures onto God we are seeing our own face in God. God reaches us through our projections onto God. For Nicholas he sees God as the essential whatness, the 'can be' of whatever is. That power to be is God. Hence to see God as this or that is God using our images to communicate who God is through these most personal pictures we create of God. We are not seeing our projections onto God, but instead, because God's face is the truth, the image of all faces, we are seeing our own truth: "Thus, O Lord, I comprehend that your face precedes every formable face, that it is the exemplar and truth of all faces and that all are images of your face ... therefore, which can behold your face sees nothing that is other or different from itself, because it sees there its own truth" (Nicholas of Cusa 1453 "On the Vision of God' in Bond 1977 6: 18, p. 243).

Nicholas also notes about God, what Jung notes about the unconscious: the face we turn toward the unconscious is the face the unconscious turns toward us. Nicholas says of God "whoever looks at you with a loving face will find only your face looking on oneself with love ... Whoever looks on you with anger will likewise find your face angry ... if a lion were to attribute a face to you, it would judge it only as a lion's face" (ibid, 6:19, pp. 243-244). In other words, as the excellent translator and introducer H. Lawrence Bond puts it, "we may perceive how we who look upon God do not give God form but see ourselves in God, because from God we receive what God is. Whatever we seem to project into the form of God is in fact God's gift to us" (ibid, p. 49).

I understand this to mean that through our projected pictures onto God we discern the truth that is God. We are not the subject searching after God; we are the object searching after the subject who is already there. We search and find God through sorting through our projections which are the means through which God draws us. In a sense God gives us through our projections pictures of ourselves and pictures of God's eternal truth through the small conditions of each of our way of being. We climb one rung of Jacob's ladder at a time which God accommodates. Our projections do not create God but act as gestures toward the "all power to be" (ibid, 15: 62, p. 263). "You receive the form of whoever beholds you, then you lift me up that I may see how one looking at you does not give you form, but rather one sees oneself in you, for one receives from you that which one is. Thus, what you seem to receive from one who looks on you is your gift, as if you were the living mirror of eternity, which is the form of forms" (ibid, 6:63, pp. 263-264).

If we project parts of us onto God, God reaches us through those projections: we see ourselves needing a protecting God, or we see our destructiveness in a persecuting God. We see ourselves through what we project onto God. For example, if we projectively identify God with what is unconscious in us, asking, in effect, for God to carry what we are not yet able to, we now identify God with those parts of ourselves. Identifying God with our hate or fear, we will combat God through those emotions. If we project onto God beneficence beyond our conscious experience, then we will communicate in and through a balm, if not from Gilead, then from the Bronx, or from a lost corner of our own personality we now find.

If we notice through our projections that they are projections and God is other than a bundle of projections, and we too are a subject separate from these projections that move through us, and we notice that in the midst of them is an imago, a nugget of our experience of Self, of what we have called God, and of a symbol that has its own rich history, we are living a threefold way God draws us to closer communion. We might notice, for example, to which figure of the Trinity we pray, to which emblem of the divine in Hebrew Bible draws us in, which name for Allah of the thousand names keeps coming to mind and lips.

If we use projection as cover for events – positive or negative – then God might appear in synchronistic meanings; we are drawn closer through that image, that window, that door. If projection is of our notion of goodness then it is goodness that brings us near to being enfolded in God's presence. In all the functions of projection we are not distorting reality by imposing subjective contents in its place, but finding a meeting place with a reality named God. Meeting occurs between and within one's subjectivity with objective, ultimate reality in the specific fashion of our own projections. It helps to remember right here Jung's point that projection is not loss or separation from the contents hurled out of us. Projection is the first step out of unconscious state of identity with the projected content moving toward consciousness of it. Our relation to it changes in this process of becoming more aware of what is projected.

To see our projection onto God of as God's gift to us – what an astounding idea that is! Paradox confronts us. We thought psychic and social hygiene means only to get rid of projections, to stop polluting the shared atmosphere with what we repudiate in ourselves. That is true and a contribution to social peace. But the soul and psyche's project wants more. We must also accept what we thought we had to get rid of. What we thought we had to get over turns out to be part of the path to go forward, nearer, dearer, into the heart of the real.

This chapter was presented originally to The Washington D.C. Jungian Society June 2017, Portland Maine Jungian Society May 2018, Jung on the Hudson July 2019, Portland Oregon Jung Society February 2020, and candidates in New York Jungian Psychoanalytical Association February 2020.

References

Abram, J. 2013. Ed. *Donald Winnicott Today. London and New York: Routledge.*

— 2012. "D.W.W.'s notes or the Vienna Congress 1971: a consideration and interpretation of Winnicott's theory of aggression and an interpretation of the clinical implications. *Donald Winnicott Today*" pp. 302-331

Bond, J.L. 1997. *Nicholas of Cusa Selected Spiritual Writings.* Trans. and Ed. H. Lawrence Bond New York and Mahwah N.J.: Paulist Press.

Dupre, L. 1996. "The Mystical Theology of Nicholas of Cusa's *De Visione Dei.*" Eds. Gerald Christianson and Thomas H. Izbicki. 1996. *Nicholas of Cusa on Christ and the Church. Leiden, New York, Koln: E.J. Brill,* pp. 205-221.

Eidelberg, L. 1968. *Encyclopedia of Psychoanalysis.* New York: The Free Press.

Freud, S. 1911/ 1973. "The Case of Schreber" *Standard Edition XII.* Trans and Ed. James Strachey. London: Hogarth Press, pp. 3-85.

— 1920/1973. "Totem and Taboo" *Standard Edition XIII.* Trans. and Ed. James Strachey. London: Hogarth Press, pp. 1-162.

Hinsie, L.E. and Campbell, R.J. 1974. *Psychiatric Dictionary.* New York: Oxford University Press.

Hopkins, J. 1978. *A Concise Introduction to the Philosophy of Nicholas of Cusa.* Minneapolis: University of Minnesota.

Houck-Loomis, T. 2018. *History Through Trauma, History and Counter-History in the Hebrew Bible.* Eugene Oregon: Pickwick Publications.

Jaspers, K. 1964. *Anselm and Nicholas of Cusa.* Ed. Hannah Arendt. Trans. Ralph Manheim. New York and London: Harcourt, Brace and Jovanovich.

Johnson, R.A. 2008. *Inner Gold.* Kihei, Hawaii: Koa Books.

Joseph, B. "Projective Identification: Some Clinical Aspects" Eds. Elizabeth Spillius and Edna O'Shaughnessy, 2012. *Projective Identification, The Fate of a Concept*. London: Routledge, chapter 6.

Jung, C.G. 1921. *Psychological Types Collected Works 6*. Trans. R. F. C. Hull. Princeton N.J.: Princeton University Press.

— 1946/1954. "The Psychology of the Transference" *The Practice of Psychotherapy Collected Works Collected Works* 16. Trans. R. F. C. Hull. Princeton N. J.: Princeton University Press, paras 353-530.

— 1948/1960. "General Aspects of Dream Psychology" *The Structure and Dynamics of the* Psyche *Collected Works* 8. Trans. R.F.C Hull. Princeton N.J.: Princeton University Press, paras 443-529.

— 1952. "Synchronicity: An Acausal Connecting Principle" *The Structure and Dynamics of the Psyche Collective Works* 8, paras 816-968.

— 1953. *Psychology and Alchemy Collected Works* 12. Princeton N.J.: Princeton University Press.

— 1963. *Memories, Dreams, Reflections Recorded and Edited by Aniela Jaffé. Trans. Richard and Clara Winston. New York: Pantheon Books Random House.*

— 2009. *The Red Book, Liber Novus*. Ed. Sonu Shamdasani. Trans. Mark Kyburz, John Peck and Sonu Shamdasani. New York: W.W. Norton.

Klein, M. 1952/1975. "Some Theoretical Conclusions Regarding the Emotional Life of the Infant" *Envy and Gratitude and Other Works 1946-1963*. Delacorte Press/ Seymour Lawrence, pp. 61-94.

— 1955/1975. "On Identification" *Envy and Gratitude & Other Works 1946-1963*. New York: Delacorte Press/ Seymour Lawrence, pp. 141-176.

— 1959/1975. "Our Adult World and its Roots in Infancy" *Envy and Gratitude and Other Works 1946-1963*. New York: Delacorte Press/ Seymour Lawrence, pp. 247-264.

Ogden, T.H. 1979/2012. "On Projective Identification" Eds. Elizabeth Spillius and Edna O'Shaughnessy, *Projective Identification, The Fate of a Concept*. London: Routledge. 2012, chapter 17.

— 1982. *Projective Identification & Psychoanalytic Technique*. New York: Jason Aronson.

The Prophecy of Baruch. 1950. The Holy Bible. Translated from the Latin Vulgate in the light of the Hebrew and Originals, Authorized by the Hierarchies of England, Wales and Scotland. New York: Sheed and Ward, pp. 737-744.

Ricoeur, P. 1967. *The Symbolism of Evil*. Trans. Emerson Buchanan. New York: Harper & Row.

— 1970. *Freud and Philosophy: An Essay on Interpretation.* Trans. Dennis Savage. New Haven, Ct.: Yale University Press.

Shamdasani, S. 2021. Zoom lecture on Jung's *The Black Books,* June 6.

Steiner, J. 1993. *Psychic Retreats Pathological Organization in Psychotic, Neurotic and Borderline Patients.* London and New York: Routledge.

— 2011. *Seeing and Being Seen Emerging from Psychic Retreat.* London and New York: Routledge.

Ulanov A. and Ulanov B. 1975. "Intercession" *Religion and the Unconscious.* Louisville: John Knox/Westminster Press, pp. 218-243.

Ulanov, A.B. 1996. "Disguises of the Anima" and "Vicissitudes of Living in the Self" in *The Functioning Transcendent.* Wilmette, Il.: Chiron, chapters 9 and 10.

— 2001. *Finding Space*: Winnicott, *God and Psychic Reality.* Louisville; John Knox/Westminster Press.

— 2007. "Evil" *The Unshuttered Heart, Opening to Aliveness and Deadness in the Self.* Nashville, Tn.: Abingdon Press, chapter 6.

Winnicott, D.W. 1967/2013. "D.W. on D.W." Ed. J. Abram, *Donald Winnicott Today.* London and New York: Routledge, 2013, pp. 29-46.

— 1968. "The Use of an Object and Relating through Identifications" Eds. Clare Winnicott, Ray Shepherd, Madeleine Davis, D.W. Winnicott, *Psycho-Analytic Explorations.* 1989. London: Karnac.

— 2012. "D.W.W.'s notes for the Vienna Congress 1971: a consideration and interpretation of Winnicot's theory of aggression and an interpretation of the clinical implications" Ed. Jan Abram *Donald Winnicott Today* 2013, pp. 302-331.

Chapter 7:

Trauma and Transcendence

I. Introduction

Transcendence flings the door wide – what is meaning? What is my emotional purpose? How am I to live after this trauma or even think about it? Trauma taught I may not live but bleed forever from this wound. What is big enough to gather me up as I circle it? Trauma explodes clear ways of being, shoves us into other ontological realms. It makes us ask finally, what do I love, care about; is it there?

For clinicians all these questions come up – the beyond piercing the here and now problem the analysand presents, and the space/time barriers of the here and now piercing into the beyond. What do we find? As a clinician I move from experience to theory and agree with Jung that truth of spirit "is nothing if it cannot live" (Jung 1926/1960 para 648). But trauma wrecks living, and transcendence, if fake, can encapsulate trauma instead of working it through. Yet if transcendence is authentic it can burn us not out, but up. For how to live transcendence in daily space-time limits when it blazes and beckons us beyond those borders?

Further, to the one of trauma and the two of transcendence I add a third of psychoid processes of unconscious that Jung describes as piercing space/time boundaries: "Under certain conditions it [psyche] could even break through the barriers of space and time precisely because of a quality essential to it ... its relatively trans-spatial and trans-temporal nature" (Jung 1934/1960, para 813; see also Ulanov 2017, p. 7). Contact with unconscious psychoid processes touches the madness that trauma threatens, and makes, I suggest, more possible our transcending those wounds that feel beyond repair. Contact with psychoid processes within us is another source of healing, I suggest, even toward trauma, and may promote living connection with what transcends it.

But such growth does not come in continuous predictable manner, even though our assimilating it is gradual. It comes in a leap to a new way of conceiving and perceiving, indeed, a metaphysics related to the physics of quantum mechanics, thus affecting how we know (epistemology), what we know (ontology), what we do in analysis (clinical work), and finally what we believe is the real (theology). Trauma and transcendence is thus a dangerous topic – it lassos in the all in all and induces swooning away.

Trauma

Trauma shatters the ego, and we can ask a Jungian question: does it shatter the Self? Whatever we answer, trauma is terrible. It plunges us into No-thingness, destroying hum-drum space and time that supports our finite life. Trauma steals our ordinary spaces by substituting for them the No-place where we left body and soul and fell into abysmal confusion. Trauma interrupts our time sense of going-on-being – with sieges of weeping, blanked silences, breath-stopping anxiety that brings no rest between words, only agitation. Kidnapped into a far country we feel ejected from safe spaces of security. Trauma can even obliterate future time: we never know when we will be liberated from this exiled state. Trauma pokes holes into our space/time parameters of ego living. Through those holes we can feel pushed toward the oncoming subway train, or to seize the kitchen knife in our hand from cutting vegetables to thrust it into our gut.

But Jung sees our psyche also has capacity to pierce space/time barriers through which piercings the infinite flows. Through experiences of psychoid process and related synchronistic experiences the impact of meaningfulness is bestowed that ushers us into wholeness of the whole that Jung calls the *Unus Mundus*. We transcend meaninglessness and space/time limits. We rise above them in the traditional definition of transcendence as ascending beyond material existence and our usual categories of understanding.

Transcendence

In his usual style Jung gives various meanings of transcendence and uses them interchangeably. Transcendence describes anything beyond the boundaries of conscious ego life, so anything unconscious can be transcendent to our ego perspective. For example, I am shocked to discover a different departure point living in me alien to my conscious sense of identity. Who is this blabbermouth speaking publicly that my introversion eschews? Yet Jung describes God as the other standpoint within us as "where we are not" and he knows it is God by the "unshakeableness of the experience" (Jung 2009, pp. 234, 299). Hence if we turn our ego attention toward this animus personification so he speaks *to* us, not stepping in front of our egos spouting certainties in public, we may discover truth as spirit by which to live (Jung 1953, para 232-233; see also Jung 1931/1976, para 1292).

Jung also describes transcendence as a function: it makes a bridge between rivaling opposites: "There is nothing mysterious or metaphysical about the term 'transcendent function.' It means a psychological function comparable to a mathematical function … which is a function of real or imaginary numbers. The psychological 'transcendent function' arises from the union of conscious and unconscious contents" (Jung 1916/1960, para 131). This third element bridges the former one and two of conflicting elements but surpasses them with a new life of its own that we know we did not construct or invent, yet it comes through us enlisting a function we somehow possess. Its arrival amazes and moves us as profoundly meaningful, giving evidence that meaning exists external to us as well as including something we contribute to its arrival. He stresses that just because something is a psychic function does not mean that what the function makes accessible is psychic (Jung 1954/1976, para 1538). Its psychoid nature remains mysterious, other, and we register its impact as profoundly meaningful. Jung says it can feel like the voice of God.

Jung says many images for God exist and he has no doubt that there is an original beyond those images. Why not call this original God as everyone knows what that means (Jung 1956-57/1976. para 1589)? Indeed, Jung asserts, we have capacity for conscious relation, not knowledge, but relationship to deity (Jung 1953, para 11). Jung's comment that God does not usually speak to us through the telephone but always through the psyche does not mean that God is psyche, nor that psyche is God, anymore than the intellectual hypothesis about the nature of reality means the reality it posits is intellectual.

Trauma, however, detonates any and all of these meanings of transcendence in the maelstrom of suffering it inflicts, whether in acute or chronic form. Jung expands the meanings of transcendence saying it is necessary to include the realm of the Below and that is usually where trauma delivers us. What is the Below? It is transcendence going down as well as up, down into our incapacity, meaninglessness, ambiguity, absurdity, ugliness, nonsense, for they abide with the meaningful, the beautiful, true and good (Jung 2009, pp. 235, 240, 247, 250, 272).

Can we transcend downward into the body's interior darkness, into matter in its multiple forms – like Jung's stone carvings and Wallace Stevens' "Rock" – into what matters, indeed, into the mystery of being alive? Can we transcend downward beneath the splitting in our psyche, beneath the analyst-analysand relationship, beneath dissociated chunks of us, beneath our obdurate defenses, and yield to the humming along of psychoid processes? Jung says he gives up all personal striving and becomes, from the perspective of men and things, a "dead man" in order "to save the immortal in me," thus linking the Below downward to the transcendent God Above. (ibid, pp. 323, and pp. 291, 300).

Psychoid

We must add unconscious psychoid process to our focus on trauma and transcendence and look into what each adds to the other. Psychoid processes are unconscious, not caused by repression but there already, beneath Freud's primary process and Jung's nondirected thinking, going on all the time beneath even ravages of trauma.

Psychoid processes are unrepresentable in word or image, yet are liveable but not knowable in customary style of epistemology. Like the archetype that Jung also deems psychoid, we know its processes through derivative behaviors, emotions, images. Jung calls the psyche itself psychoid because we do not perceive it straightforwardly; "on account of its 'unrepresentable' nature I have called it 'psychoid' (Jung 1952/1960, para 840).

Psychoid processes and archetypes that Jung also deems psychoid, manifest physically and psychically simultaneously, not as two separate or parallel tracks, but rather like two sides of the same coin. Thus our conscious experiences of opposing elements – matter and spirit, flesh and mind, physical and psychical – link through a continuum of consciousness extending from predominance of instinctual at one end to spiritual at the other (Jung 1954/1960, para 408).

Our experiences of both psychoid processes and of synchronicity open to what Jung calls the *Unus Mundus*, the one entire world where our ego's familiar binary categories no longer obtain (Jung 1963, paras 464-465, 766-770). Synchronistic experience of elements or events noncausally related but coinciding elements or events impact us with tremendous sense of meaning, indicating it exists independent of our constructing it (Jung 1952/1960, para 942). The reality of meaningfulness is present and presses us for acknowledgement and the living of it.

In contrast, our actual experience of psychoid processes is apt to be disorienting, upending binary distinctions of our customary reality. Psychic and physical boundaries dissolve into an all in all, everything at once, as do usual spatial references of here and there and temporal references of past, present and future. Differentiated roles fade but remain in the present all at once. Piercing space/time barriers we are both our adult self in our analyst's office right now and our nine-year-old self, climbing out of our bedroom window at night "to escape a house that will kill me if I can't get out" (to cite a patient). We might even feel right now as if also in future time, experiencing we will die alone and no one will notice. Contradictions that we usually differentiate as separated, rivaling, or in sequence are not cancelled nor merged as in primary process nondirected thinking, but exist distinct and both present here and now. It makes me grasp Kierkegaard's sentence: For A not to be also non-A is so much twaddle.

Elements in psychoid processes are distinct though jumbled together. Affects of many kinds bundle into our awareness, their vivid oppositions not rescinded – love and hate, passion and nonattachment. We experience both opposites as separate, diverse, unmitigated and simultaneously present. Thus elements different and all together happen in a timeless/spaceless surround, as differentiated and mutually exclusive rivalries of inner/outer, then/now, here/there, us/them, even me/you. The jumble can be lived but not known or represented.

The elements transgress former boundaries, like painters whose colors go onto the frame and sometimes even into the empty space around it, for psychoid processes or archetypes are not found exclusively in psychic sphere or the physical sphere but in both coincidentally. For example, Hockney is known for his flattened paintings of swimming pools and bathers, inspired, he says, by magazine and billboard advertisements, and executed with precise defining lines. But in a few paintings he transgresses borders of the frame itself by carrying over from a corner of the canvas a marvel of dotted colors, recalling Seurat's pointillism, but more jumbled together like an impressionist's palette that suggests further light illumining the painting from beyond the canvas, frame and all (Hockney 2017). Can we say psychoid processes and synchronistic experiences transcend ordinary finitude both downward into the Below of primordial instinctual and spiritual promptings and upward and outward piercing limits of time and space? (Ulanov 2017, pp. 20 ff, 23).

In touch with psychoid processes we can feel frightened or liberated or both. We may feel panic – what is going on? In clinical sessions everything floods in and can unhinge us so that usual markers fade. Which level of interpretation is happening here – subjective or objective level of countertransference, or intersubjective level, or all of them at once? We may defend against this all in all and grasp for intellectual understanding to regain our footing by reinstating our categories of inner/outer, you/me. Is the analyst functioning as transference object of parental projections or as one who teaches about otherness, or present as one human being to another, or all of those at once? But that grasping blocks our experience of this bigger terrain. Defending against unraveling of usual categories of understanding can leave analyst and analysand defeated, feeling evicted from dwelling together in an ordinary session and a numinous event happening at the same time (Ulanov 2017, pp. 19, 21).

In touch with psychoid processes we can also feel liberated, unencumbered, ushered into a larger world that synchronicity often unveils. Our roles as analyst and analysand still pertain but are not dominant, though not annulled either. Their relationship is more equal as two humans sharing this remarkable encounter with the bigger surround (reality) in the humdrum session. This larger reality presses to be lived in our awareness showing at once the congruence of the small with the large, and calls to mind the relevance of physics and metaphysics right in the midst of working on the particular problem presented in the analysand's material.

Here is the amazing fact that we humans, tiny dots in the multitude of universes, yet able, especially by the geniuses among us, to envision cosmos as a whole. Physicists evolve theories about the nature of reality and hold contradictory theories about it simultaneously – that light is particle and wave, that theory of relativity and theory of quantum mechanics both prove experimentally viable, yet contradict each other about space and time, and as yet no new theory adequately reconciles them. Physics includes paradox of the small envisioning large and of living in the midst of opposing truths. Physics is like the psychoid level where everything is present simultaneously.

Individuals' processes of individuation possess the same quality of paradox. We the tiny dot can feel the insistence of impersonal instinctual drive to become who we are, but also simultaneously see our free consent is necessary for individuation to fulfill its aim. We hold in awareness opposite contradictory views, each valid: individuation processes will occur whether we agree or not, and individuation will not come to pass fully unless we consent and participate. Consciousness concurrently meets its limits and surpasses them – an example of psychoid processes of touching all in all. And when we consent to nudges of individuation, just as when we evolve theories of physics about the cosmos, what unfolds is various and diverse and each show a truth even though those truths conflict. We live from this jumble that enlivens tolerance and curiosity about other people's views and experiences, an attitude that furthers social justice among us. It also makes us mull about what is the source of this great reality with so many variations within it; psychology and physics prompt metaphysics.

Experience of the psychoid level, can also, I suggest, proffer healing. Simply the presence of beholding all alternatives at once, both disorientating and liberating, may pull us loose from stubborn hidden narcissism, and from obstructing complexes that kick in automatically dunning us with such convictions as "I am doomed to failure" as one man said, or "I am unwanted and unwantable" as one woman said. The sheer amplitude of the psychoid processes suck the life out of such fixating complexes. Being touched by the plenty of everything simultaneously granting a vision of the whole, present here/now, may free us to see this plenty from which we choose our focus. What we need is already here, as an analysand heard on his journey to this space: "There is nothing wrong with you" or what Bion calls O and Jung the bliss of experiences of God of which he may not speak.

Other Theorists

I see a parallel interest in theories of Bion, Matte Blanco and Lombardi in this psychoid level. They substitute the words infinite and finite for unconscious and conscious and investigate their differing logics. Bion focuses on the infinite unrepresentable O of the unconscious expressed in the as yet unrepresentable and assaulting beta elements that may or may not transform into the alpha function of consciousness where we can think in the presence of emotion. He maps the development of thinking with feeling to wrest a life from formlessness to become one with "ultimate reality, absolute truth, the godhead, the infinite, the thing-in-itself" which he calls O (Bion 1970, p. 26).

Matte Blanco, like Bion using mathematics as his conversation partner, contrasts the infinite symmetrical logic of unconscious emotion that multiplies and overwhelms the person with spaceless, timeless intensity of emotion, versus asymmetrical logic of finite consciousness, differentiated and communicable in word and image (Matte Blanco 1988, pp. 288-306). For example, the famous cigar that may or may not be a cigar, in unconscious symmetrical logic is identical to all other items of the same class of rounded elongated objects that come to a curved point - submarines, poles, fat pencils. So if a patient caught in the unfolding of infinite sets of emotion wants to put a Billy Club into a woman's vagina, it is the same as putting a penis there. Reality sense is lost. Discriminating separate and different objects is washed away in an infinity of identities of item with the class to which it belongs and the expanding intensity of emotion overwhelms the patient into psychosis.

The finiteness of conscious asymmetrical logic limits items from multiplying indefinitely by using word or image to name-define the item and develop thinking with which to control emotion and rescue us back into sanity (ibid, pp. 17-24, 46-58). A homely example was when I fell down when pregnant when my flat leather sandal slipped on a smooth downward sloping sidewalk. This was traumatic. Intense fear gripped me: will the baby fall out? be damaged, lost? The doctor said, oh those are the seven-month pregnancy anxieties and I felt an immediate return to sanity: this is fantasy, not reality, fear, not fact; this is time to get rubber soled shoes.

Riccardo Lombardi a contemporary psychiatrist-analyst influenced by Bion and Matte Blanco, sees the body as the corporeal foundation for psychic reality. The mind-body core of personality is the *sine qua non* of development. Attention to bodily sensations stimulates perceptions of the mind's capacities to think and thus establish personal existence within finite spatial/temporal limits (Lombardi 2016, pp. 20-26, 88-91). The patient kidnapped into "formless infinity" of psychosis recovers existence grounded in her body and is rescued into finitude to live a personal life.

Lombardi aims to get emotions "divested of their infinite features" within space/time boundaries rescued from the trauma of obliteration of those limits and falling into "infinite formlessness," subject then to acting out destructive impulses on others or self in cutting or eating disorders or bleak challenging silences in therapy sessions. He believes attention to the mind/body split is the central therapeutic issue. Focusing on analyst-analysand relationship comes later as does any use of the analyst as transferential parental object or agent of relatedness. Without the body-mind connection there is no finite life (ibid, pp. 91-92; see also Lombardi 2017, pp. 23, 25-26, 28-30).

All three theorists follow Freud in speaking of the unrepressed unconscious. Freud writes "The Ucs. does not coincide with the repressed; it is still true that all that is repressed is unconscious, but not that all that is unconscious is repressed" (Freud 1923/1973, p. 18). Each of these three theorists treat mainly psychotic patients. My practice falls into another category agreeing with Bion's insight that we all have both psychotic and nonpsychotic parts. Dealing with trauma and transcendence takes us right into the thicket of these parts of both kinds and usually with their mixing up and psychotic parts dominating.

Jung's notion of the psychoid is akin to the unrepressed unconscious, but with some significant differences. I emphasize these theories and their connections and differences because our clinical work is influenced by how we perceive what goes on in analysis. Like psychoid processes, the unrepressed unconscious is there already to be drawn upon as source of energy in the psyche. The three thinkers tend to focus more on negative effects of overwhelm by unconscious into psychosis that inflicts loss of ability to think with feeling and can induce catastrophic anxiety when we are confronted with the blast of reality itself that can mentally paralyze us or imbue us with fear of falling into the "dimensionless abyss" (Lombardi 2016, pp. 147, 162).

Jung sees the danger of psychosis, indeed experiences its threat himself in *The Red Book* ventures. But he also equally emphasizes the unconscious along with instincts as the root of life, through which flows a self-replenishing fountainhead that is source and resource of ongoing aliveness (Jung 1946/1954, para 366). Further, Jung explicitly recognizes the spiritual as legitimate and inescapable root and aim of life, seeking how to translate it into living. The God who is to Come includes transcendence of Below of psychic reality and personal struggle to integrate flesh, spirit, nature and mind, as well as transcendence of Above – blissful joy. The living of spirit means facing both forces of destructiveness and creativity. The psychoid processes and synchronicity experiences drive us toward wholeness of the whole that includes meaninglessness and meaningfulness in collective as well as personal terms.

Clinical Example

A dreadful severance of soul from body at an earliest age left the woman I shall call Lulu, now in her seventh decade, yelling out in a session, "I have wasted my life!" She elaborates, "How separated I've been from my own life experiences; my body is my life experience and I have avoided it, removed myself from it, not allowed myself to feel it. Instead a sleepiness comes over me when I get close to it – a hole I'm afraid of falling into, into the entirety of my experience, the Void if I allowed myself to be who I am. My own being a Void terrifies me, so lost and sad and alone. I abandoned this child in me who also then says, 'Leave me alone! I'm tired and want to go to sleep.'"

Lulu retreated from the world when her book about her bi-cultural life was rejected by a publisher; she let it go: "I did not mourn what I tried and failed; I just let it go." She married happily but let unsuccessful pregnancy efforts go unmourned. (These events happened years before we began analysis.) She wrote again and in current rereading a pivotal chapter written seven years ago the whole severance from her soul burst upon her now as an immediate living experience between us, not a knowing about. I felt a climaxing of a long analysis that had included many insights but this was a leap, in a rush of energy to a new event. She recalled her active imagination of herself facing the Void, the frightening 'It' and succumbing to sleepiness when nearing it, but struggled to talk to it. Engaging again in active imagination she struggled to talk to the 'It' and force the confrontation into specificity of words, but then discovered what had blocked her in previous efforts: "I can't go there because I will be annihilated."

What looms in the room at this precise moment is a piercing of time: I felt the unspoken word "again" as if it was announced. Heidegger's words came to my mind, "The dreadful has already happened." Lulu *was* annihilated in her earliest years and right now felt its blow. Her terror says she cannot survive it again. Indeed, she now in her seventies perceives years and years of her life "wasted." She could not risk being rubbed out, erased again. How do I know that the word 'again' was announced some way between us? I do not know; perhaps because boiling up through our session came my own brush with obliterating certainties. We were at the same time analysand and analyst as well as two women facing the threat of annihilation, each arriving there by our own personal routes. The psychoid all in allness is not a result of *participation mystique* nor of projective identification, though could include and surpass them.

Is 'again' spoken by Lulu or me? I find it hard to remember because of the outpouring of her associations. "Why am I so frightened?" She asks the It. "Because it will shake up your whole life" It answers. Indeed she finds her writing bland because of "something missing" and sees her whole book "upended." She continues in the present: "My inability to go into the Void is also because of all the hate and a ferocity of anger I could not hold in my body, so I left my body and took on an ultra-sweet persona because I could not handle this animal savagery within me. It is almost a relief to see so much I was unable to look at, always saying (which was true in every session), 'I don't understand'" (and we would have to go over what was said in previous sessions). "I wrote this chapter seven years ago and had knowledge of what it describes but I could not live it." Hence the piercing of time back and forward finally to incarnate the present living of the emotions.

Lulu continues in the session to bring back what she sees now over the arc of her decades, hence transcending the conflict but now admitting the Below. She returns to an event in her crib that she now refers to as the 'crib dream.' Her mother told her of it and she discusses it with her elderly mother now. Her mother dressed her up in special finery as her parents were taking her out, their first born, to greet company. Mother puts her back in the crib and goes to get dressed. Lulu stands in the crib, with active arms and hands, not yet walking hence less than a year old, 8-9 months? When mother and father return, she finds her daughter covered with 'poop' her childhood name for bowel movements. A giant bowel movement has occurred and Lulu smears it all over the special dress, crib railings, mattress. Her first dream when seeking analysis features poop in a taxi and she discretely wipes herself and tries to wrap it in a plastic bag and tells the driver she tried to be neat. In a second dream dogs poop all over and "a little boy wants to help clean it up but he taunts me and smears it over everything. I scold him and tell him he is dirty and making more work for us."

Many dreams of ensuing years feature poop – where to put it to get rid of it, finding no toilet, shit on the floor from overflowing toilets, pooping in her underwear and carrying it around with her. We garnered much meaning of the poop theme about unlived aggression to get out in the world, about unlived creativity, and experiences of arousal. Rushing in was also her distress that her long devoted spiritual practice combining Hindu and Christian meditation, chanting, yoga, praying, went upwards to seek her soul without her body. She declares in this session in response to the crib scene: "That is when and where I left my body, in that crib; I have wandered like a ghost my whole life since. I was looking for my soul."

We pierced space and time, going backwards to less than a year old when separation from her embodied soul was annihilation. Except now, annihilation of soul and the terror it invoked of being annihilated once again was matched in this session by an embodied urgent intent to live her soul. That necessity to live her soul matched her terror of being annihilated again. Then and now are both present: annihilation through severance of body/soul and assertion through owning soul in body; terror of being rubbed out becoming a ghost and feeling alive in joy all existed at once, distinct and together. That is the plenty of the psychoid level of challenge.

Annihilation that happened years ago and terror it could happen again right now coexists with emotionally claiming soul in body – a leap to unfolding a more whole self not rent apart by defensive splitting. This is not knowing about but simultaneously inhabiting space of small girl and coincident space of advanced adult age. The past time of early annihilation due to split of body from soul that resulted in experience of feeling decades of wasted time as a ghost looking for lost soul, coexists with future time that transcends the waste because of the present joining of soul with body and feeling the aliveness that bestows.

I was with Lulu in the penetrating possibility to claim her soul in the midst of threat of being once again wiped out in terror. I was trying to make mental space for her story to unfold while my analogous experiences of splits and terrors insists to be lived. I thought of the charcoal drawings of facing death of Kathe Kollwitz and of Emily Dickinson's words, "Because I could not stop for Death/ he kindly stopped for me" (Johnson 1929/1960, #712 p. 359).

Still in this present session as well as subsequent ones, another shoe dropped making as vivid as the traumatic severance of soul from body the arousal of tremendous fury as a small girl toward her mother, and her mother's fury, though denied and then evacuated onto the small daughter. They loved each other in these episodes and do still, decades of relationship going on, and they arouse hate in each other as well which my patient acknowledges and her mother protests. My patient remembers her mother's overwhelm in the crib scene though her mother denies it, just as she annuls her rage at increasing dependency that her aging imposes. For example, she resents her children finding an assisted living home for her, acting as if she had been kidnapped despite her falling and seeing she cannot manage a house anymore on her own. Previous attempts of two of her children to bring her to live in their homes with provisions for her independence did not decrease her negativity about getting old nor advance her accepting it, and hence did not succeed. She tended to blame her children for not spending more time with her instead, as if that would erase increasing limitations.

Discussing the crib scene her mother, now in her mid-90's, says she just wanted to protect her daughter, take care of her, which my analysand remembers not liking at all, wanting to express herself in the world, explore, or form independent opinions. But then her mother withdrew utterly and my patient felt she had to placate her mother to get the loving connection again. For example, in wanting to be independent and walk outside alone, her mother cut her loose without markers or advising a safe distance. Lulu remembers going a long way and finding herself in the midline between traffic, scared, not knowing which way to go, as if abandoned. In our session recalling this, Lulu exclaims, "I hate her for squashing my soul! I could not say anything critical or negative about her without her pouncing on me, saying, "How could you? How dare you! That is not nice of you." Then I'd feel bad. I wanted to make her happy.

Mother said from the beginning I had strong wishes and opinions and she wanted to protect me and that mind of my own. But I got her back. I did not like her telling me what to do and not supporting what I wanted to do. I would stick a knife in her back. She described me sitting in my highchair with a small cup of milk in my hand looking at her as I poured the milk on the floor. I knew how to needle her and she would not be able to curb her angry response. But I always let it go, "Everything will be ok Mommy; I'll be nice" and I locked up my anger and could not use my aggression to get out in the world and succeed in my opinions. And that energy is missing from my writing; it is boring and bland. My book is upended. She had demands on me and I felt stifled. I wanted her to be happy and I could never make her happy. I could never live my life and I am furious at myself for letting my life go. In my spiritual meditations I was always trying to go up above this ferocious anger which now I must include.

Lulu sees to get rid of the pain of loss of connection to mother, and the pain of severance of her body from soul, and the pain of her hatred and anger she carried in her body, she made her body disappear. She cut psyche from soma to survive. She became a ghost wandering through life spending the bulk of hours every day alone in her house writing, meditating, doing her spiritual practice but not feeling real, able. Her terror of being rubbed out in the past accumulated as unlived life over decades. She loved her mother but felt her own soul life went unmothered.

Looking back, I can see all this slowly came to climax in the pivotal session of "I wasted my life and I found my soul now." One instance of something emerging that startled me was her strong interest in joining out in the world at a gym a rigorous exercise class, she in her seventies, other members in their twenties. Her body was staking its claim; she persisted in making this happen. Unlike her mother who let her go unsupported out in the street and sidewalks, she accompanied this mad idea of exercise by looking for her own right pace and being willing to go slowly and safely. It worked. Over months of classes, her body acquired muscle strength and definition. She felt strong.

Another detail caught my attention in this pivotal session of our going over the crib dream, as she called it: she *played* with her poop. Its smearable, smellable, stickable nature engendered her experience of a capacity to create something from inside herself that pushed outside herself into the world. She made things with it on the dress, the crib railings, mattress. In this pivotal session, Lulu exclaims she wants her body back and her love of her God in her body and to live the aliveness of that small soul inhabiting her as an adult woman. She mourns loss of years separated from her body because she feels enlivened in her soul coming back into her body, no longer leaving her a ghost wandering in search of it. Mourning severance of body from soul and registering joy of body with soul coincide; transcendence goes down as well as up; at a psychoid level she mourns and celebrates simultaneously.

II. Ways of Knowing

Epistemology

Experiences of analyzing trauma that involve transcendence and psychoid processes open up our assumed ways of knowing to unknowing. Epistemology concerns how we know what we know and changes radically. Our linear, logical, verbal, communicable knowledge gives way to mulling, imagining, pondering. Gone is the primacy and exclusivity of rational procedure of getting items in order and reaching defining conclusions. Lulu felt an inrush of multi-perspectives, mutually exclusive alternatives concurrently. "I've wasted my life and now I have found my soul and am now in my body!" These emotional insights did not cancel each other but enhanced each other.

Seeing blanks of unknowing – the letting go of unmourned rejection of her book, of pregnancy efforts failing, letting go of "my experiences of my life in my body," also brought realization that in facing the gaps, she was not annihilated but energized. Gone was that sleepiness that pulled her under, and sometimes me too, unable to face this hole of annihilation lest it erase her again. She faced losses of decades of not being bodily in her experiences and she felt full of gratitude to be able to do so now. Opposites existed together.

I found myself mulling where had the losses gone? lived? What sheltered them? I remembered how often Lulu spoke of body rigidity along her left side especially. Were they hiding there, guarded from their emotional neglect in body stiffness? Where did the impulse come from, so uncharacteristic of Lulu, to enroll in a public gym exercise course? She fought the initial rejection of her husband as impractical and expensive. What before were opposing elements – body versus soul, private versus public, compliance versus fighting for, asserting her agency – all those elements now existed together as a plenty from which she could choose her focus, and they transcended the splitting when she was less than a year old. Transcending meant a bigger picture bringing the ghost looking for soul, the gaps of unlived life pressing her, despite her terror, to face into them.

If we accept that Lulu's experience of trauma, or anyone's if looked into carefully, teaches us about ourselves and our wounds, then we learn about the whole of reality and its source in theological terms. Trauma reveals such gaps and may teach us to accept them as belonging to the whole, leading somewhere, not just hurting us deeply. I thought of Philosopher Richard Kearney hazarding 'The God Who May Be' which means then

> "there is a free space gaping at the very core of divinity; the space of the possible. It is this divine gap which renders all things possible which would be otherwise impossible to us – including the kingdom of justice and love. But because God is *posse* (the possibility of being) rather than *esse* (the actuality of being as fait accompli), the promise remains powerless until and unless we *respond* to it. Transfiguring the possible into the actual, and thereby enabling the coming kingdom to come into being, is not just something God does for us but also something we do for God." (Kearney 2001, p. 4; see also pp. 8, 27)

If we allow the gap of unknowing in our ways of knowing, the ramifications reach all the way to whatever we believe is the source of our existence and of reality and our signal role in what ordinary life may turn out to be, including love and justice or evading them. Our theology changes from a traditional static being of God to a contemporary hypothesis of "The God Who May Be" that interdepends on how we respond, or refuse. My point is that in trauma we are pressed down to this wide, deep scope of the transcendence of Below and that healing depends on responding to it with all our heart, soul, mind, strength, even if we choose no.

This new way of knowing by including gaps of unknowing, is akin to what has occurred in 20th century physics. A leap similar to Lulu's coincident experience of I have wasted my life and it is right here now to be lived in uniting soul and body, is a leap from one exclusive theory to holding opposite theory simultaneously. We leap from the elegance of the General Theory of Relativity that offers coherent vision that the gravitational field is space-time itself. Reality is not contained in the fixed shell of space and time as if they are different from matter; space is one of the material components of the world and is an entity "that undulates, flexes, curves, twists" (Rovelli 2014/2015, pp. 6, 56).

Time does not exist objectively containing reality like a shell even though we experience the flow of time from past to present to future. As Einstein said, "the distinction made between past, present and future is nothing more than a persistent, stubborn illusion" (cited in Rovelli 2014, p. 58). We live in time but our present does not exist objectively and Rovelli hazards that for a "hypothetical supersensible being" that is, not like us living in the experience of time flowing, "the universe would be a single block of past, present, and future" (ibid, p. 60; see also Greene 2004, pp. 139-145). This idea co-mingled in my mind with an idea we can pray backwards – for example, for Christ on the cross, or for those fleeing burning up by jumping to their deaths from New York City office buildings attacked by terrorist planes on 9/11/01. We can pray for future students of our school, or lives yet to unfold of our children, grandchildren (Ulanov and Ulanov 1982).

We leap to the contradicting theory (this theory is held simultaneously with its contradicting neighbor) of quantum physics that says no time or space exists. Atoms meet, collide, go out of existence: their interaction is reality. They exist only when leaping from one system to another without any predictable manner. Only the probability of their appearance here or there, then or now can be calculated (Rovelli 2014, pp. 1516). They have no specific space or locale nor prediction of time of appearance. Both contradicting theories are experimentally viable, true, and, so far, cannot be reconciled to each other. Both exist together. We can imagine psychological parallels.

The first, the Theory of Relativity, associates to our experiences of synchronicity that unveil a meaningfulness that exists external to us but is not real to us unless we interact with it. The second, the Quantum Theory that asserts that only interaction is the real, associates to our individuation process when the functioning transcendent leaps to a new attitude or symbol that transforms the heartrending conflict of two opposed elements with a new sense of the real but only if we consciously participate in this process.

The epistemological question now asks, how do we come to know something that disrupts our ways of knowing? Contradictions coexist as in psychoid process where we can see chaos is also plenty. That beckons us to see a larger circumference already there that we just now discover. Jacob Boehme names it 'Ungrund'; Nicholas of Cusa calls it the 'Whatness in everything' – his most fulfilling God-Image that conferred great happiness on his last years. Jung calls it *Unus Mundus.* Our ways of knowing are penetrated by but exceed our 'personal equation', that is, our particular viewpoint, our God-Image, the theory with which we are identified that inevitably skews our seeing the reality accurately as well as leading us to look at the whole through our particular slant. Our time-space perspective from which we observe the universe influences what we see and think we know. But this new way of holding in mind contradictory views that are distinct, not merged, just as in an analytic session analysand and analyst are distinct yet may feel merged or mixed-up in *participation mystique* or in projective identification, yields a sense of interplay of different ways of seeing reality. We might say all those ways of pre-judgment enunciated in our theories interpenetrate with the transcending wholeness of the whole that does not annul them or its entirety.

Paul Ricoeur says of course we reify our profound perceptions; we want to make them flesh to hold onto them, and we identify with them as if they want to step over into finite (daily) life (Ricoeur 1970, pp. 530-533; see also Ricoeur 1967, pp. 351-357). But he also says we must de-reify our views and see even our most precious moments of seeing the real as belonging to the whole but not defining it. For that reductive definition leads to the most awful results, such as the pilot locked into identification with his suicidal and homicidal complex and its archetypal mandate, locks the cockpit door against crew and passengers in order to fly the plane straight into a mountain face. But at its best, both believing in our most real event and seeing it as a lens through which the real is spied but not contained nor defined, adds to the richness of living the mysterious, the boundless in the particular.

Further, we might want to hear our neighbor's different view that shows an added perspective of the plenty of the whole reality. Does this land us in neither/nor relativism? No. It allows us to embrace our particular lens of seeing and accept that others do the same and all together we make up the whole – a community of knowers who include the gaps of unknowing and depend on each other to see more of what transcends us Above and Below.

Ontology

From such experiences we are led back to trauma and to three kinds of being, in effect, to ontology. Now our focus is not on *how* do we know what we know – epistemology – but on *what* do we know; what is it? What shows itself? The Oxford Dictionary defines ontology as "metaphysics concerned with the essence of things" (Concise Oxford Dictionary 1964). Three types of being, not fixed essences but epiphanies of being surface in clinical work, not esoteric but hum-drum, just not usually named as perceptions of ontology. Lulu introduces the ontological level by presenting her problem of how to go on being when annihilation of being, that is, non-being threatens. She lived her answer: as a ghost. She avoided the hole, the Void facing her, the annihilation that occurred when she severed body from soul at a very early age. She knew she felt unalive. That was the problem and her solution of appealing to transcendence by offering herself to God through her guru, though sincere, also felt unalive. Where was the real? How to understand it? Hence the clinician must mull about being versus nonbeing underneath symptoms of depression, sleepiness, nasty moods of resentment, and deep sadness that does not yield. My reflections described three ontological realms.

Beingness comprises the first, all we treasure individually and together as the wonders of this ego life in the world – its multiplicity of corners, nests, birds' colors, big padded furry creatures, the variety of persons' shapes, weights, textures of skin, human genius of inventing can-openers, elegant mathematical equations, new melodies, spices, sports, and simple acts of kindness that change everything. Think of all you love about this life and still there is more. Wondrous, diverse, people even creating in abysmal suffering of dreadful physical illness, cut-off mid-life, yet edifying the rest of us with their dignity and truth-seeking (Ritvo 2016; Ulanov 1994). Let alone the courage people show in suffering unavoidable horrific injustice, displaying heroism and humility. I like very much Jung's endorsement of ego life – to be lived, enjoyed, explored, including our mistakes which belong to the whole. Children in the holocaust walled city of Terezin writing poetry, still alive in the maws of unspeakable death (Volavkove 1993). A whole tradition of praying has developed, the Cataphatic, to pray to the beyond through specific beings of this world – this earth, leopards, our beloved dog, Mozart, dreams, African carvings, Byzantine icons, stark desert hues. We pray through elements of beingness that manifest the transcendent.

Nonbeing evidences in terrible suffering that people experience when plunged into homeless refugee status, stateless citizens, finding no country that welcomes them, or people confronted by others who seek to expunge them with their different beliefs from this earth, hunting them down to kill. 'Africa Town' in America's Alabama near Mobile shows a history of a community's effort to make a town where they could breathe free. But others used it as a dumping ground for chemical waste, sewage waste, whole cemeteries ploughed under to make their own highway wider. Even the town's momentous discovery of the last slave ship to America is denied and discounted. Injustice of one of us to another of us, in crime, prejudice, cheating, stealing and maiming delivers us into hopelessness of finding where to breathe free and safe.

Trauma on a personal psychological level flings us, sometimes as small children, into the abhorrent, to be trapped there for years. Such suffering hurls us into nonbeing – no life, no succor, no one to heed or help. This is no-time, no-space, of paralysis, of shock simultaneously with strain as if treading water constantly moving your limbs to keep your nose above water that could take you under and out to sea. Cast into void, here No-thing exists, No-one, No-where; nothing grows, like an exaggerated Anselm Kieffer painting of the sucking, stinking mud of war's no-man's land with scraps of straw stuck into thick paint in the canvas, portraying rotting deadness.

Lulu felt as if she had no town to live freely in, and shunned community and felt it shunned her. She could not find her place of admittance. Even with her close family and siblings, she had to check her texts to them with her husband lest they upset people. This was the ferocious unacknowledged anger she feared would slip out. She did not know this but simply behaved as if she did, acting without really understanding it, hence always wanting to go back go over previous actions, previous sessions, to make sure she understood. Lulu's soul was left behind in nonbeing as a ghost as result of severance of body and soul at her earliest age.

I found myself asking, where had her soul gone? Jung asks the same question in his *Red Book* of his lost soul, where has she been hiding, but he does not pursue it once she appears from a dark shaft (Jung 2009, p. 233). My question expanded: how does this part of us stay alive all these years – for Lulu many decades. What keeps it still living? It is the part that knows about nonbeing. But I have wondered if through the nonbeing state, as if inching along in a dark place, the soul comes to another realm of being, so different from both being and nonbeing.

In Lulu's life poop was the link between the abandoned small girl, her split-off soul and body, and the adult woman trying to live her life only half alive. Poop kept messages coming through from the soul all these decades and in our long analysis.

Other Than Human Being is the name I use to describe this other kind of aliveness, so different from both being and nonbeing. It is hard to find words to express its existence (See chapter 3 pp. 29-30). I find it a less personal realm, less linked to our idiosyncratic biographical and cultural influences. Here are wonderings about the whole nature of existing as persons singly and as together in shared life. I think of Lao-tzu enjoining us to see the whole and live from that root. He describes sanity as accepting

> "life as a whole, as it is ... the measureless untouchable source ... while it appears as dark emptiness,/Brims with quick force" (#21, p. 370). "Though there can be no name for it,/I have called it 'the way of life'"(#25, p. 40). "The man of stamina stays with the root" (#38, p. 49). "On a root for growing by" (#39, p. 50). "An ever-living root of it: The seeing root, whose eye is infinite" (#59, p. 63). (Bynner 1944)

This realm precedes and postdates our differentiation into consciousness' binary structures and space/time limits. Laotzu's "whole life" is not the preconscious world of early childhood but the advanced realm where through differentiation we bring consciousness to the large whole, see the shared collective symbols of the ages, the world of personality number 2 of Jung's perception, and the nonhuman aliveness of all that transcends particular human life and society. This level of reality is always penetrating from the root and we need to anchor there beneath and beyond what has hurt us and see the wholeness going on.

This level interplays with beingness and nonbeing and displays the whole – expressed by humans in theories of the cosmos, envisioning the nature of reality itself. This might be the transcendent in seeing the human as but one small part of the bigger surround, in seeing the constant but irregular colliding of matter and anti-matter particles and both in a flash go out of existence, so that reality is the deepest level to do with life itself always there proliferating and destroying despite trauma and the jumble of the psychoid plenty and chaos. This scope of being is amplitude, bigness, like the Japanese paintings of tiny people in the realm of the vast mountain, woods, sea. We abide in a kind of being that includes us but is other than human. Our mistakes and epiphanies belong there but are not the center.

My point here is this other than human realm of being exists different from the human, perhaps best described as the formless forming the painter Paul Klee writes about in the images that grow into visibility in his paintings (Klee 2017, pp. 93, 155). Or the painter Agnes Martin, afflicted by trauma of schizophrenia, who got herself back and painted scenes of happiness in her last work with pale colors and thin intricate lines. (Martin 2015, pp. 170-171, 182-185). We live the force of living penetrated by the beyond, our personal striving put in smallest proportion to the totality of which we are a part, like my sister facing the death of her daughter in her twenties in a car accident. She *only* found solace in looking at the endless rhythm of ocean waves coming in and going out. She no longer attended any funerals.

Clinical Work Again

Lulu invited her mother to live with them without stating any endpoint to the visit. Her conviction about the rightness of this decision was impervious to any reality testing. Jungians might name this our being identified with a complex that overtakes our ego and substitutes its rightness for any uncertainty. Lulu believed her compassion fed by her spiritual devotion would supervene any negativity in her mother; Mother would be happy living with them. One result of their eventual blowup ending was Lulu coming full face with what she later identified as her ferocious animal anger. We had to tread delicately so that it did not wipe out her compassion that was real and heartfelt.

Epistemologically, not-knowing is integral to knowing what is going on in the analytical process, especially with the gap imposed by trauma. Further, reflections on being, nonbeing, other than being do not contain each other so much as interpenetrate. Our reflections on these aspects of being alive influence what we can see, think, feel in the clinical work of doing analysis. The presence of truth brings its own authentication that we register in living experience – the dream clicks, the reflection goes to the core. This is the experience of letting psychic events happen, not engineering them, not being so identified with our theories, what Bion calls saturation, that we fit the patient to the theory instead of accepting the gap of our unknowing. Our understanding is always provisional.

We become alert not to overdo the symbolic level – what Jung calls putting aside our learning – as it can impede natural process of symbol formation. We are cautious not to idolize what relational theories rightly call the central importance of the relationship between analyst and analysand, nor seeing the analyst as the primary authority of the analysis teaching us how to be a subject with an other who is also a subject and different from us, lest we get caught in an omnipotence of a know-it-all attitude or hidden narcissism of the analyst. We, like our analysands, sit in helplessness in the face of forces of destructiveness exhibited in trauma. And we, like our analysands, need not be defined by trauma. We depend on the transcendent shining through.

In Lulu's transference I learned that trying to cut through the fog with confronting remarks left Lulu feeling a small girl once more discounted and left alone in scary darkness. I learned not to be lured into appearing the too good mother, for then Lulu put into me the authority she hunted for herself. When she could protest my failures to attune and be angry at me as the bad mother and I did not pounce nor withdraw, and she did not get all-sweet to cover up this fierce anger, we inched along to what became the climaxing insight she now described in her reinvigorated writing. Increasingly we became two women facing forces of loss and of life, not only relating through the mother transference. Another way to put it is that I was the lens of a mother of a different kind, fostering her individuating into her ownmost self, her path, more than a lap mother.

She wrote in the voice of her soul speaking to Lulu in the guise of the small girl severed from her body in the crib so long ago: "We have lived sadness in this life. I want to cry." (Lulu could never cry.) "You gave me up for our mother. It was more important to make her happy than to make me happy. In the crib something uncomfortable in me, warm, brown, smelly came out of my body. I mushed it in my hands and spread it around. I was enjoying myself making something special with this brown mushy stuff that was special to me. And then it happened. Our mother and father walked in. I saw our mother was unhappy with this smelly stuff that came out of my body. My body must be bad. I must be bad. From that day we left our body and became a ghost. Leaving our body, you also left me, along with our mother. I was left alone, floating in scary darkness outside my body without you and without our mother. I felt anger and fear and terrible sadness that scared me. I would have to hide my anger to make our mother happy again, agreeing with her by being very sweet. She stepped on me like a mouse and mushed me, stopped my play in life, playing with the mushy stuff coming out of me."

This voice of the soul, at first through the wounded small girl, called our attention to a detail not emphasized until now. It was the detail of the little girl *playing* with her poop. In her reinvigorated writing, Lulu calls this soul play. She sees it has also been going on in her adult life in the exercise class she took up, in a public gym, she in her 70's, her classmates in their twenties. In addition, she plans ballet classes to find her own feminine grace. Play, she says, is the life of her soul; her spiritual meditation takes on gladness over dutiful faithfulness. Spontaneity toward her husband infuses sexual-body-based awareness that she names her 'Bela-Being' that recalls her to her short-lived happiness living in Polynesia, a country that accented body, when her father's job took them there. She understands now her strong sobbing on the plane taking them away from that emotional climate due to his transfer to another post. Therapy now changes to excitement, awakeness to pleasure, sexual feelings, spontaneous imaginings and actions, loving with vigor and compassion and limits with her mother.

In clinical work, trauma and transcendence coexist and contribute to each other. Transcendence as the vast Above and Below is needed to penetrate the severance of trauma. Glimpses of a larger entirety mediate that something more than trauma exists. Trauma destroys a small or fixed view of transcendence that we identify with and then use as a weapon against ourselves – how bad we are in our body or saying as trauma sufferer that we must have done something wrong and if we pray this way or get conscious that way things might get better. Like Job's friends we get caught in omnipotence because we feel so helpless and pronounce as if we know, when in fact we do not know. Accepting the gap of not-knowing makes space outside trauma where something might come in. We need Job as intercessor as the Lord appointed him to be for his friends.

I want to emphasize that the opposites of trauma and transcendence do not contain each other but interpenetrate in their co-existence. Knowing includes unknowing. Containing, container/contained is an image in fashion now for how analysis works and should not be ignored. I would put next to it images of interplay, interdependence, interpenetration as clinical work shows me that characterizes living experience that brings healing. Trauma and transcendence weave in and out; creative and destructive forces collide.

The analysand may keep to new ways of perceiving while also struggling to integrate and dismantle old ways. We discover the hurt is not beyond repair, though we still feel it. The leap is like the physics leap to another theory that contradicts the former theory that is also still viable. Both give evidence experimentally of their truth just as we experience the psychoid level of opposite elements simultaneously present and valid. I think of Jung saying we must extend this perception to mistakes that happen to us and that we make. We see our vexing symptom from its other side, that it too is part of the totality that composes us, a jigsaw piece that fits into the mystery of the whole puzzle of us: "We must make our mistakes. We must live out our own visions of life. And there will be error. If you avoid error, you do not live; in a sense it can be said every life is a mistake, for no one has found the truth" (Jung 1933/1977, p. 98).

The clinical experience of transference/countertransference changes when we perceive this totality of being human. Greater equality of analysand and analyst obtains. Like two sisters, two refugees, two ones privileged to be doing analysis, we look together at interpenetrating levels of being and knowing in the long arc of our life, or seeing the moment of anger also exists as if in its own right as well as in each of us. Sorting through personal motives, how do we understand the force of destructiveness itself in life? What do we make together of the wonder of seeing right now everything afresh, as we partake in the origin of livingness?

Jung saw this, I believe, in his peculiar and insistent perception that the primary object of analysis is the psyche itself. The analyst is the first witness to trauma and essential to the telling of it; the second witness is the psyche itself. Psyche has its own agenda to which we must pay attention. In touch with the psychoid process we pierce the space/time barriers of ordinary living. The Self focus exists alongside the ego focus and they interplay, do not contain each other. The psyche tosses up symptoms, flashes of insight, archetypal images. Jung asks,

> "What if there were a living agency beyond the everyday human world – something even more purposeful than electrons? Do we delude ourselves in thinking that we possess

> and control our own psyches … but [psyche is] rather … a door that opens upon the human world from a world beyond, allowing unknown and mysterious powers to act upon a man and carry him on the wings of the night to a more than personal destiny?" (Jung 1933/1966, para 148).

Theology

Our relation to the real, whether patchy or exegeted, bears on the work of analysis. What we believe is real and what we call it – our God image, or what we put in place of God bears upon dealing with the impact of trauma and all its wreckage. I do not believe real itself is wrecked. Our connecting to it may stir in us such gratitude that it reaches repair of the brunt of traumatic events. Or our not connecting to it may evoke a despair so deep that even the genius Paul Celan walks into the Seine all alone and drowns, even though he was a strong swimmer, his body discovered days later.

Clinical work is not usually explicitly concerned with creed. It is imbued with faith in experience of the ineffable that happens right in our office. That raises questions about the whole of reality – what is its source? What is the emotional purpose of my life? What do I serve? What must I face as my slipping off, remaining derelict, careless, inhospitable to the gods that stop by Abraham's and Sarah's tent, Baucis' and Philemon's hut? Or have I thrown God out like trash? Jung writes, "Let us … be for God limitation in time and space, an earthly tabernacle" (Jung 1973, p. 66).

Two things stand out about the theological, even amongst different belief systems: the particular and incarnation. By particular I mean odd things that belong to each of us, those images that convey to us the transcendent, that for Lulu were in her meditation corner including an altar displaying symbols of life and guru. Particular means scraps – the dream detail that opens the meaning of the dream that we could not invent, but only detect; a hunch that shows right now the next step that makes the process of individuation feel real and our own. Lulu had insights over the years of analysis and in her writing, but none with the clarity and energy of, 'I have wasted my life' and the power of soul reentering her life and the role of poop that kept her soul messages coming, addressing her. Everything opened and she felt the power to choose, to reflect, make her own, even when the tug of denying her body threatened again. She saw the tug, or I did, and she saw why and rejected it. Particular means unsuspected scraps, throw-aways, as well as Lulu's piercing moment of rising above space and time and perceiving the whole arc of her life and its broken thread and using her receptive aggression to take back soul, embody it, unghost it down to where it was hiding in her poop, the Below leading the way.

Incarnation means the ego world matters; it is the space/time means through which the transcendent, transspatial, transtemporal appear. The finite is necessary for the infinite to be perceived. Our reception of what comes is necessary for the infinite to be real to us. Plotinus seeking simplicity does not disparage the finite body, or anything finite. He only loosens our fixing upon it to the distraction of the spiritual which we unconsciously live. We need to pay it heed: Plotinian love "waits for ecstasy ... establishing the soul's faculties in complete repose ... as to be completely ready for divine invasion ..."; "a gratuitous surplus" (Hadot 1993/1998, pp. 8, 9).

Incarnation means stepping over into space and time and body life, into soul and the beyond it points to, available to our present living. Knowing-about helps in acknowledging how traumatic events inflicted suffering on me. A living experience with another, often the analyst, for who else would get the meaning of the craziness that we stitch together into defenses that protect us, or the leap to new encounter with reality that brings its own authority to receive the good? We see good seeping in, there for the taking, as uncaused by me as is the dreadful that already happened, granting the possibility of living with joy.

I divided this chapter into two parts, for the convenience of the reader (I. and II.) I presented this material at the Conference on Trauma and Transcendence at Pacifica Graduate Institute Carpenteria California, April 2019, and at the 14th Odyssey Annual Conference "Rupture and Repair: Minding Crippling Emotions" in Vitznau Switzerland Hotel Flora Alpina Lake Lucerne May 2019.

References

Bion, W.R. 1970. *Attention and Interpretation*. London: Tavistock.

Bynner, W. 1944. *The Way of Life According to Laotzu, An American Version*. New York: The John Day Company.

Dickinson, E. 1929/1960. # 712, see below T.H. Johnson.

Freud, S. 1923/1973. "The Ego and the Id" Standard Edition XIX. Trans. James Strachey. London: Hogarth Press and the Institute of Psycho-Analysis, pp. 3-69.

Greene, B. 2004. *The Fabric of the Cosmos*. New York: Vintage Books.

Hadot, P. 1993/1998. *Plotinus or The Simplicity of Vision*. Trans. Michael Chase. Chicago and London: The University of Chicago Press.

Hockney, D. 1974/2017. "Contrejour in the French Style (Against the Day dans le Style Français)" Ludwig Museum-Museum of Contemporary Art Budapest. Metropolitan Museum of Art Retrospective December 8 2017.

Johnson, T.H. 1960. Ed. *The Complete Poems of Emily Dickinson*. Boston: Little, Brown, and Company.

Jung, C.G. 1926/1960. "Life and Spirit" *The Structure and the Dynamics of the Psyche Collected Works* 8. Trans. R.F.C. Hull. Princeton N.J.: Princeton University Press, paras 601-648.

— 1931/1976. "Foreword to *Seelenprobleme der Gegenwart*" lst edition. *The Symbolic Life Collected Works* 18. Trans. R.F.C. Hull. Princeton N.J.: Princeton University Press, paras 1292-1295.

— 1933/1977. "Is analytical psychology a religion?" Eds. William McGuire and R.F.C. Hull, 1977. *C.G. Jung Speaking*. Princeton, N.J.: Princeton University Press. pp. 94-99.

— 1946/1954. "The psychology of the transference" *The Practice of Psychotherapy Collected Works* 16. Trans. R.F.C. Hull. Princeton, N.J.: Princeton University Press.

— 1950/1966. "Psychology and Literature" *The Spirit in Man, Art, and Literature Collected Works* 15. Trans. R.F.C. Hull. Princeton N.J.: Princeton University Press, paras 133-162.

— 1952/1960. "Synchronicity: an acausal connecting principle" CW 8. paras 816-997.

— 1953. *Psychology and Alchemy Collected Works* 12. Trans. R.F.C. Hull. Princeton N.J.: Princeton University Press.

— 1954/1960. "On the nature of the psyche" CW 8, paras 343-442.

— 1954/1976. "Letter to Pere Lachat" *The Symbolic Life*" *CW* 18, paras 1532-1557.

— 1956-57/1976. "Jung and religious belief: *The Symbolic Life CW* 18, paras 1532-1690.

— 1963. *Mysterium Coniunctionis Collected Works* 14. Trans. R.F.C. Hull. Princeton N.J.: Princeton University Press.

— 1973. "Letter to Walter Robert Corti 30 April 1929" *Letters*. Vol 1 of 2. Eds Gerhard Adler and Aniela Jaffé. Trans. R.F.C. Hull. Princeton N.J.: Princeton University Press.

— 2009. *The Red Book Liber Novus*. Ed. Sonu Shamdasani. Trans. Mark Kyburz, John Peck, Sonu Shamdasani. New York: W. W. Norton.

— 2020. *The Black Books 1913-1932 Notebooks of Transformation*. Vol 2 of 7. Ed. Sonu Shamdasani. Trans. Martin Liebscher, John Peck, and Sonu Shamdasani. Philemon Series. New York: W.W Norton.

Kearney, R. 2001. *The God Who May* Be: *Hermeneutics of Religion*. Bloomington and Indianapolis: Indiana University Press.

Kierkegaard, S.K., 1936. *Philosophical Fragments or a Fragment of Philosophy*. Trans. David Swenson. Princeton, N.J.: Princeton University Press.

Klee, P. 2017. *Ten Americans After Paul Klee*. Munich, London, New York: Prestel.

Martin, A. 2015. *Agnes Martin.* Eds. Frances Morris and Tiffany Bell. Millbank, London: Tate Publishing of Tate Enterprises Ltd.

Matte Blanco. 1988. *Thinking, Feeling, and Being.* London: Routledge.

Ricoeur, P. 1967. *The Symbolism of Evil.* Trans. Emerson Buchanan. New York: Harper & Row.

— 1970. *Freud and Philosophy: An Essay on Interpretation.* Trans. Dennis Savage. New Haven, Ct.: Yale University Press.

Ritvo, M. 2016. *Four Incarnations.* Minneapolis, Minn.: Milkweed Editions.

Rovelli, C. 2014. *Seven Brief Lessons on Physics.* Trans. Simon Carnell and Erica Segre. Penguin Random House Books UK.

Ulanov A.B. and Ulanov B. 1982. *Primary Speech: A Psychology of Prayer.* Louisville, Ky: John Knox/Westminster Press.

Ulanov, A.B. 1994. *The Wizards' Gate, Picturing Consciousness.* Einsiedeln, Switzerland: Daimon Verlag.

— 2017. *The Psychoid, Soul and Psyche: Piercing Space/Time Barriers.* Einsiedeln, Switzerland: Daimon Verlag.

Volavkove, H. 1993. Ed. *I Never Saw Another Butterfly Children's Drawings and Poems from Terezin Concentration Camp 1942-1944.* New York: Shocken Books.

Chapter 8:

The Nexus Point

The Meeting of the Two Viewpoints

If we consider the two projects going on in an individuation process – our ego's own and our psyche's own – (chapter 1), and the lure of destructive fascination with one to the exclusion of the other (chapter 2), with the consequence of dissociating chunks of our personality (chapter 3), and falling into a hole with a helplessness at the bottom of such sufficient effect that space is made to sense something beyond our efforts (chapter 4), so we consent to the agony of integration as unavoidable necessity (chapter 5), then sudden moments of illumination occur. This is what I call the nexus point. It happens and it remarks us as much as we remark it. It happens more than once, sometimes often enough to feel it is now a regularity, though unpredictable when exactly, hence always a welcome surprise, an unexpected recognition.

Two horizons meet and show off their secret intercourse. Emily Dickinson's famous poem aptly advises: "Tell all the Truth but tell it slant – / Success in Circuit lies," (Dickinson

1129 Johnson 1955) "... one is linear, coming at an angle and the other curvilinear, working around a circumference" (Cameron 1979, p. 4). Jung's method of circumambulation comes to mind, circling round and round an image or a problem, until the core emerges into visibility.

The personal project of individuation needs sustained narrative to recognize the archetypal in the historical, with space/place and time/sequence to tell the story of what went amiss that makes one show up in an analyst's office to find it and instantiate it again in actual living with oneself and with others. The psyche's project circles round the center so it emerges and appears everywhere and in everytime, there to be found – the cheapest and the most treasured thing, needing symbols to render it visible. When the two projects' horizons meet in the flash of nexus point, we feel a fullness, a certitude, a this is it, this is what it is all about.

An example of the difference and similarity between the two projects is illustrated by the approaches to analysis of Thomas Ogden and Wilfred Bion. Ogden writes of intersubjective space constructed and found by the analyst/analysand pair. Two personal paths interchange and build up a space/time in which both participate and transform. Each contributes their individual reverie as they listen to the other. Even the dreams of each arise out of and fold back into their analytic conversation and shared gesture, pause, restlessness, ease, body breathing and holding one's breath to create this intersubjective third that is unique to this analysis and is, I suggest, to borrow Jung's insight, its 'subtle body.'

This intersubjective third is composed of imagination and hum-drum passing thoughts – Ogden's garage appointment right after the session to pick up his repaired car, his idle noticing the fancy label on his patient's coat so casually flung on the floor as she lies down on the couch. From the patient's side similar bits of thought re the details of daily life before and after the analytic appointment mix with the surprising experience of the gap of missing life in her childhood that always canceled any liveliness of before and after. Here it is now, right here, this gap that made life dead. How did that happen? The narrative with all its interruptions, sidelines, past memories and future promises plays the witness to whom you have become - from whence and toward where. The personal narrative of each of the pair - voiced and conscious and unvoiced and felt unconsciously, co-construct the connection to each other. They create the shape that is specifically their own analytic relationship (Ogden 1999, pp. 9-11, 29-32, 116-119; Ogden 2016, pp. 173-177).

Finitude includes excitement about coming to an end, a completion. Sometimes the flash flashes in the nexus point and we register something decisive for our whole life. Stories have beginnings, middles, and ends and push toward a completion that blooms (or withers), like Dorothea Brooke gaining liberation from Casaubon when she sees she had endowed him with talents of a scholarly mythographer, only to discover he was a fraud, hiding out in mists of myths untranslated into living because he did not grasp their meanings (see Cameron 1979, p. 56). Or take the 1980 Olympic ice hockey match when the amateur U.S. team beats the professional Soviets and defeating one more team go on to win the gold; Goliath falls and David wins! Or take the fairytale suitor who deciphers the riddle and wins the princess. Or take Psyche who risks keeping for herself the beauty cream she finds to please her lover Eros rather than handing it over as instructed to the goddess Aphrodite her mother-in law (see Ulanov 1971, pp. 237-238). Without all these finite turns and corners and paths opening, the plot does not get lived. It remains disincarnate knowledge and makes no actual difference.

The project of psyche circumambulating a center that is always there, what Bion calls O ("ultimate reality … the 'thing in itself'") and counsels us to look for in every session, means laying aside memory of facts of the analysand's life, and laying aside the analyst's desire to be of help to the analysand (Bion 1970 pp. 26, 41, 42). The presence of O – the Godhead – affects and gathers analyst and patient into an emotional field that each experiences with resistance and transformation. Is the patient married? Bion answers, in the present moment he does not appear to be wedded or act as if married. Do not reduce him to biographical facts that obstruct perception how O right now engineers connection or exposes our evasion of it. Do not cloud that openness with the analyst's need to prove useful or, even worse, a good fellow offering neighborly aid. Bion says once, I don't know why he (the patient) is mad at me; I did not try to help him (Bion 1970, pp. 26, 30-31, 87-89; Bion 1993, pp. 108-109; 1997, pp. 32-35, 37-38).

The psyche's project's language is not words so much as affect in the emotional field the analytic pair create and find between them – fugitive bits of thought, impulsive gestures, images, sounds, textures, even scents. All that can wrap up into an abiding symbol attached to an object that emerges – that center again. Jung and Bion can be seen as both finding O or Self influence clinical sessions and bring healing energy into range of small or large personal problems. Whatever the specific way Self or O moves this analytic pair, the repeated direction is to translate an outer shock of trauma into an inner psychic realization. The terror can lose its defining power and be emotionally held within each person's expanding insights and healing experience. Or a dream points somehow to that center – sometimes a note of music, or a smell of freshly baked bread, or delicate fragrance on a lovely woman's throat drawing the lips of her lover to where her pulse beats.

Dreams can point to that center as if it waits to be found, as long as we do not interpret the dream upwards into ego terms telling us what to do or not do, nor downwards into archetypal resonances now become fixities that define us. Jung suggests, "imagine a dream as like a conversation you overhear on the radio or the phone … and now you should reconstruct what has been said … It is always a 'listening in" (Jung 2008, p. 359). A dream often evidences both the daily concern of ego and the general difficulty of being human. Jung is helpful here with his insistence to stick to the image, to the phenomenon of the dream, not its translation (ibid, p. 194). In a dream the personal and the collective meet. In so far as the collective speaks of the immortal of the ages – the pattern of meaningfulness that endures – the dream evokes questions – am I living right, all I can live? Those queries in the dream contrast to puzzling over immediate mortal tasks like paying taxes or do I go back to the office in the wane of the pandemic or be safer by still working from home?

A dream can show the intersecting of personal and collective giving the flash of the nexus point – a sudden seeing how each fits with the other. Such a spark defies loneliness and ushers in realization that we share in solitude. We dream out of our environment; its problems enforce our personal ones (ibid, p. 86). Jung writes, "This is the secret of dreams – that we do not dream, but rather we are dreamt. The dream is dreamed to us. We are the object of the dream, not its maker … We simply find ourselves put into a situation … We can only try to understand what the dream offers" (ibid, p. 159).

The Personal and the Collective

For example, in the midst of the pandemic, a radical racial crime occurred in Minneapolis Minnesota and was as nationally compelling in the U.S. as was the virus. A crowd saw in person and hundreds more soon saw on video film in social media and then on television news the killing of Mr. George Floyd by a policeman setting his knee on George Floyd's neck and cutting off his breathing. Despite outcries from the people watching and from Mr. Floyd gasping I can't breathe numerous times and finally calling for his mother, the cop's knee held its pressure for almost nine seconds and suffocated Mr. Floyd, killing him.

The racial wound in the U.S. broke open wider and deeper. It was as if now two viruses swelled across airways and city demonstrations here and abroad. Collective consciousness of the sickness of the pandemic and of the snuffing of a black man's life penetrated into the collective unconscious and both reigned in two directions – inwardly in people's imaginations, and outwardly in talk shows, protests, in television and radio interviews, and in conversations from the corner barber shop to the U.S. government.

An analysand's dream brought the environment problems into personal issues and the reverse too. Woken up, as many were, to a deepened awareness of the systemic nature of racism in which we all dwell, this patient said, "I dreamt I was white in a black family and I was black in a white family." The dreamer is dreamt into the social problem flooding the environment and retains the personal issue of always feeling the outsider, not at ease fitting into either family but showing up visibly, unavoidably, a different color from the family members.

Listening to this dream, I heard again in my mind people on the radio reporting, 'I saw my son's, my brother's, my father's face under that policeman's knee; I saw my own face,' evidencing the public problem existed now in personal pictures. I felt my horror imagining that scene, as if one of the crowd now become witnesses. Would I have rushed forward to push the cop's knee away from George Floyd's neck? Or stood there dumbstruck, paralyzed by shock then dread I would be shot if I rushed forward, or many of us would be shot if some of us together rushed forward? What was the cop thinking? Ruining his own life as he murdered this man's life? My fantasy matched many people's fantasy of rescue for a man's life and of overwhelm by helplessness to save it.

The power of technology in phone and photo catching the crime as it is being committed and witnessed, making it available to thousands of viewers in their personal imagination is a new fact of our shared existence. We are relocated, drawn into what we cannot keep out, not distant, not detachable but flooded with what a black man is subjected to. We are transmogrified from observers, then spectators into participants involved personally. The white public now catches up to the public of color and particularly the black public who have had to participate as involved sufferers all along because of numerous instances of the same murder. The power of technology makes a difference. We are there, not distant in another city hearing about something happening elsewhere. Elsewhere is now where we are, this space and time. Piercing those usual barriers exposes us all as together in this crime.

The analysand's personal problem is included and maybe surpassed by this dream – standing still as outsider, not like the other family members and identified as one of them but shown as visibly different with a different accumulated history. This 'exile' persists and still shows need for attention, working through to possibilities of closer relationship different from a state of identity or easy identification with family members. The dream also raises general human questions. Must difference exile loving closeness, or can it shape it? How to be close as the different one that one is? Does the dream hint that all-togetherness is possible including one who looks different, from either side, as a true family member? Does the dream relocate the 'problem' by transcending 'outsiderness' in family love?

Consent

The nexus point requires our consent to be registered as happening, to incarnate itself in our living. Otherwise, it remains at best an intellectual knowing of some interest, but making little difference in living. Or we exploit our mind to use such insight as defense against the prick of certitude we have to change our life, as Rilke says in his startling poem results from beholding the arresting beauty of Apollo's statue (Rilke 1908: 'Archaic Torso of Apollo').

The last two stanzas read:

> Or else this stone would not stand so intact
> beneath the shoulders' through-seen cataract
> and would not glisten like a wild beast's skin;
>
> and would not keep from all its contours giving
> light like a star: for there's no place therein
> That does not see you. You must change your living.
> (Leishman 1960, p. 143)

Often the nexus point may be preceded by opposites conflicting where the personal preferences of I want X versus I do not want X usher us into deeper themes of conflict like conscious-unconscious, mortal-immortal, good-evil. Opposites also may meet where we feel a fullness, a certitude, a "this is it; all that matters is present here."

Consent to the flash of opposites meeting in a nexus point means our being made vulnerable, undoing our defense of dissociation, dismantling the protecting wall of schizoid armor, giving up the wholesale effect of denial. Consent means admitting I saw the spark, the flash, and let it impact me with startle, surprise, curiosity, or even more – that something more which I do not invent poked me, addressed me. I risk registering that and its coming for me, me coming for it, open. I take my chance crossing the Rubicon and take the full risk to be penetrated. It begins something. I grow a habit of attentiveness, that may deepen into devotion.

The Opposites Simultaneously

Jung describes one form of response in his early essay, "The Transcendent Function" left unpublished for decades, and then taking a pivotal place in his entire oeuvre (Jung 1916/1960, paras 131-193). The specific conflict burdening us demands careful review of each opposing side of it. We become aware of two different projects going on in us that contrast mortal and immortal, our personal problem and our psyche's pushing the Self viewpoint and, even harder to accept, what the Self points to beyond itself. The ego center of consciousness must take in the bigger Self center of the whole conscious and unconscious psyche, and, further, our entire personality must take in, notice, that it revolves around a still bigger center within and beyond us, we a small part in its orbit, along with everyone else.

Such examining work screws the tension up a notch of holding both opposites in awareness simultaneously. The question is, can we bear this strain and the vulnerability it opens in us? We feel helpless to solve the dilemma between these opposing sides; we feel frightened, we feel mad. If trauma is also part of it, we feel the deadly coldness of the extinction point (see above Chapter 5 pp. 4ff, 12) momentarily tossing us out of existence, its few seconds as if final, punctuated with a period.

The two sides seemingly opposed betray their secret handshake the deeper we consent to their bothness. Each are valid, have a right to exist, cannot be gotten rid of. How to climb over the razor-sharp edge of their either/or contention? Yet it happens. Something about our voluntary readiness to recognize the validity of each draws our attention to their simultaneity not yet recognized. I remember years ago an analysand so distressed to find himself inescapably drawn to a woman outside his marriage as if the survival of his soul was at stake. This urgent demand existed in antagonism to the care with which he had vowed and built his marriage to his wife including adoption of an immigrant child whose troubled acclimation required his father's steady presence, also a soul-demand of the first order. He was so distressed he walked out of the office mid-session. The proximity of the two women and soul on both sides and their simultaneous rivaling demands he found unbearable.

When he returned to the next session we started with the difficulty of living soul and its untameable nature. Soul was the third thing that appeared. Its demands set the conflict of the two opposing sides in a larger territory and that brought relief, if not immediate solution. The arrival of this third felt like a larger perspective, as real as both sides of the conflict; that happens and neither he nor I invented it or thought it up, nor had a ready solution. The opposition is lifted by a new thing to a new level that so alters the previous either/or conflict that sometimes it dissolves, just melts away, and other times refers itself to a deeper opposition seeking reconciliation.

What bedevils us so much at the start seems now as if the doorway into a larger territory of a human problem, not just my humiliating one, but one the human family suffers and struggles with. That softens our shame and guilt for being snagged by such antagonism. But further, now the task of solving dilemmas includes this third thing, in this case, called soul, and that changes everything. Jung writes of it: "When a man has lost his soul, he does not live … The discovery of that lost treasure means the greatest discovery man can make, for in finding it he finds the totality of his life and existence … It is a temenos, that sacred, delimited space in which the god dwells" (Jung 2019, p. 186). Jung describes it: "a movement out of the suspension between opposites, a living birth that leads to a new level of being, a new situation" (Jung 1916/1960, para 189). "These are experiences we cannot rationalize. Neither can we argue with them" (Jung 2008, p. 299.)

We each have to find and accept being found by our particular personal route into the general human difficulty. Then, with decrease of obstacles of humiliation, guilt and shame, we have energy for the work to find our personal solution to an age-old human problem. We feel supported by an intimation that in making a contribution to its unraveling we make a difference; we are part of a whole. This is the beginning or the reinforcement of the symbolic attitude where even this most personal heartbreaking conflict shows its symbolic function of representing the crosses of human struggle – love for the young son and his soul in trouble, horrified questions what happened to the verve of the marriage, its soul, that made them dare to take on such responsibility for a new young life, and how did this unexpected other appear to address his soul life with that aliveness that makes us dare to take it as offered lest we go dead before we actually die?

Questions of ethics, metaphysics, spirituality, theology crowd in – what god do we feel summoned by? Evil threatens as does being judged selfish re another's well-being. All these devilish questions implode, inundate. No wonder he walked out of the office!

Contra criticism of Jung as overly emphasizing the archetypal as the real thing separate from personal daily life and overly taking the introverted route to the exclusion of social activism (Saban 2019, pp. 220, 234-235) is my emphasis on the interpenetration of the two always going on. Note here that both sides of the conflict land the man of my example in social, economic, cultural environment, with practical and spiritual issues – with the new woman, with the wife, with the child whose immigration from trauma of social conditions impacted his young son's violent energy, his talent in potential, and his stability. We cannot separate the person from the society, the collective environment from the individual object relations, the everyday from the spiritual meaning. They form a total psychological situation. We feel pressure from both sides, outer and inner. Jung got hold of this soul role that lives in both archetypal and personal situations that enliven and support or try to snuff soul. That, I suggest, is an inestimable contribution to social action.

An example of the pressure the social exerts on the individual is the influence of the decisive change in western society with the advent of Scholasticism. That Jung describes as "a form of education which enabled thinkers to detach their spiritual ideas from objects … to think without objects … it was no longer the object that was of importance, but the thought." This "release of the mind from its attachment to objects" enabled advances in abstract thinking, but with the consequence it is hard to understand psychology. This lack is made worse by the positive eventual return in science to the object studied but it has

> "become rather concrete, so that we are often unable to think without an object … which makes us … unfit to understand psychology … [where] you have an invisible object, for thoughts themselves are the object of psychology, and when you deal with invisible things which you cannot touch, then you easily begin to imagine that you are dealing with mere inventions … that psychology is a mere invention of certain thoughts invented for certain purposes; that you can really only observe those objects that are outside yourself – a very concrete experience … [and] science can exist only where you deal with the real object and … thought is never a real object, but an invention." (Jung 2019, p. 143)

The objectivity of the unconscious is then hard to credit, let alone the validity of symbolic thinking. Even a mind as great as physicist and Nobel Prize laureate Wolfgang Pauli's had trouble countenancing the veracity of his dream images and the symbols that appeared to him (see ibid, pp. 190-192; see also Jung 2008, p. 303). The fact that this larger perspective just occurs without our manufacturing it so unseats the basis of our ethics that we can be frightened. Are we rationalizing and evading something more here? What is its source?

Further, even if a new level is reached and the pleasure real and solid of a resolution all around, there is no purity that lasts. Right then the other side pops up, personified by the devil, "the disintegrator par excellence, the destroyer" (Jung 2019, p. 260). Jung writes,

> "The divine spark between the opposites has hardly flared up before the evil, the devil, interferes in the form of instinct, of the physical body. This is ... the admixture of diabolical fraud. It becomes evident that there is no such thing as complete purity, that things are mixed with the impure, with matter, and that, therefore, the burning ensues. The purification occurs in the fire, so that the pure being may rise into heaven, while the ashes fall down to earth." (Jung 2008, p. 189)

The One and the Many

The devil symbolizes the reduction of the One to the literalized, the concretized, the objectified. Jung says in *The Red Book* (p. 322) if we do not recognize the serpent in us, making its serpentine way through our living, now toward this side of the conflict, now to its opposite, then we eject the bad outside us as if into the devil. Then the devil has us in his grasp. If we accept the serpent in us, the devil has no power over us. We work with our shadow, suffer it, find place for it (see Ulanov 2017, "The Really Bad," p. 83).

Paul Klee's painting, *The Serpent Goddess and Her Enemy* makes visible the attack of the literalized: only this is the *right* word; of the concretized: only this is the *right* action; of the objectified other who is only defined as the *enemy* we then exploit or kill. The many possibilities get reified into a false One. It appears as a dictatorial obligation that shoots down anything different. We get trapped in the cage of our definition of the One. We lose the sparks, or recoil in terror of the flash now like lightning that could electrocute, set us ablaze. What then? What saves us?

The reality of the nexus point stands against this fragmenting chaos. The nexus point is there but remains outside our vision which has narrowed. Sometimes only great suffering rescues us, by blowing up the barricades around us. A person told me in intermission between my lectures of the most extraordinary rescue a man experienced and later worked on when he went to her for therapy. He told her he had squandered his relationships, his career, his resources in excessive destructive behaviors and he could not stop it. A terrible accident (with farm machinery?) occurred that landed him in a quadraplegic state. He told her he felt gratitude for what happened: "I couldn't stop the destructiveness, and this terrible accident stopped me." I understood him to be saying to her, "I can find a life now."

The reality of the nexus point stands against such tyranny of a complex and the consequent flagrant squandering of one's life. It is the meeting of the timeless and the now, of extension into the spaceless and the here. That flash of connection we register as meaningful. What we do or fail to do with it makes a difference, conferring on the present moment a sense of eternal significance, bestowing on this specific place a sense of belonging to the ages.

Experiences of the flash, the sparks of the nexus point may occur often and even more often if we consent to attend them. If not, they become irregular with much time and big spaces between their happenings. If we attend the capacity for symbolic representation in thought or feeling, that capacity increases. We notice more. Our sense of the many and its mysterious nearness to our sense of the One persisting throughout each instance grows more evident. The more we notice this pearl and that one, the more we discover that the several turn into scores, the various into the numerous, the ample into heaps. The sheer muchness, like the swarm of fireflies lighting up the dark opens a child to wonder, the muchness of objects in the world that can elicit our consciousness amazes, impresses, offers itself to be explored. The child who discovers books, or the many angles from which to shoot a basketball, or our first love who sees through the eyes of the beloved our self-loathed faults in an entirely different way, opens our sealed-up state, liberating our unfolding.

Many possibilities occur, many choices; how to select? Even in dire circumstances a tiny choice abides with decisive results as Victor Frankl made clear in recounting his deathcamp peril. Upon entrance he was stripped of everything, even his body hair shaved away and then shoved from one deprivation – food, drink – to the next – rest, cleanliness, company. He dared not think of food lest his longing set his body into disorder and augment his starvation. But even treated as no-thing, to be ordered about, tyrannized, dispatched on marches or to labor, to be at any moment rubbed out by random gunshot or by slower death intended with torture, he said as human we still have attitudinal freedom, to choose our attitude to what was unavoidably and horribly happening to us (Frankl 1948/1975, pp. 125f; Frankl 1978, pp. 48-49).

Other survivors scoffed and repudiated this idea, feeling totally victimized in and by their surroundings. But he persisted, thus showing the glimpse of the One in the many degradations, the One still gleaming there in re-calling and re-feeling I can choose, no matter to what small degree, my own attitude and response. The victimizing is to and in me, but I am not in it, despite appearances to the contrary. After liberation from the camp he wrote of this tiniest wedge of freedom and built his subsequent understanding of therapy around it (Frankl 1946/1959, 1948/1975, 1969).

When we see who we are in our bodily and psychic reality, then, with Jung we may say of the many, "I have all of them in me … one has become universal" (Jung 2008, p. 68). That holds for the luminous nexus point experiences too. Through this specific event into which I dive deep to take the risk entirely to engage it, all the luminous events of my life are present. 'This is it': the One – origin and arrival in everything – dwells here; we dare to take it as offered, and generate that possibility in others.

In collective consciousness, the many are the multiplicity of choices from which to select what to try, which possibility to pursue, what attitude to shape in our finite life. We cannot do everything; the many underline our personal limits and the limits of our cultural environment. That is the positive: abundance and limitation. The negative is multiplicity as overwhelm, excess, glut. Copiousness disseminates into separate tiny fragments scattered near and afar; no glue; no unity or accord, no affiliation or cooperation with others, just surplus; profusion floods us. Consciousness then decenters and disperses like a swarm of insects: "If you fall prey to the many, you will be dissolved … we have lost the unity of the personality. If we are at one with ourselves, the other will face us" (Jung 2008, p. 216). When consciousness no longer is a process reposing in itself, "The motif of multiplicity indicates a splitting of the soul" (ibid, p. 156). A simpler way to put it is we take a part for the whole and infect others with the chaos that results. We lose the soul meaningfulness that life is precious and worth living.

In the collective unconscious the negative of the many and the One is that the One is lost. At best its vigor and robust brawn might be identified with one part of the whole. We cling to that part as to a life raft, dictate it to others and bruck no disagreement. If others protest, we attack them with iron grip and pretense of invincibility. But our consciousness enforcing only this one part dissolves. We dwell in the one part; the One does not dwell in us.

We can suffer a negative experience of the psychoid level of the unconscious as teeming chaos where everything is everything else, swelling tides going back and forth, infiltrating everything. Consciousness thus unsupported disseminates into tiny separated units (Jung 2019, pp. 271, 322). There is no temporal succession but everything all at once engulfing us; no spatial order nor alignment, only surplus or gap. Thrashing, flailing, demanding first this and then backtracking to its opposite, we become the medium of chaos in the world and feel always persecuted by others refusing to recognize us as the One who knows, acts, and must be revered. The negative of synchronicity is paranoia: every tiny bit of the many looking at us with menace. Instead of the positive sense of unconscious as plenty, as bounty always alive beneath consciousness, it is chaos threatening to drag us into its darkest corner of tumult. We suffer the many as fragmentation. Failing to connect to the One, we deny it exists (see Ulanov 2010/2014/2020, pp. 145-159).

In the positive manifestation of the One, we know it exists. The orthodox Christian belief names it "The Existing One." Jung writes of his experience of the One in his *Black Books:* "Forever denied, it exists forever. Recurring in all forms, forever the same, this one precious vessel ... It is the One and the Many. A path leading ... across mountains and valleys, a guiding star on the ocean, in you and always ahead of you" (Jung 2020 vol 7, p. 193).

The One shows in the varieties of the many and is never rigidified nor captive to our needs, wishes, insights. It is: we participate in its livingness. This ushers us into a sacred here and now where we see we belong. We experience this point of conjunction but can never define it, only gesture, dance, stammer, behold, living its connecting to us, never entirely knowing it. We glimpse we each are shareholders in its large forming that shows in many forms, diverse, spontaneous as well as worked. We craft and create our point of view and recognize the different views of others.

We become neighbors in such creative perception. Individual details that differ link us to our particular environments and to such details of others. Such finite details mark the limits of what we can see and do and indicate the huge diversity beyond our limits. No universals are imposed, but rather we see a "process of universalization, of making specific differences relate as stand-ins for all the world's variety" (Skeritt 2016, p. 17, see also pp. 9-18.)

Contemporary Aboriginal women painters know this and show it in their paintings (ibid, passim). The common theme of linking thrums through their community without blurring over their distinct individuality.

> "The detail lays bare the limits of representation. Unlike the fragment – which suggests a break from the whole – the detail constantly pronounces its connectivity … as such, it has power to relate links between disparate realities, without requiring movement toward a universalizing homogeneity." (ibid, p. 13)

We learn from these painters that borders between us distinguish us and are not broken nor reduced, but rather come into play among us. This play points to primal creativeness, welcoming its multiple variations, like the stars of the sky shown to Abraham as symbols of his many descendants (See Glissant 2010, pp. 13-21). Meeting such big forces includes the brutality of nature too, along with the terrific power of the creative. Nexus points reveal the reality that is behind visible things. We need the specific things through which to see that reality, the

One in and through the many. We need the many, the details and specificities, to see the One in and among them.

In the positive manifestation of the One and the many we recognize the psychoid level of unconscious, an ongoing formlessness from which many forms emerge. They are fashioned by the social collective consciousness and by our personal consciousness and selections, never finished, always capable of flexible change into more, or a more discovered by a subtraction instead of endless addition. The painter removes the extra items on the table and Morandi's bottles show an order whose revelatory effect is bearable, not a clutter that distracts and disperses. The bottles and cup and bowl glow. We see in the single line of Matisse the intense pleasure of a woman's cheek, the line of brow leading to outline of her eye, the swell of breast or buttock conveying a receivable generosity. In social terms we are astonished by the One shown in an act of simple kindness to a stranger with its softening of excluding lines and its bracing courage-giving effects. We feel the whole point of living: this is what matters. We recognize the existence of each other, and of the One in the many of us.

In psychological terms, the One shows forth in the two: our self in relation to outer others, and inwardly in the two of ego and Self achieving the three in their alignment. Like a symbolic bridge, that alignment points to what is beyond the three as the fourth. It raises the question what shows the difference of the beginning of this process of transformation from its end? Jung writes,

> "The One is the unconscious; everything is still unseparated. The Two is the appearance of the opposites, of male and female. The Two creates the ... child, and this is the fiery spark ... the divine spark already contains the burning ... But then what is the difference between the original and the final states? What happens when things are burned? ... The

> smoke carries the images, the subtle bodies of the things, up again to the seats of the gods … transported back again into eternity in the form of images. But the original and final states are not the same. In the original state we are victims of the events … In the end … the whole richness of our experiences, returns in the smoke to the gods." (Jung 2008, pp. 187-188)

Jung refers to "ancient patterns" that turn up in dreams as if referring to cosmogonic forms like stages of transformation from animal to human (ibid, p. 362). He notes, "the principle of *fourness* appears … which is always the symbol of composition … to bring order into the chaotic plenitude of phenomena. The division into four is a *principium individuationis*; it means to become one or a whole in the face of the many figures that carry the danger of destruction in them" (ibid, p. 372).

God Images

From the plenty of collective consciousness and of the collective unconscious we are graced with perceptions of the many phenomena external to ourselves and inwardly with perceptions of the many images, sounds, motifs, sensations, bodily instincts – indeed an abundance from within ourselves. The nexus points, those sparks, scintilla, flash the meeting of inner and outer, of many and One, of phenomena that are personal to us like flashbacks of trauma or of beauty that stunned us meeting up with collective motifs that portray the destructive and creative forces of life in fairy tale bits, mythic heroines, epic battles, religious rituals.

From this plethora of nexus points God images are born. These are pictures we create and find of the wholeness of the whole, of the Source of the source, of the core of reality.

Our pictures try to point to the God the image mirrors, but never captures. Indeed, trauma can occur if the God image is abruptly broken or harshly betrayed. We lose connection to our picture for God and fear we never will get it back nor be found by a better one. We lose the deep link to the core of reality itself. Thus we lose contact with the core of ourselves that was gathered up in this image of the center of being and nonbeing. This perceiving through image is a drive, a fact of our nature, a knowing in the dark as "a life process ... an inner need ... like water seeping into dry ground ... Knowledge stemming from blood ... the stone ... is found in blood-filled veins" (Jung 2008, p 260).*

The image of the god means everything to us. Yet a danger lures us to equate our 'icon' with what it represents. Then we plunge into identification of our picture with what it points to and believe we can thus define God, bag God in the net of our knowing. Icon becomes idol (Marion 1991, pp. 14-18).

Another danger is to drain our God image of its aliveness by conceiving of it and what it points to in one-sided intellectualism and leave out what Jung calls 'The Below' – "the thinking out of the bowels, out of the depths" (Jung 2008, p. 260). This is dead knowing-about, and the devil jumps in right here to replace the aliveness that dogma with its many God images vivifies. But change of fundamental God images happens in times of cultural and collective upset, as in the worldwide 2020 pandemic, or in social or political protests not made up of looters and rioters but of families, children, elderly, protesting the murder of Mr. George Floyd, or in a foreign country repeated crowds

* For simplicity's sake I use the word 'image.' But the pivotal god-indicator may be a sound, a scent, an indisputable feeling tone, or a hard fact. An example of the latter is an announcement of a word in a dream addressed to the dreamer that convinced her she would survive her serious cancer. The dream: "You are adamantine." Her gathered associations uncovered a certitude: "You are hard like a stone, a rock. Enduring."

who yell to a dictator of many decades who rigged the recent election to show himself the victor, "Go Away! Go Away!"

Without God images that religions of the world and of history bequeath us we feel rudderless, or over the abyss. Jung refers to the image the prophet Zechariah uses (Zechariah: 4:10): "the eyes of the Lord run to and fro through the whole earth" and links it to the psychological point: "the eye is also the self-perception of an unconscious illuminated or capable of being illuminated ... From such inner perceptions stem the images of God ... The commonness of these experiential processes has also led to the fact that we find concordant God images in the most various places" (Jung 2008, p. 261).

We all have God images (see Ulanov 2001, pp. 22-36; 1986, pp. 164-184; Ulanov and Ulanov 1999, pp. 153-162). Psychologically, they function as the central reference point to our personality both conscious and unconscious and may not be explicitly religious or sacred. In negative terms, the central reference point around which we revolve and to which we repeatedly refer could be our drinking problem, our inferiority complex, our drive for power or money. Or it can be positive as our cause for justice, our love for our child, a particular religious ritual, or our devotion to beauty, to art, or scientific method. Something holds this space of center and when we investigate it, it moves, changes, influenced by and influencing our social movements and politics. Moved by deep emotion and sense of sacred we engage. If the word 'God' skewers us, or causes allergic reactions, then ask what do we revere as the ultimate value, or more simply, what do we love best. That is where God is hiding, as well as in our incapacity, our undeveloped function that presses to be developed. Jung describes his *Red Book* journey, "one blunders into the work of redemption" (Jung 2009, p. 338; see Ulanov 2018, passim). We will find a central point or issue or complex around which we revolve, that functions as our repeated reference.

One of the gifts of working as an analyst is you get, eventually, to hear of this secret, sacred reception, both good and wondrous, and bad and ensnaring.

This chapter was written for this book during the pandemic. Some of its material was given to the Montreal Jungian Society April 2021, to senior analytic candidates of San Francisco C.G. Jung Institute of San Francisco May 2021, to Jung on the Hudson July 2021. All these presentations were on zoom.

References

Bion, W.R. 1970. *Attention and Interpretation.* London: Tavistock Publications.

— 1993. *Second Thoughts.* London: Karnac.

— 1997. *Taming Wild Thoughts.* Ed. Francesca Bion. London: Karnac.

Cameron, S. 1979. *Lyric Time, Emily Dickinson and the Limits of the Genre.* Baltimore: John Hopkins University Press.

Frankl, V.E. 1946/1962. *Man's Search for Meaning From Death-Camp to Existentialism.* Trans. Ilse Lasch. Boston: Beacon Press.

— 1975. *The Unconscious God Psychotherapy and Theology.* New York: Simon and Schuster.

— 1978. *The Unheard Cry for Meaning: Psychotherapy and Humanism.* New York: Simon and Schuster.

Glissant, E. 2010. *Poetics of Relation.* Trans. Betsy Wing. Ann Arbor Michigan: University of Michigan Press.

Johnson, T.H. 1955. *The Poems of Emily Dickinson,* 3 vols. Cambridge, Mass. Harvard University Press.

Jung, C.G. 1916/1960. "The Transcendent Function" *The Structure and Dynamics of the Psyche Collected Works* vol 8. Princeton N.J.: Princeton University Press, paras. 131-193.

— 2008. *Children's Dreams: Notes from the Seminar Given in 1936-1940.* Philemon Series. Princeton N.J.: Princeton University Press.

— 2019. *Dream Symbols of the Individuation Process.* Ed. Suzanne Gieser. Philemon Series. Princeton, N. J.: Princeton University Press.

— 2009. *The Red Book Liber Novus.* Ed. Sonu Shamdasani. Trans. Mark Kyburz, John Peck, Sonu Shamdashani. New York: W.W. Norton.

— 2020. *The Black Books 1913-1932: Notebooks of Transformation.* Ed. Sonu Shamdasani. Trans. M. Liebscher, J. Peck & S. Shamdasani. Philemon Series. New York & London: W.W. Norton & Co. 7 volumes.

Klee, Paul. 1940. 317. "*The Serpent Goddess and Her Enemy.*" *Ten Americans After Paul Klee.* Munich, London and New York: Prestel, p. 99.

Marion, J.L. 1991. "The idol and the icon" *God Without Being.* Chicago Il.: University of Chicago Press, pp. 7-25.

Ogden, T.H. 1999. *Reverie and Interpretation.* London: Karnac.

— 2016. *Reclaiming Unlived Life.* London and New York: Routledge.

Rilke, R.M. 1908. "The Archaic Torso of Apollo" Trans. J. B. Leishman *Rainer Maria Rilke Selected Works* vol. 2. New York: A New Directions Book Hogarth Press, 1960, p. 143.

Skerrit, H.F. 2016. "Marking the Infinite" *Marking the Infinite Contemporary Women Artists from Aboriginal Australia.* Munich, London, New York: Delmonico Books, Prestel, pp. 9-19.

— 2016. Ed. Henry F. Skeritt. *Marking the Infinite, Contemporary Artists from Aboriginal Australia, From the Debra and Dennis Scholl Collection.* Munich, London, New York: Delmonico Books, Prestel.

Ulanov, A.B. and Ulanov, B. 1999. *The Healing Imagination.* Einsiedeln, Switzerland: Daimon.

Ulanov, A.B. 1971. *The Feminine in Jungian Psychology and in Christian Theology.* Evanston, Ill.: Northwestern University Press.

— 1986. *Picturing God.* Einsiedeln, Switzerland: Daimon.

— 1996. *The Functioning Transcendent.* Asheville N.C.: Chiron.

— 2001. *Winnicott, God and Psychic Reality.* Louisville, Ky.: John Knox Westminster Press.

— 2010/2014/2020. "The Many in the One, The One, in the Many" *Knots and Their Untying: Essays on Psychological Dilemmas.* Einsiedeln, Switzerland: Daimon, pp. 145-159.

— 2018. "Blundering into the work of redemption" Eds. Murray Stein and Thomas Artz. *The Red Book For Our Time* vol. 2. Asheville, N.C: Chiron.

Chapter 9:

Simultaneity

Simultaneity is an odd word to use in a final chapter. Its meanings include coeval, coexistent, coincident, concurrent that convey an all-roundness that suggests differing elements appearing together and at once, a recognition of space and time and a piercing of their barriers. It makes me think of geometry, a branch of mathematics concerned with points, lines, surfaces and solids in space and Hobbe's opinion that geometry is the only science bestowed by God (cited in Cameron 1979, p. 31: Hobbes, The Leviathan, Part I Chapter IV). Geometry made me remember Edna St Vincent Millay's describing its inventor, or discoverer: "Euclid alone has looked on Beauty bare."* That gaze recalls Rilke's connecting it to the marvel of beauty: "For Beauty's nothing/but the beginning of Terror we're still just able to bear" (Rilke 1912, "The First" in Leishman and Spender 1939, p. 21). The majesty of space holds everything: even an

* By Edna St. Vincent Millay. I cite its last seven lines:
O blinding hour, O holy, terrible day,
When first the shaft into his vision shone
Of light anatomized! Euclid alone
Has looked on Beauty bare. Fortunate they
Who, though once only and then but far away,
Have heard her massive sandal set on stone.

interval of time (the space of an hour) or the silent rests between musical notes, or the landscape we love best, or holds nothing: the loss that leaves us staggering, the nowhere of depression that crushes us. Time stands still is such moments of beauty or loss: all that *is* is here now, including the paradox that time is illusory and felt as intensely real.

Psychoid and Simultaneity

Simultaneity calls up Jung's notion of the psychoid level of the unconscious. There everything appears – the mists of unconscious perceptions forming and not yet formed, body instincts and senses of smell and touch and shape of others, let alone conscious experiences left to drift back into unconsciousness yet retrievable, of wondrous phenomena in the world – adamantine rocks, furry creatures, flashes of mind apprehending colors, the pleasures of taste, touching a shiny leaf, let alone emotions of sorrow and anger suffered by individuals and whole groups of people, as well as the grace of out-loud laughing that blows clean the soul and puts everything into proportion and strengthens the muscles of compassion to face the worst harm we do to each other.

Simultaneity brings to mind space and time, the design of spaces in geometric forms and the instance of time, here, now, immediate. Our experiences of simultaneity cross barriers of space and time while harkening to them. A full expanse in space makes room for time as its fourth dimension, and temporality grants a way to think of next to and far from. Both modes call up into our imaginations the phenomena of the world and of our own interiority, the thusness of animals and the scent of fir trees, the red hawk's bossy cry, the tiniest yellow flowers ringing the center of a zinnia, the fleeting thought that lights up the knot we work to untie, the feeling yes, it is all right. In addition, we might feel the soul of the world, animating the world into life and us too when it sparks or flashes in nexus points. Soul brings space and time – the ability to live in this locale and moment with zest and meaning – and transgresses those barriers, pointing to something transcendent. Any opposite we can think of dwells in the all-roundness and calls upon the round as symbol of the whole. It calls to mind Augustine's illumination of the immutable radiance of God that Jung appropriated for his notion of Self as the "circle whose center is everywhere and circumference is nowhere."

This every-whereness and every-hereness makes the god, and the Self and soul that point to the beyond, portable, not stuck in a hidden complex within, nor a rigid rule without, nor in the horror of separating immigrant children from their parents as a way to discourage the family's seeking admittance to a safe country. The radiating center is movable, found in the byways and highways, on different altars, undivided (the One) yet in the many diverse moments of illumination – in the blank of pain, in the "loaded gun" of rage (Dickinson #754, see Cameron 1979, pp. 65-69), and in heart-stopping awe. Yet as well that center lights up as the tiny boy utters syllables, pronounceable only to himself, in the naming of his grandfather, what he will call him. Looking right at this big man the small boy announces, "Bwu Bwu." And the older man accepts this as his name; it expresses the recognition and love between himself and this precious grandson now verbal.

In psychological language simultaneity marks the psychoid level, where exists everything in teeming formlessness from which forms emerge to be shaped in particular ways by each of us as we articulate our meeting with them. From those nexus points of spark and flash and scintilla in the dark darkness of this deep unconscious, we conceive of things and name them, like Freud who names 'mystical' in a dream the "unplumable navel … that is its point of contact with the unknown" (Freud

1900/1958, p. 143). It is truly unconscious and remains so beneath and through our various concepts for it.

We grow bodily senses of the shape of the forms. We come to see this other emerging as external outside ourselves and as inside ourselves as internal other. Jung thinks we fear this other and would do anything to avoid meeting it. Its claim on us exerts a direction we would not choose, preferring our ego plan. This other takes different forms, of the shadow, for example, the stuff we disown and only come to recognize as belonging to us, hence unavoidable.

The personal and the archetypal meet in trying to understand, for example, what the dream image means, or what the meaning of the repetitive symptom may be. This is not substituting archetypal amplification for action in the world but drawing on it to discern the direction of one's action in the world. The converse happens as well; our action in the world introduces us into the self we are. The threatening snake in a dream becomes a lion and calls up the image that between the lion and the snake in Mithraic ritual is revealed a deep vessel, the Krater. Then, Jung says, it is clear what to do: "Hurry down … dive into your vessel … and hurry up again to your kind, to your *genus*, to your lineage, to your relatives, that is, to what one actually is" (Jung 2008, p. 224). And that owning – of the personal and the psychic projects – sparks a new level of being.* Jung's symbolic concept of Self embodies the One found in the

* Paul Klee makes the same point about the spark that renders the origin of the 'work' of making a painting. He too emphasizes that origin point must meet with response of willingness and ability to master the artistic demands of painting. "The history of the work, which is first and foremost genesis, can be described briefly in broad strokes as a hidden spark from somewhere that, glowing, ignites the human spirit, moves the human hand and from there is transmitted as movement of matter; it becomes work" (Klee, P. 2016. "Contributions to the Theory of Pictorial form" Madrid: Fundacion Juan March cited in Fabienne Eggelhofer, 2018. "Paul Klee: pictorial writing" in Ten Americans: After Paul Klee. 2018. Zentrum Paul Klee Bern and The Phillips Collection, Washington DC, p. 93 of pp. 93-123).

boundless possibilities of soul and in multiple perceptions and attractions to actual phenomena in the world.

Roundness is a symbol of "complete fulfillment" (Jung, 2008, p. 185) that combines world and self, not one excluding the other, but joining in their simultaneous appearance. But, that *coniunctio* does not last. It "represents a climatic point in life, which, however, will soon fade. The revelation of the deity is immediately followed by an enantiodromia, turning it into its opposite to reach a new climatic point again" (ibid, p. 186). What springs us from immersion, repetition and imitating the general – the many – instead of living our original way, is finding our particular path and style to engage outer and inner living beings. We find and create our particular experience of the One speaking through us, unique and irreplaceable. Without that push of individuation we rise and fall with the cycle and become like everybody else of the many, not distinctly ourselves.

Experience of psychoid level of unconscious presents us with paradox: we are each of the opposites at once. One fears "what in the deepest sense belongs to one … .and yet wants it at the same time … I don't mean 'I,' but fear of the Other in us, the Self … a superior force of which one knows: 'It belongs to me, and I belong to it'" (ibid, p. 263). To claim it we must dare our uniqueness, however small the light shines in us; that is our original experience of light. Yet to claim it we must also depersonalize it, know that light is universal, belonging to everyone everywhere, As Mandela said "It is our light, not our darkness that most frightens us" (Mandela 10/11/1983).

In engaging the psychoid paradox of all opposites together, we shape both conflicting sides – light and dark, self and other, inside and outside, if we get either. Take Jung's notion of Self as sum of conscious and unconscious for example. For the Self to be real to us it must be *my* experience of Self. For God to be real to us, it must be *my* experience of that universal symbol. Pascal marks the specific time – the day, hour, and the particular feast in the liturgical calendar. He marks the specific space in which his revelation occurs and then where precisely he places his recounting of it under his doublet. He has a made a fine copy on parchment and a copy for himself on ordinary paper. The universal One who saves us all, breaks into the time and space of this particular man. In the meeting of the One in itself for the many, in the breaking of space/time barriers and occurring in his specific times and spaces, Pascal marks exactly where and when the 'immutable radiance' found him (B. Ulanov 1960, pp. 188-189).

Yet the opposites meeting bring to vivid awareness that what we encounter is general and universal as well as arriving through the particular and banal, the One and the many, the personal project and the psyche's project (so to speak) of setting wholeness of the personality in the wholeness of the whole of reality that exceeds our individual path. Central to that path is to admit to consciousness we are part of a larger group, society, and a larger time and space than our limited personal journey. The universal and the particular emerge from a different origin point and cannot be substituted for each other. Both are real. Individuation cannot be reduced to personal fulfillment; it is rather the full filling of the whole; we take our part in what is beyond us and feel our service to that. Others benefit or suffer from what we do.

Anyone who enters analysis to deal with her or his personal entanglement will soon be ushered to confront life and death issues, such as good and evil. For example, what to do with being hurt badly that arouses rage and vengeance? How to house destructive emotions without repressing them as bad, off limits, and without acting them out toward the other in actions intended to hurt or in attitudes that are murderous and thus poison the shared atmosphere of everyone?

Jung is criticized for reifying his terms and for privileging inner over outer life in the world. That leads to making analytical psychology a dead zone, stultifying its evolution (See Saban 2019, pp. 154-155). I prefer to focus on the flashes in Jung's writing where he stresses the unfolding going on of each opposite and the emergence (the transcendent function) of a third item that lifts the conflict to a new level and configuration that appears to happen under 'the shadow of the fourth' – the wholeness of the personality taking shape (Jung 1916/1960; Ulanov 2007b, pp. 505-606; see earlier version 2007a, pp. 157-186).

Jung says in the future someone will fashion another vocabulary. He offers his 'subjective' view, even a 'confession' of his experience of psyche. The nub, the beginning place, is the experience from which issues the vocabulary. That's the flash (the nexus point) the reader feels in Jung's writing. Something happened to him and he tries to spell it out. The fact of it happening is the point. The old and the new go on meeting for him:

> "I admit that this may be a new kind of symbolical language by which we are continuing the process of human thought … every new race or new civilization will invent a new terminology … we must find a terminology, a way of envisaging things, that really expresses the structure of the human mind, so we are forced to use archetypal terms. If we were to invent an entirely new theory of the mind, it would perhaps only explain the most recent and superficial psychological layer … the uppermost layer of up-to-date consciousness, but nothing about these structural elements. The unconscious does not follow them unless they contain an archetypal pattern … You only feel that something has gone home, has hit the nail on the head, when the archetype is sufficiently expressed. Otherwise it has no appeal at all." (Jung 2019, p. 293)

He gives as example dreaming of a mandala:

> "it simply means that the process of integration or individuation is about ... it is perhaps advisable to do something, but the dream does not say so ... Dreams don't tell you what you should do with them, and they don't give you advice. The dream is not a sort of well-meaning teacher ... who tells you what you ought to do. The dream is a symptom, a manifestation, a natural event ... much like a compass ... It doesn't even tell you where north is. It simply moves ... You must know the degrees of declination of the compass ... It is just a natural phenomenon, and if you learn to make the right use of it, it is useful. But there is no 'ought to'." (ibid, pp. 293-294)

Instead of a clear line to follow in space directing the next step to take and indicating clear temporal stages of succession of this first, then that, we perceive in astonishment the simultaneity of life's elements as always there, and the psychoid deep level as a moving basis from which forms emerge according to the rhythms of the total situation in which we find ourselves. That situation encompasses others we depend on, good and bad, the time in history we live in, which cultural images are dominant, and what brutal social facts, like poverty, and what wondrous facts, like community, influence our consciousness, and whether the archetypal fundaments are on the move, as in such life-changing events for everyone of the pandemic in 2020-2022, or of 9/11 U.S. catastrophe twenty years before. Instead of certain directions to follow, we become alert to nudges, hints, and take 'idle' thoughts seriously. With luck it may be from a nexus point of flash where we see in this moment the next step to take, the next space to traverse, symbolized in dream or imagination by vehicles of transition – a train, a car, a subway, a boat, a bike, a horse carrying us, a portable iPhone showing in GPS the direction to follow. The opposites engage and a new level is reached and right away a new opposite accumulates. We move toward another climatic point, the 'end of the world' as we know it. For example, the grocery store clerk says to me, 'after this covid thing we will not go back to the old normal; it's over.'

Opposites

Clinically, I have learned from listening to the knots – the psyche's dilemmas – that people bring into analysis, to imagine the specific set of opposites that steadily appear in each person's living experiences (Ulanov 2013). Those repeating opposites show the two points of view I have been describing. The psyche's project shows itself in the general human theme of opposites, the conflicting elements that besiege us and that generate energy. The personal project of individuation shows the idiosyncratic aspects of their own opposites – in the woman with a wide open wonder of a child mind that is also extremely vulnerable vying with the opposite of the dried up hag unalive before she is dead and armored with tough defenses; in the man with a strategy of compliance versus rebellion that enables him to steal some real life but leaves him feeling never on firm ground in himself; or in a genius like Wittgenstein who suffered, I suggest, a schizoid condition with accompanying acute depression, feeling separated from others by a "pane of glass." His isolation from others and from the reality of the world left him with a life without meaning, only barely "keeping on his feet" (Eilenberger 2020, p. 64). Yet struggling with this desperate condition, he also engaged the opposite of radical creative insight into the "linguistic roots of our relationship with the world" (ibid p. 255). He invented a ground breaking theory of language stripped of false meanings, declaring language as never saying anything let alone proving it. Language can only show (ibid, p. 171).

Healing

What has all this to do with healing? Everything, and still healing remains unexplained. Its processes can sometimes be described, but never defined nor summed up in guarantee. Perhaps the best word is improvised; we contrive, dream-up, spontaneously find the unpremeditated and originate. In most examples, we can note the two viewpoints activated. What bedevils us? What specific hook am I hoisted on that the psyche might portray as at Erishkegal's mercy in the underworld? The horrible jolt, the shock of trauma when someone does something to us they should not, or someone fails to do something for us they should do, we jerk awake to not mattering to the other or, in the larger scheme of things, to the horror we could at any moment not be. This jolt is like a sudden shove between our shoulder blades; down we plunge into the open manhole. We hope in treatment to see that repeating stark undigestible shock slowly transform into a psychological image of it, now once removed from its initial concretization. That step toward depersonalization helps us deal with trauma better. A small space begins to emerge between us and it.

Harry Wilmer gives examples from veterans with PTSD who were members of Harry's dream groups in a psychiatric hospital, Harry being the first doctor to ask for dreams (Wilmer, 1982; 1986; 1986; see also Ulanov and Ulanov 1991, p. 131). The vet begins to dream not the exact repetition of the surprise attack that wipes out his entire battalion, because now the dream ego moves around to different agents in the trauma. The dreamer is the attacker; the dreamer is one of his slain buddies; the dreamer is merged with Harry listening to the dream. When I gave this article of Harry's to the woman who cleaned my house, I suggested she just leave it lying around in their home. Marking the day of his war trauma, her husband disappeared every winter on that date, sometimes for few weeks, with their only car, leaving her stranded from her jobs. He seemed compelled to go off and drink to blot out he was the sole survivor because he carried the large radio on his back that protected him from being shot. We think her husband picked up Harry's article and read it as that year and none since he ceased disappearing, stranding her. Conscious and unconscious begin to work on the wound.

Or another example, an analysand awoke transfixed in terror. Slowly an image was recalled from a dream that transformed the blind terror into a scene where he was lined up in a bunch of men against a wall in a restaurant, held hostage by men with guns. Who? Why? Waiting for what? Never explained. The agent behind this had yet to arrive. Awaking in terror but now transformed to a hostage restaurant scene, made the terrifying fright slightly more bearable. Jung notes, the unconscious attempts to "to integrate the shock psychically," so instead of gunmen the next rendition might picture the men together finding the secret to effect an heroic escape. The drama gets mythified, and in a way even depersonalized. He is one of a band, not all by himself; imagination gets to work. He can look at the scene with less panicked paralysis, more elbow room, even to look into it with curiosity.

Or another analysand's dream pictured the individual plight as part of collective plight – one of a crowd of refugees. The collective image and a piece of mythology gives not an intellectual escape but a way to exist in space and time from a more collective, less personal point of view. The person's suffering is part of group suffering: I am one of many. Jung comments that "the psychotherapeutic system of the past, namely, the religions, always tried to heal man through depersonalizing his psychology ... take Christianity ... It would say, 'Sure you suffer, you are sick; but look at the wounds of Christ ... He was healed and now he heals you ... many people suffer; look at them; and they are healed by Christ.' That is depersonalization of personal suffering" (Jung 2019, p. 244).

If caught in too personal a psychology, emotions and animal impulses dominate us. Caught in entanglements of personal relations we can go round and round with no exit. Nature shows in the dream the general impersonal elements at work, a helpful power. Like the body that attempts to balance and compensate in self-regulatory system, so does the psyche. Using alchemical images we might say, put the whole personal haggle back into the bath, into the unconscious and wait; see what evolves. At times Jung goes even further, writing that the impersonal elements are the immortal parts of us:

> "the collective unconscious is the immortal substance in man. Conscious is mortal; we shall discover that there will remain nothing of that which our consciousness has acquired. But our mind is based upon a layer of the psyche that is everywhere and always there. So long as there are living beings, human beings, there will be the collective unconscious, and so we might call it the immortal part of man." (Jung 2019, p. 315)

Connecting to the level of psyche that abides and is not pushed up and down by personal strivings can happen at young ages too. It may be an initiation where a link is forged to authority beyond the individual; one sees the event and is not caught up in personal triumph or humiliation. A young man of fifteen had a noisy and adamant showdown with his father who had betrayed him by secretly paying the fee to enroll his son in a day school the father wanted after agreeing to and then annulling the boy's own choice for a boarding school away from home. Confronting his father, the father admitted his ploy of going behind his son's back. After the father's confession and much back and forth, they agreed to the son trying out the day school for a year on the condition he could then move to the boarding school if he so desired. It was a kind of initiation where the son broke from his father's authority into his own.

Unexpectedly the son then used in public his now consciously claimed authority that included his capacity to see two sides of a conflict just now experienced in his confrontation with his father, but also long honed by living in an atmosphere of constant fighting between his parents every one of his 15 years. Yet he knew each parent loved him and that obtained a space of his own outside the parents' embroilments. He grew a capacity of seeing both sides of a passionate difference of viewpoint. Along with claiming his own authority, this capacity bloomed in an unguessed public space and time in front of his whole new school in their custom of every faculty and student member partaking in public debate. To everyone's surprise, including his own, this new-boy spoke from his own authority at the end of school debate. He stood up without anxiety and summed up the debate's two points of view and what was implied for the school from each perspective. He spoke without judgement but with acuity and respect. He won the prize of the day, an award never given in the school's long history to a new freshman.

Near and far reaches of healing appear in its processes. A cyclic circularity – the processes seemingly endlessly repeating themselves – can trap us unless we connect with the inferior in us, what the shadow shows, as do the opposites we wrestle with. Change, if it happens, is subtle, almost like a preview of what Jung calls the subtle body that appears in later phases. But beginning with what we fear and reject, what angers us, what humiliates us, the symptom that does not go away but persists in hiding its emotional truth, this confrontation is the basis of all human relations Jung says:

"We like to think that our human relations are chiefly based upon achievements ... but as a matter of fact, real human relations are based upon our inferior function. Where we are really related is where we are really dependent ... It is very disagreeable to admit we are dependent somewhere … In our strength we can stand alone. We don't need other people … we prefer to act by ourselves and we are capable of so doing, but where we are weak, where we are dependent … uncertain … there we even have a vital need of other people, and there we are related" (Jung 2019, pp. 321-322).

Acknowledgment of dependence slows everything down. We become aware of how much we lack and need what the other supplies, whether it is the other person, or a different point of view, or collective society, or spirit beyond that makes its power felt here and now. I laughed out loud in recognition of the truth of Jung saying, "only differentiated functions can leap. Inferior functions can't jump; they creep like snails" (ibid, p. 123).

Then there is the mess we find ourselves in – a heap of stuff both personally and together in society with others. How will we ever find a way out or through? Healing seems far off if it is up to us and our feeble powers. There, again, is the hole we fall into and miss as also a country misses the opportunity to stand up on our own feet. The new leaders always succumb to the temptation of riches and pervert the gift of funds to buy masks in the pandemic, for example. They take the money and also sell the masks for personal profit, corrupted by the glint of having golden bathroom faucets. The monies are squandered and the chance of strengthening their country's health is wasted.

Such debasement shows in local incidents too. A small energy-supplying company boosted their fees two to three times over former bills and the regulation committee in the state also took the easy rubberstamp reaction, not the work of investigation if this was just. It was not. Customers' protests called the company to account and they lowered their rates the next billing, but they kept the money they had unethically acquired and resisted repayment. This leaves the customer enraged and dispirited. It's like being robbed: the thief gets caught stealing the victim's money. But the thief is allowed to keep the money he stole for himself instead of returning it to his victim. The power company keeps the overpayment and does not return it to the customers. That small example is inflated to egregious examples where greed takes millions that are not restored to the people whose taxes was their source, nor are the donated masks reclaimed and distributed to the intended recipients in the pandemic even though the perpetrators were caught.

We feel our dependence on something bigger than us to help us. We need liberation from the condition of half-truths, greed, rapacious power for personal gratification. This is perception of need for something coming from outside ourselves. The heap of our messes is the dissociated, unintegrated aggregated stuff that needs backbone (courage) to correct it, what the ancients might call "more snake." Jung cites a dream of Pauli where the task is to recreate "the instinctive man, which is a unity … give him a backbone" and comments "this is a genuine re-creation of an archetypal image … They exist in the blood … in the very structure of the brain, so that he produces the same ideas that were always made use of under such conditions" (Jung 2019, p. 231). Further, it comes from outside our personal entanglement: "He doesn't do it; I don't do it; it happens; it is done as if by a superhuman agency or superhuman consciousness" (ibid p. 232).

An example of liberation from outside our efforts relates to the heap of *massa confusa* when we experience the psychoid level that way, not as plenty or abundance, but a pile of everything mixed and contaminated with everything else. Jung draws on alchemists' notion of 'primordial chaos' as "understood to be a remnant of the original matter which existed, when, in the beginning, the spirit of God incubated the waters of the world … the idea was this original matter contained the living breath of God … the constant originator of new life" (ibid, pp. 299-300). Our mess and our heap of messes in common is a remnant of this original matter *still* housing the *living* breath of

God. The breath of God, to repeat, "as the constant originator of new life" stirs over and through our unconscious as it did over the waters of the deep in creating this wondrous planet in the huge cosmos. Only an image can hint at the extraordinary link here – the going on of going on toward thriving and wellbeing.

People know this experience of being dead and now alive, of receiving 'amazing grace' for the wretches we are. This regeneration of life *happens* and healing needs to note it. We need to take the diving breath to breathe in this living breath, rely upon it. The Spirit that brooded over the primal waters of the earth lives now hovering over and in the waters of our unconscious, stirring the remnant of living matter in the messes we are in, individually and all together. We live in such a time now and can read in ancient papyri our forebears also suffering their messes and calling on the gods for help.

Help comes from outside the ego realm, breaking in. Then living comes again to life, radical change happens yet gradual and all but indiscernible until one knows one feels different. We feel less strained, surprised by compassion for a former enemy, able in *Red Book* terms to own the serpent in ourself that brings evil to consciousness and not blame evil on everything and everyone outside oneself, but accept it there in our growing (Jung 2009, p. 322). We carry in our awareness the bug-like monster of our hate and *the presiding of the Serpent Goddess* in Klee's painting. Jung shares his insight about good and evil: as long as we are growing, evil and good are together in us and in the world; when we stop growing, they fall apart again into hostile rivalry. Healing is always in process.

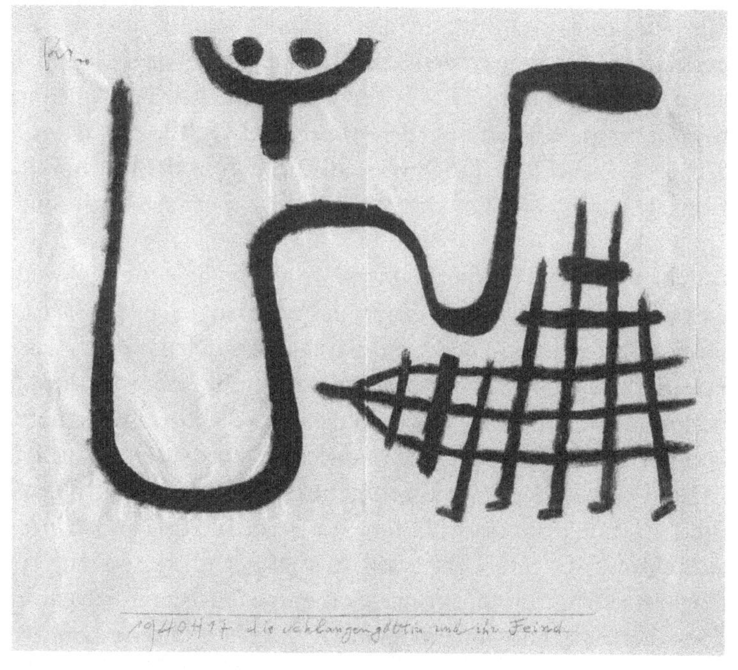

Paul Klee, "die Schlangengöttin und ihr Feind", 1940, 317
The Serpent Goddess and Her Enemy, 1940, 317
coloured paste on paper on cardboard
29,6 x 42 cm
Zentrum Paul Klee, Bern, Private collection/Switzerland
Image credits: Zentrum Paul Klee, Bern, Image archive

Subtle Body and Mirroring

If healing is a process never ending and if there are those two projects – personal individuation and impersonal reaching of the psyche itself, so to speak, for wholeness of the whole and our place in it, and if we include the holes we fall into and the destructiveness that lures us, and the heap of dissociation and agony of integration, what is the difference then between the beginning and the end of these processes? On the impersonal archetypal level it is, Jung avers, all there from the beginning. Consciousness is what makes the difference between beginning and end.

Consciousness of what? Of who we are, what we are, to what we belong. We arrive at this awareness. We can tell by the transformation felt in our body and psyche: less defensiveness, less knee-jerk reactions, more ease, more humor, more nearness, not hiding or stiff, more relaxation, pleasure, content with more and less knowledge, not super knowledge; more surety, security. Change comes gradually, but sometimes it comes violently. Like the fairy tale princess who does not want the frog in her bed and throws it against the wall! In that act of aggression the frog transforms into the prince. Sometimes such aggressiveness does the trick, not slow understanding, but a bursting out or into.

We grow familiar with anchoring in what transcends us, the beyond ego of the collective parts of our psyche, and the purposiveness that goes beyond our personal strivings. We register the wounds, the trauma even as it now exists in us as emotional memory, as grief that can still bleed. It is in us, we are not engulfed in it. We are not thrashing around, flailing in its hurt done to us, but sobered by the pain that can still quicken but no longer define us. We are mindful of those who erased us as if we did not matter, of no account, but we are not erased. Instead, there is a hovering with that Spirit brooding over the waters, over our unfinished healing of intermittent vengeful thoughts toward those who hurt us and over our inability to sincerely wish them well. That is a cross we carry, hoping to be liberated from its weight, but still embroiled in its burden. But it is ours to actively hold within us, not to act it out on our neighbor nor act in against ourselves.

I remember an analysand telling of a freedom that rose up in her when taking up yoga. The teacher proposed a non-violent attitude in her pupils. She explained: no violence toward yourselves by saying you should be better at yoga than you are, farther along in its poses and silent moments; no violence by comparing yourselves to your neighbor who does better than you do; greet your body and let it be as it is, acceptance not measurement against a judgmental standard that captivates you. The difference at the end from the beginning of healing process is that we are not the victim.

In the beginning everything is already there in a sort of blueprint, psyche here like the body with its basic plan, not in a "strict causality" but with "an interwoven action of conditions ... with a connection open to many interpretations ... causality ... adapted to the multilayered material of life ... determined by *unconscious purposiveness*" (Jung 2008, p. 4). Chronological order gives way to "a radial one ... from a center" (ibid, p. 10). What makes the difference is that on the way to the end, we know about this center, have nexus points of experiencing its coincidence with our daily preoccupations, and with our searchings for meaning. At the end of *The Red Book,* Philemon, the Self figure, tells Jung that the God-image we each find and create is the God we pray to, is our companion and a bridge across death (Jung 2009, p. 354; see also Ulanov 2011, pp. 60-62).

For Jung, we know God as an image, not God's self. In the end of our personal individuation process all becomes as image and 'returns to the Gods'. We undergo a kind of detachment from such images, no longer enthrall to them. The adamantine stone, the *lapis* "is at the beginning, in the middle, and at the end" (Jung 2008, p. 226). The primordial opposites of masculine and feminine that sum up all life's opposites, are joined, interpenetrate "not the male or female *in corpore* ... but it is a fine subtle body, an extract ... It is not the man and the woman that are unified, but the male and the female, in a subtle, psychic form" (ibid, p. 228). Something is being made more unified and whole that is not concretely applied to men and woman as defining them. It is an image of interpenetration: "they should function together" (ibid, p. 229). Other images of opposites make the same point – wild "devouring desire contains light in itself ... an intensification of consciousness" (ibid, p. 229). Another example is the figure of Christ "as lion he is ... the glorious king, and as lamb he is the victim" (ibid, p. 231).

Healing then involves living connected to the ages in the finitude of personality number 1. The space in between finite and infinite is recommended: "The place or medium of realization is neither mind nor matter, but that intermediate realm of subtle reality that can be adequately expressed [only] by the symbol" (Jung 1953, para 394 cited in Jung 2008, p. 287). How do we know we are living this goal? By our ordinary experience of the extraordinary we participate in, a meaningful life as part of the whole and yet still ourselves, with doubts and troubles and joys and gladness. Further,

> "the fulfillment of the meaning of life is linked to the idea of immortality. This does not tell us anything about immortality, as such. We only state that human beings have this emotion ... It is simply a psychological fact. In all of life's highest points in which we face life *completely,* we also have the feeling of the meaningfulness of life, and this feeling is always linked to the feeling of eternity." (ibid, p. 202)

Alchemy associates this meaningfulness to the "second body, the incorruptible body" which is not immaterial will of the wisp, but as something corporeal, a subtle body, semi-spiritual in nature. Alchemy associates it with images of the *corpus glorificationis,* to a process of healing that extends beyond the personal to the social and beyond the social to all of life here and beyond.

The nexus point is critical; there flashes the spark that ignites the fire and fire is always at the center: "In this cycle of rise and fall, the end of the world is ... depicted also as a *fire ending*" (Jung 2008, p. 186). Jung cites Heraclitus for whom "life itself is a flow of fire, the 'everliving fire'" (ibid, and p. 189). The One in the beginning is the unconscious and the Two means things cross over into consciousness which differentiates them so we can relate to them in their opposite forms. From transcending their conflict and bearing their mating comes the Three, sometimes called "the son, the child, and this is the fiery spark" (ibid, p. 187).

We connect with the image of the thing, the *res* and feel the all in the small, the beyond in the here and now. That kindles imagination and facing the big human problems – good and evil, life and death, power and devotion, joy and despair. Yet "the divine spark already contains the burning ... This burning leads from the Three to the Four, to the whole. This desired state, however, is at the same time the original one" (ibid).

But the difference of the end process is that what burns goes up in smoke:

> "The smoke carries the images, the subtle bodies of the things, up again to the seats of the gods. The original One is transported back again into eternity in the form of images ... In the original state we are victims of the events, we are not detached from them, we do not have any vision. In the end, however, the whole richness of our experiences, returns in the smoke to the gods." (ibid, pp. 187-188)

This giving back made me think of the poet Hopkins' poem "The Leaden Echo and the Golden Echo," his ecstasy before beauty and what to do with it (1948, p. 96).

> "Give beauty back, beauty, beauty, beauty,
> back to God, beauty's
> self and beauty's giver.
> ...
> A care kept. Where kept? Do but tell us
> Where kept, where. –
> Yonder. – What high as that! We follow, now
> We follow. –
>   Yonder, yes yonder, yonder,
> Yonder.

Mirroring seems to be the point, the old idea that our job here is to mirror the work of God there. We witness its reality though it exceeds our comprehension. Its manifestation breaking into our awareness happens of itself, in the dark, not in the full light of our consciousness. Jung even cautions not look too directly:

> "There is no way we could unify the opposites with clear, conscious reason – *tertium non datur* – but in reality, there is always a third, because otherwise we would be eternally stuck in the contradiction. Practically speaking, we are able to bring the Yes and No together, only we must not look too closely and be so terribly precise, just look the other way a bit." (Jung 2008, p. 214)

It happens outside our awareness, in the dark, yielding a sense of the sacred here and now originating there beyond our scope: "The transformation occurs when that inner growth with all its original values and implicit meanings, enters into the empirical world" (ibid, p. 298). We do not know it; we live it.

We happen to ourselves and mirror the creative force of the god. That link, that spark becomes a flame, that giving it back now doubles the mirroring. We give back to the gods; we feed the gods as they feed us.

We cooked our experiences in forming images of them and living their meaning in our ordinary lives and thus we give them back to the gods. Like a doubling of the Christian eucharist, we now feed the God who feeds us. With the body of our existence, including especially the subtle body, we fuel the god. Not a burnt offering and bloody sacrifice, but a living devotion full of life's blood. We feed the god with our process of receiving all we are given to be and give back all that God would receive from us.

This chapter was written during the pandemic for this book.

References

Cameron, S. 1979. *Lyric Time, Dickinson and the Limits of the Genre.* Baltimore and London; Johns Hopkins University Press.

Freud, S. 1950/1958. *The Interpretation of Dreams* Standard edition vols IV and V. London: Hogarth Press.

Hobbes, *The Leviathan,* Part I, chapter IV, cited in Cameron op.cit. p. 31.

Hopkins, G.M. "The Leaden Echo and the Golden Echo." *Poems of Gerard Manley Hopkins,* Ed. W.H. Gardner. New York: Oxford University Press, 1948, p. 96.

Eilenberger, W. 2020. *Time of the Magicians.* New York: Penguin Press.

Jung, C.G. 1953. *Psychology and Alchemy Collected Works,* 12. Trans. R.F.C. Hull. Princeton, N. J.: Princeton University Press.

— 2008. *Children's Dreams: Notes from the Seminar Given in 1936-1940.* Eds. Lorenz Jung and Maria Meyer-Grass. Trans. Ernst Felzeder with the collaboration of Tony Woolfson. Philemon Series, Princeton, N.J.: Princeton University Press.

— 2019. *Dream Symbols of the Individuation Process: Notes of Seminars on Wolfgang Pauli's Dreams*. Ed. Suzanne Gieser. Princeton N.J. and Oxford: Princeton University Press.

Mandela, N. 1983. South Africa, Johannesburg, Inaugural Speech 10/11/1983.

Saban, M. 2019. *Two Souls Alas: Jung's Two Personalities and the Making of Analytical Psychology*. Asheville, N.C.: Chiron.

Ulanov, B. 1960. *Sources and Resources, The Literary Tradition of Christian Humanism*. Westminster, Md.: The Newman Press.

Ulanov, A.B. and Ulanov, B. 1991. *The Healing Imagination: The Meeting of Psyche and Soul*. Einsiedeln Switzerland: Daimon Verlag.

Ulanov, A.B. 2007b. "The third in the shadow of the fourth" *Journal of Analytical Psychology* vol. 52, no. 5, pp. 585-606; see also earlier version 2007a in *The Unshuttered Heart: Opening to Aliveness and Deadness in the Self*. Nashville, Tn: Abingdon Press, pp. 157-186.

— 2011. "Encountering Jung Being Encountered" *Jung Journal Culture & Psyche* vol 5, no. 3, pp. 54-62.

— 2014/2020. *Knots and Their Untying, Essays on Psychological Dilemmas*. Einsiedeln, Switzerland: Daimon.

Wilmer, H.A. 1982."Vietnam and madness: dreams of schizophrenic veterans" *Journal of the American Academy of Psychoanalysis*, 10, 1, 1982; Wilmer 1985, "War nightmares in decade after Vietnam" in Eds. James F. Veniga and Harry Wilmer *Vietnam in Remission*. College Station, Tx: Texas A & M University Press; Wilmer 1986."The healing nightmare: a study of war dreams of Vietnam combat veterans" *Quadrant*, 19, 1986; Wilmer 1986. "Combat nightmares, toward a therapy of violence" *Spring* 1986.

Ann Ulanov

The Psychoid, Soul and Psyche: Piercing Space-Time Barriers

This book offers a collection of many new ideas: connection with the psychoid processes of the unconscious is a source of healing, especially in relation to trauma; fresh interpretation of the bedeviling flashbacks of trauma; addition of an alternative interpenetrating matrix to the container model of healing; sum of the insights of Nicholas of Cusa and their implications for Jung's complex around freedom and relation to the Divine.

117 pages, ISBN 978-3-85630-768-4

Encounters with C.G. Jung
The Journal of Sabi Tauber (1951–1961)

Edited by Andreas Gerber & Irene Gerber

This volume presents the journal notes of Sabi Tauber, a young Swiss woman who recorded the experience of her encounters with C.G. Jung. She conscientiously noted Jung's responses to her questions and his comments on her dreams, mostly related to love, the creative principle, and the shadow. In the years 1951–1961, Sabi Tauber often visited Jung in Küsnacht and in his secluded tower in Bollingen. Jung also went to her home in Winterthur a few times, where he spontaneously explained his views in the circle of the Tauber family and their friends.

A reader today will immediately be touched by C.G. Jung's living spirit, just as Sabi Tauber was then. While addressing her personal situation, Jung also repeatedly points to the archetype that he recognizes behind each problem. In this way, the scientific precision of Jung's thoughts is imbued with a unique feeling quality.

248 pages, hardbound, illustrated in color, ISBN 978-3-85630-784-4

English Titles from Daimon

Ruth Ammann	- *The Enchantment of Gardens*
Susan R. Bach	- *Life Paints its Own Span*
Diana Baynes Jansen	- *Jung's Apprentice: A Biography of Helton Godwin Baynes*
John Beebe (Ed.)	- *Terror, Violence and the Impulse to Destroy*
E.A. Bennet	- *Meetings with Jung*
W.H. Bleek / L.C. Lloyd (Ed.)	- *Specimens of Bushman Folklore*
Tess Castleman	- *Threads, Knots, Tapestries*
	- *Sacred Dream Circles*
Renate Daniel	- *Taking the Fear out of the Night*
	- *The Self: Quest for Meaning in a Changing World*
	- *Psyche and Soma*
Eranos Yearbook 69	- *Eranos Reborn*
Eranos Yearbook 70	- *Love on a Fragile Thread*
Eranos Yearbook 71	- *Beyond Masters*
Eranos Yearbook 72	- *Soul between Enchantment and Disenchantment*
Eranos Yearbook 73	- *The World and its Shadow*
Eranos Yearbook 74	- *The Age of Immediacy at the Test of Meaning*
Michael Escamilla	- *Bleuler, Jung, and the Schizophrenias*
Heinrich Karl Fierz	- *Jungian Psychiatry*
John Fraim	- *Battle of Symbols*
Liliane Frey-Rohn	- *Friedrich Nietzsche, A Psychological Approach*
Marion Gallbach	- *Learning from Dreams*
Ralph Goldstein (Ed.)	- *Images, Meanings & Connections: Essays in Memory of Susan Bach*
Yael Haft	- *Hands: Archetypal Chirology*
Irene & Andreas Gerber	- *Encounters with C.G. Jung. The Journal of Sabi Tauber*
Fred Gustafson	- *The Black Madonna of Einsiedeln*
Daniel Hell	- *Soul-Hunger: The Feeling Human Being and the Life-Sciences*
Siegmund Hurwitz	- *Lilith, the first Eve*
Aniela Jaffé	- *The Myth of Meaning*
	- *Was C.G. Jung a Mystic?*
	- *From the Life and Work of C.G. Jung*
	- *Death Dreams and Ghosts*
C.G. Jung	- *The Solar Myths and Opicinus de Canistris*
Verena Kast	- *A Time to Mourn*
	- *Sisyphus*
Hayao Kawai	- *Dreams, Myths and Fairy Tales in Japan*
James Kirsch	- *The Reluctant Prophet*
Eva Langley-Dános	- *Prison on Wheels: Ravensbrück to Burgau*
Rivkah Schärf Kluger	- *The Gilgamesh Epic*
Yehezkel Kluger & *Nomi Kluger-Nash*	- *RUTH in the Light of Mythology, Legend and Kabbalah*
Paul Kugler (Ed.)	- *Jungian Perspectives on Clinical Supervision*
Paul Kugler	- *The Alchemy of Discourse*
Rafael López-Pedraza	- *Cultural Anxiety*
	- *Hermes and his Children*
Alan McGlashan	- *The Savage and Beautiful Country*
	- *Gravity & Levity*
Gregory McNamee (Ed.)	- *The Girl Who Made Stars: Bushman Folklore*
	- *The North Wind and the Sun & Other Fables of Aesop*
Gitta Mallasz / Hanna Dallos	- *Talking with Angels*
C.A. Meier	- *Healing Dream and Ritual*
	- *A Testament to the Wilderness*
	- *Personality: The Individuation Process*
Haruki Murakami	- *Haruki Murakami Goes to Meet Hayao Kawai*

English Titles from Daimon

Eva Pattis Zoja (Ed.) - *Sandplay Therapy*
Laurens van der Post - *The Rock Rabbit and the Rainbow*
Jane Reid - *Jung, My Mother and I: The Analytic Diaries of Catharine Rush Cabot*
R.M. Rilke - *Duino Elegies*
A. Schweizer / R. Schweizer-Vüllers - *Stone by Stone: Reflections on Jung*
- *Wisdom has Built her House*
Miguel Serrano - *C.G. Jung and Hermann Hesse*
Helene Shulman - *Living at the Edge of Chaos*
D. Slattery / G. Slater (Eds.) - *Varieties of Mythic Experience*
David Tacey - *Edge of the Sacred: Jung, Psyche, Earth*
Susan Tiberghien - *Looking for Gold*
Ann Ulanov - *Spiritual Aspects of Clinical Work*
- *The Female Ancestors of Christ*
- *Healing Imagination*
- *Picturing God*
- *Receiving Woman*
- *Spirit in Jung*
- *The Wisdom of the Psyche*
- *The Wizards' Gate, Picturing Consciousness*
- *The Psychoid, Soul and Psyche*
- *Knots and their Untying*
Ann & Barry Ulanov - *Cinderella and her Sisters*
Eva Wertenschlag-Birkhäuser - *Windows on Eternity: The Paintings of Peter Birkhäuser*
Harry Wilmer - *How Dreams Help*
- *Quest for Silence*
Luigi Zoja - *Drugs, Addiction and Initiation*
Luigi Zoja & Donald Williams - *Jungian Reflections on September 11*
Jungian Congress Papers - *Jerusalem 1983: Symbolic & Clinical Approaches*
- *Berlin 1986: Archetype of Shadow in a Split World*
- *Paris 1989: Dynamics in Relationship*
- *Chicago 1992: The Transcendent Function*
- *Zürich 1995: Open Questions*
- *Florence 1998: Destruction and Creation*
- *Cambridge 2001*
- *Barcelona 2004: Edges of Experience*
- *Cape Town 2007: Journeys, Encounters*
- *Montreal 2010: Facing Multiplicity*
- *Copenhagen 2013: 100 Years on*
- *Kyoto 2016: Anima Mundi in Transition*
- *Vienna 2019: Encountering the Other*

Our books are available from your bookstore or from our distributors:

Baker & Taylor
30 Amberwood Parkway
Ashland OH 44805, USA
Phone: 419-281-5100
Fax: 419-281-0200
www.btpubservices.com

Gazelle Book Services Ltd.
White Cross Mills, High Town
Lancaster LA1 4XS, UK
Tel: +44 1524 528500
Email: sales@gazellebookservices.co.uk
www.gazellebookservices.co.uk

Daimon Verlag - Hauptstrasse 85 - CH-8840 Einsiedeln - Switzerland
Phone: (41)(55) 412 2266
Email: info@daimon.ch
Visit our website: **www.daimon.ch** or write for our complete catalog